Democracy against Development

South Asia Across the Disciplines
Edited by Muzaffar Alam, Robert Goldman, and Gauri Viswanathan
Dipesh Chakrabarty, Sheldon Pollock, and Sanjay Subrahmanyam, Founding Editors

Funded by a grant from the Andrew W. Mellon Foundation and jointly published by the University of California Press, the University of Chicago Press, and Columbia University Press.

Also in the series:

THE POWERFUL EPHEMERAL: EVERYDAY HEALING IN AN AMBIGUOUSLY ISLAMIC PLACE *by Carla Bellamy (California)*

EXTREME POETRY: THE SOUTH ASIAN MOVEMENT OF SIMULTANEOUS NARRATION *by Yigal Bronner (Columbia)*

BODY OF VICTIM, BODY OF WARRIOR: REFUGEE FAMILIES AND THE MAKING OF KASHMIRI JIHADISTS *by Cabeiri deBergh Robinson (California)*

CONJUGATIONS: MARRIAGE AND FORM IN NEW BOLLYWOOD CINEMA *by Sangita Gopal (Chicago)*

CUT-PIECES: CELLULOID OBSCENITY AND POPULAR CINEMA IN BANGLADESH *by Lotte Hoek (Columbia)*

SECULARIZING ISLAMISTS? JAMA'AT-E-ISLAMI AND JAMA'AT-UD-DA'WA IN URBAN PAKISTAN *by Humeira Iqtidar (Chicago)*

RECEPTACLE OF THE SACRED: ILLUSTRATED MANUSCRIPTS AND THE BUDDHIST BOOK CULT IN SOUTH ASIA *by Jinah Kim (California)*

THE SOCIAL SPACE OF LANGUAGE: VERNACULAR CULTURE IN BRITISH COLONIAL PUNJAB *by Farina Mir (California)*

THE MILLENNIAL SOVEREIGN: SACRED KINGSHIP AND SAINTHOOD IN ISLAM *by A. Azfar Moin (Columbia)*

UNIFYING HINDUISM: PHILOSOPHY AND IDENTITY IN INDIAN INTELLECTUAL HISTORY *by Andrew J. Nicholson (Columbia)*

FROM TEXT TO TRADITION: THE *NAISADHĪYACARITA* AND LITERARY COMMUNITY IN SOUTH ASIA *by Deven M. Patel (Columbia)*

THE YOGIN AND THE MADMAN: READING THE BIOGRAPHICAL CORPUS OF TIBET'S GREAT SAINT MILAREPA *by Andrew Quintman (Columbia)*

DOCUMENT RAJ: WRITING AND SCRIBES IN EARLY COLONIAL SOUTH INDIA *by Bhavani Raman (Chicago)*

ISLAM TRANSLATED: LITERATURE, CONVERSION, AND THE ARABIC COSMOPOLIS OF SOUTH AND SOUTHEAST ASIA *by Ronit Ricci (Chicago)*

UNFINISHED GESTURES: DEVADĀSĪS, MEMORY, AND MODERNITY IN SOUTH INDIA *by Davesh Soneji (Chicago)*

MAKING SENSE OF TANTRIC BUDDHISM: HISTORY, SEMIOLOGY, AND TRANSGRESSION IN THE INDIAN TRADITIONS *by Christian K. Wedemeyer (Columbia)*

South Asia Across the Disciplines is a series devoted to publishing first books across a wide range of South Asian studies, including art, history, philology or textual studies, philosophy, religion, and the interpretive social sciences. Series authors all share the goal of opening up new archives and suggesting new methods and approaches, while demonstrating that South Asian scholarship can be at once deep in expertise and broad in appeal.

Democracy against Development

Lower-Caste Politics and Political Modernity in Postcolonial India

JEFFREY WITSOE

THE UNIVERSITY OF CHICAGO PRESS   CHICAGO AND LONDON

JEFFREY WITSOE is assistant professor of anthropology at Union College in Schenectady, NY.

The University of Chicago Press, Chicago 60637
The University of Chicago Press, Ltd., London
© 2013 by The University of Chicago
All rights reserved. Published 2013.
Printed in the United States of America
22 21 20 19 18 17 16 15 14 13   1 2 3 4 5

ISBN-13: 978-0-226-06316-4 (cloth)
ISBN-13: 978-0-226-06347-8 (paper)
ISBN-13: 978-0-226-06350-8 (e-book)
DOI: 10.7208/chicago/9780226063508.001.0001

Library of Congress Cataloging-in-Publication Data
Witsoe, Jeffrey, author.
    Democracy against development : lower-caste politics and political modernity in
postcolonial India / Jeffrey Witsoe.
        pages cm. — (South Asia across the disciplines)
    ISBN 978-0-226-06316-4 (cloth : alkaline paper) — ISBN 978-0-226-06347-8 (paperback :
alkaline paper) — ISBN 978-0-226-06350-8 (e-book) 1. Caste—Political aspects—India—
Bihar. 2. Bihar (India)—Politics and government. I. Title. II. Series: South Asia across the
disciplines.
    DS422.C3W58 2013
    305.5'60954123—dc23

                                                                                2013008859

♾ This paper meets the requirements of ANSI/NISO Z39.48-1992 (Permanence of Paper).

To Tara

Contents

Acknowledgments

I must begin by thanking my many friends in Bihar, whose extraordinary hospitality made this research both possible and enjoyable. First and foremost, Shri P. K. Thakur, Shrimati Usha Thakur, and Sachin Shankar Thakur, without whom this work would not have even begun. I want to specially thank all of the residents of "Rajnagar" for their very warm hospitality and stimulating conversation over the years, and especially my host Jafar and his family. Sanjay Singh also provided generous hospitality. In Patna, Akhilesh Kumar's tireless assistance and dedication to research contributed substantially to this work. The Ghosh family provided warm hospitality and friendship. The Asian Development Research Institute (ADRI) has continued to be my intellectual home in Patna. I thank everyone at ADRI, P. P. Ghosh, and especially Shaibal Gupta, who taught me a great deal of what I know about politics in Bihar. I benefited from many discussions with Manoj Shrivastava in Bihar and London and with Shrikant in Patna. There are many other people in Bihar whom I don't have space to mention. Thank you, all!

The research for this book began at the University of Cambridge. I'd like to give a special acknowledgement to Susan Bayly for her guidance, insightful critique, and continued support. I thank Caroline Humphrey, Marilyn Strathern, and the participants of the writing-up seminar for their helpful feedback. I also thank Mukulika Banerjee for very helpful comments.

The Center for the Advanced Study of India at the University of Pennsylvania provided an ideal intellectual environment for the completion of the later parts of this book. Francine Frankel's in-depth feedback on several chapters shaped this book in important ways and taught me a great deal about Indian politics. I thank Devesh Kapur for his continued encouragement, support, and intellectual engagement. I also want to thank Atul Kohli for his insightful comments on parts of the book and also Mekhala Krishnamurthy.

John Harriss supported this work from the beginning. F. G. Bailey provided encouragement and wise advice. I thank my colleagues at Union College for supporting the final stages of this project. I would also like to thank the three anonymous reviewers for their insightful comments.

The following funding bodies supported this research, listed in the order received: Gates Scholarship (Gates Cambridge Trust); Smuts Research Award (Smuts Trust); Ling Roth Scholarship (Ling Roth Trust); a grant from Clare Hall, Cambridge; funding from the Center for the Advanced Study of India; and funding from Union College. Finally, I thank my family and especially my parents for supporting me throughout this remarkable journey.

Introduction

Democracy and the Politics of Caste

A political rally on April 30, 2003, drew tens of thousands of villagers to the sprawling Gandhi Maidan field in the center of Patna, the capital of Bihar, a populous state in the "Hindi belt" of north India. The event was called the "*laathi* rally," as Lalu Prasad Yadav, the charismatic president of the Rashtriya Janata Dal (RJD), then the ruling party in Bihar, called his mostly rural, lower-caste supporters to descend upon Patna bringing with them *laathis*, long bamboo sticks.[1] The rally's theme was *bhajpa bhagao, desh bachao* (get rid of the Bharatiya Janata Party [BJP] [then the leading party of the National Democratic Alliance government in Delhi] and save the country).[2]

The day of the rally was a breathtakingly chaotic scene, as mobs of activists, with many people carrying *laathis*, gathered in the capital. The vast majority of people came from villages; many were brought in buses by local leaders eager to show their support for the RJD, and Lalu Yadav in particular.[3] On my way to Patna to attend the rally, supporters desperate for free passage besieged my train at every station. Windows were smashed, and passengers were thrown out of their seats as masses of villagers flooded the coaches. The incoming traffic into Patna was so great that outgoing car traffic was stopped for two days to allow the massive influx to reach the capital unimpeded. Patna was completely overrun. Most shopkeepers closed their doors for fear of looting; hordes of wandering, *laathi*-wielding rallygoers blocked traffic; college students were thrown out of their hostels and their rooms occupied; and Gandhi Maidan was a sea of people, *laathis* in hand.[4]

The *laathi* was endowed with a multifaceted political symbolism reflecting the RJD's political project. The *laathi* is a quintessentially rural implement used for cow and buffalo herding, carrying an additional reference to Gandhi's walking staff.[5] "The so-called modern people have ridiculed and treated with contempt such weapons of the downtrodden as *laathi*," Lalu Yadav said before the rally.[6] The massive presence of this simple tool was an image of villagers temporarily overtaking the urban capital, demonstrating where the real source of political power in Bihar was now located.

The Vishwa Hindu Parishad, an extreme Hindu nationalist organization, had been distributing *trishals*—a three-pronged ritual implement with strong Hindu symbolic association—at their rallies, and Lalu Yadav declared in his speech that the *laathi* would destroy such "*trishals* of hatred." Supporters were told to strengthen their *laathis* by applying oil and reciting the slogan *laathi piyavan, patna lavan, bhajpa hatavan, desh bachavan* (we will oil our *laathis*, bring them to Patna, remove the BJP, and save the country), emphasizing a symbolic militancy directed against Hindu nationalism.[7]

The *laathi* is also a favored instrument of the police, who employ "*laathi* charges" in order to disperse riotous crowds. During the *laathi* rally, however, the crowds were themselves armed with *laathis*, mocking the police who watched from a safe distance, visibly uncomfortable. By using the *laathi* in such a provocative manner, the RJD activists were effectively saying, "We are the state."[8]

The *laathi* rally highlighted a long-standing tension in India between a politics of agitation and mass participation that emerged during the nationalist movement and a national project of development emphasizing public order and discipline that predominated in the decades after independence (Chakrabarty 2007). A debate in the Indian media about the desirability of huge rallies followed the Patna event. If the symbolism and participatory composition of the *laathi* rally itself told the story of Lalu Yadav's RJD, the critique of the rally characterized its opposition. The debate pitted the caste empowerment and political participation that the rally expressed against the chaos and disruption to Patna's urban population, as well as the cost of such an endeavor.[9] To draw supporters, many state legislators had arranged wild and expensive parties, some even bringing entertainers and "dancing girls" from Bombay. For the national media and Patna's middle-class residents, the *laathi* rally was an example of how excessive "politicization" had destabilized Bihar, halting development and creating lawlessness—politicians' preoccupation with such the-

atrical displays being the explanation for the lack of attention to administration and a more constructive issue-based politics.

Indeed, during the period of RJD rule, Bihar was widely considered
to be the worst-governed state in India. For part of this period (1997 and
1998), Lalu Yadav was in prison on corruption charges, continuing to effectively rule the state by cell phone after his wife was installed as chief
minister. At the same time, criminality exploded, including a large and
lucrative kidnapping industry. Between 1992 and 2005, thirty thousand
kidnappings for ransom were reported.[10] Yet even with the Bihar government's dismal performance on so many fronts, Lalu Yadav, and later
his wife, Rabri Devi, served as the chief ministers of three consecutive
state governments in 1990, 1995, and 2000, a remarkable achievement in
India where governments are routinely voted out of power for poor performance (referred to in India as the "anti-incumbency factor"). How did
the RJD manage to stay in power for so long?

The RJD government's widespread support, despite its extreme and
very visible shortcomings, reveals the centrality that a politics of lower-
caste empowerment came to occupy within Bihar's political world. Issues
concerning development, or even "law and order," were marginalized as
demands for caste-based "social justice" took prominence. For the RJD's
lower-caste supporters the *laathi* rally justified itself, serving as a practical
affirmation that they had captured the state and were now in power. And
they considered this to be the true aim of democratic politics.

Postcolonial Democracy

In this book, I examine lower-caste politics in Bihar, combining a historical analysis of the colonial and postcolonial roots of the politics of
caste with an ethnographic account based on more than three years of
fieldwork, which documents the operations of lower-caste politics at
multiple levels—in the village, in regional sites, and in the often violent
political world of the state capital. This multisited approach allows me
to draw connections between contexts—the village with larger networks
of actors, contemporary political practice with longer histories, and the
drama of state-level party politics with everyday struggles within local
sites. In doing so, I build on previous anthropological studies on the relationship between caste and democracy.[11] Whereas these studies have
taught us a great deal about the ways in which democracy has impacted

the experience of caste within village contexts (especially in the two decades after independence) and the role of late colonialism and postcolonial democracy in shaping modern caste identities, there has been much
less work in the opposite direction, that is, explorations of the ways in
which the politics of caste has shaped India's democracy. This is especially
true for the lower-caste politics that emerged with force during the 1990s.

My examination of the role of caste in shaping India's political modernity provides a framework for understanding many of the dynamics of the "world's largest democracy" that, I suggest, is also relevant for
understanding democratization in postcolonial contexts more generally.
This is an especially important enterprise considering that accompanying
the global expansion of democracy today are secular economic and geo-
political shifts that are likely resulting in a decline of American and European global dominance. If this global shift means that Europe and the
United States are in the process of being "provincialized" (Chakrabarty
1999, Knauft 2007), then the Euro-American model of liberal democracy
may also be undergoing such a process. This decline of "the West," combined with the growing awareness that democracy in much of the world
is not playing out according to liberal assumptions, means that we should
seriously explore alternative ways for understanding democracy in the
twenty-first century that go beyond the liberal democratic framework.

India is arguably the most important and instructive case of postcolonial democracy today because of its sheer size and growing global clout,
but also because of its distinct democratic experience. India's democracy
has proven remarkably resilient, especially compared with other parts of
the postcolonial world (Kohli 2001). This is despite India's being perhaps
the least likely place for democracy to take root according to standard
democratic theory, which has regarded India as an extremely large "exception." At the time of independence, India had a small middle class, a
dizzyingly heterogeneous mix of linguistic, religious, and caste-based identities, low levels of basic education, and pervasive poverty. But despite
predictions of democratic collapse, regular elections have been held,[12]
monitored by an independent election commission and often resulting in
unexpected outcomes that are nevertheless followed by peaceful transitions. India has a civilian-controlled military that does not politically in-
terfere, and, perhaps most important, and in stark contrast to Western democracies, participation among historically oppressed groups has steadily
increased (Yadav 1997). Unlike the regime transitions and periodic, and
often partial, experiments with democracy that have occurred in many

other parts of the postcolonial world, India has experienced six decades of electoral democracy, providing the temporal continuity for democratic practices to become deeply engrained in everyday life. Consequently, few people in India today think of democracy as an import. And because most new democracies are now in the postcolonial world, and most citizens living in democracies are located in postcolonial countries, India offers important lessons for understanding the present and future of democracy in much of the world.

"Liberal democracy" combines a liberalism based on individual rights with a much older and subversive concept of democracy as "rule of the people" that in fact represents "a contingent historical articulation" (Mouffe 1993, 2–3).[13] And as the political theorist Ernesto Laclau (2005, 167) observes, "Once the articulation between liberalism and democracy is considered as merely contingent ... other contingent articulations are possible, so that there are forms of democracy outside the liberal symbolic framework." Recent anthropological research has richly documented the variations of democracy in different contexts.[14] Indian realities have shaped democracy, resulting in distinct forms of democratic experience. As Micheluti (2008) demonstrates, democracy in India has been "indigenized" in relation to caste, with members of the Yadav caste, for instance, viewing themselves as a "caste of politicians," and their patron deity Krishna as the "originator of democracy."

To explain the drivers of democratic difference in India, I emphasize the importance of processes of state formation in shaping political culture (Corrigan and Sayer 1985, Joseph and Nugent 1994). David Nugent (2008), in an insightful examination of democracy in the Chachapoyas region of Peru, shows how processes of state formation that differ greatly from those that produced Western European democracies produced an "alternate" democracy. He demonstrates that examining divergent processes of state formation serves as a powerful window into understanding historically conditioned democratic difference.

Building on this work, I argue that the specificities of colonialism need to be given prominence. If, as Nugent suggests, divergent processes of state formation have resulted in the emergence of "alternate" democracies, we would expect histories of colonial rule to produce distinct democratic trajectories because the colonial project entailed the construction of very particular types of state institutions, political alliances, and forms of knowledge. Postcolonial democracies, therefore, require different frameworks of analysis—they cannot be situated along a temporal, developmental trajectory, as "advanced" versus "emerging" democracies or even as "transitional" democracies, where the implied transition is to the liberal variety (see Chatterjee 2011, 21–26). But it is also important not to push the idea of culturally driven democratic difference too far—the flawed idea of democracy as an unfolding universal should not be replaced with a cultural relativist vision of India as its own incommensurate democratic universe (even if it may seem such at times). It is instructive here to consider Fredric Jameson's (2002) critique of the notion of "alternate modernities" as obfuscating the subaltern positions produced by global capitalism by suggesting that "everyone can have their own modernity." Not only are democratic ideas and institutions appropriated and deployed in culturally specific ways, but, as I shall demonstrate, democratic possibilities are shaped by colonial encounters and their aftermath, encounters that often introduced these concepts and institutions in the first place. And if, as I argue, processes of state formation are the key to understanding democratic difference (Nugent 2008) and, as Wallerstein (1974, 402–403) has pointed out, these processes can be shown to at least partly reflect relative positioning within the "world system," then the operations of global capitalism also inevitably shape democratic difference. India's postindependence regime of import-substituting industrialization produced very different democratic possibilities than the era of structural adjustment and liberalization from 1991, and India's growing global clout in the twenty-first century is likely resulting in new democratic potentials (and limitations).

This does not, of course, imply that all postcolonial democracies are the same, or even that regions within India are the same; each is shaped by the interaction between specific colonial regimes, longer histories that predate colonialism, the particular dynamics of independence movements, and the contingencies of postcolonial political economy (Sivaramakrishnan and Agrawal 2003), but in each case contemporary democracies that experienced colonial domination may be meaningfully described as "postcolonial." Partha Chatterjee (2004, 36–37) emphasizes the impact of colonial processes of state formation on Indian democracy, noting that formal citizenship based on popular sovereignty came a century and a half after the classification, description, and enumeration of population groups had been established by a powerful administrative apparatus that continued, and even expanded, after independence in the name of a national project of development. This leads Chatterjee (2004, 2011) to describe postcolonial democracy as a "politics of the governed," contrasting what he calls "political society" with an elite-inhabited "civil society" composed of the formal legal-constitutional structure of which every citizen is in theory a member but that he argues is quite different from the realities of political life in postcolonial contexts. "Political society" operates in the interstices of governmentality, with subaltern groups manipulating governmental practices and categorizations, often in disregard of the formal legal system, to gain access to development resources and secure their often precarious positions. For instance, while movements of largely middle-class activists seeking to bridge this divide resulted in rights-based legislation in recent years endowing every Indian citizen with the right to work (2005), access to information (2005), education (2009), and food (2012), in practice these rights still often have to be secured through negotiation and struggle within political society (Harriss 2011). If "civil society" refers to the abstract ideals of liberal citizenship, then, in practice the heterogeneity of "political society" is where these ideals are actualized, or subverted, according to everyday political struggle.

I find Chatterjee's formulation to be a useful way to destabilize liberal assumptions, emphasizing the ways in which everyday political life in India—or, as Chatterjee puts it, "most of the world"—diverges from the liberal democratic normative framework, compelling us to "redefine the normative standards of modern politics in the light of the considerable accumulation of new practices that may at the present only be described in the language of exceptions but which in fact contain the core of a richer, more diverse, and inclusive set of norms" (Chatterjee 2011, 22). But Chatterjee's "political society" remains a passive category—it is a "politics of the governed" with similarities to older models of clientelism (see below). As Chatterjee (2011, 148) puts it, "Political society does not offer a transformational narrative threatening the course of capitalist development. It is not a concept of revolutionary politics." I will argue, in contrast, for the need to politicize the concept of "political society," in the sense of recognizing the potential of postcolonial democracy to be an active agent. And in Bihar, democracy did come into direct conflict with capitalist development, not just through dramatic events like the *laathi* rally, but through the very types of everyday politics that Chatterjee emphasizes (Chatterjee 2011, 149).

The recognition that democracy emerges in specific forms in postcolonial contexts, therefore, has to go beyond an emphasis on the constraints that this imposes. A positive theorization of postcolonial democracy is needed; therefore, my analysis has two parts—an elaboration of the ways in which colonial and postcolonial processes of state formation have shaped the context within which democracy plays out, and an examination of the ways in which democracy, as idea and practice, has transformed this context over time. Although India's postcolonial status has shaped the dynamics of Indian democracy, democratization is simultaneously transforming India's postcolonial context. In the following section, I outline the ways in which my analysis differs from conventional explanations of caste politics, which will delineate some of the advantages of this approach.

Understanding Lower-Caste Politics

Lower-caste politics is usually explained in two ways, both of which, I suggest, are insufficient. Endless editorializing in the Indian national media treats caste politics as the product of the polluting influence of irrational identities seen as vestiges of tradition and "backwardness" that reflect widespread illiteracy, ignorance, and political immaturity. But as this study and many others make abundantly clear, caste as political identity is a thoroughly modern phenomenon, shaped by colonialism, the postcolonial state, and democratic practice.

More sophisticated academic analyses have usually interpreted the rise of caste-based political mobilizations to be an interest-driven politics seeking access to the economic resources of an expansive public sector. Bardhan (2001, 233) writes, "As the expansion of the public sector over the years created more opportunities for secure jobs and, not infrequently, for the associated extra elicit income if the job is in some regulatory capacity, more and more mobilized groups in the democratic process have started using their low-caste status for making a claim to the loot." Brass (1990,19–20) situates caste politics as part of "an all-pervasive instrumentalism which washes away party manifestos, rhetoric, and effective implementation of policies in an unending competition for power, status, and profit.... India has adopted the model of the state which exists for its own sake."[15] In a similar vein, Chandra (2004) terms democracy in India as a "patronage democracy" wherein politicians use their discretionary control over state resources to trade votes for development resources through caste-based "vote blocks." Chhibber (1999) argues that, in the context of an "activist state" and the absence of strong "associational life," electoral strategy and competition explain the emergence of caste-based parties in India. Although these are, of course, very different works, they all suggest that the centrality of caste in Indian political life results from interest-oriented politicians or voters seeking control over an expansive state.[16]

The works cited above certainly do capture important aspects of Indian political life, but we have to ask whether there is more to the politics of lower-caste empowerment than political manipulation and "looting the state." In fact, just as neoliberal reform began to shrink the public sector after 1991, the rise of lower-caste politics intensified. By the early 1990s, Congress one-party rule had ended amid a proliferation of caste and ethnicity-based regional parties (Corbridge and Harriss 2000). In stark contrast with many liberal democracies, in which the poor and marginalized are less likely to vote, popular participation in the electoral process surged in north India during the late 1980s, especially among people from lower-caste backgrounds as well as among those in rural areas—a phenomenon that Yogendra Yadav (2000) has termed the "second democratic upsurge."[17] This upsurge in lower-caste voting turnout coincided with a progressive increase in the number of members of state legislative assemblies and members of the national parliament from lower-caste backgrounds. A political watershed occurred when V. P. Singh (prime minister under the National Front government that was elected in 1989—then only the second non-Congress government in Delhi since independence) decided to implement the recommendations of the Mandal Commission. This commission, headed by B. P. Mandal, former chief minister of Bihar, recommended reserving a portion of central government employment for what the Indian Constitution designates as "Other Backward Classes" (OBCs), an intentionally broad category that includes lower castes that did not suffer from a history of untouchablity. (The constitution has mandated employment reservations for the latter, as well as for the "Scheduled Tribes," since 1950.) This policy implementation had an explosive political impact marked by violent protests, including a number of self-immolations by upper-caste students, as well as an ensuing upsurge of lower-caste political mobilization.[18] By the mid-1990s, OBC politicians dominated the state assemblies in north India, especially in what were then the two most populous states, Uttar Pradesh and Bihar.[19]

Jaffrelot (2003) has gone so far as to refer to this upsurge of lower-caste politics—following V. P. Singh's apt expression—as a "silent revolution" in north India.[20] Likewise, Hansen (1999) argues for the need to adopt a "radical Tocquevillian framework" in order to understand recent democratic experience in India.[21] If these scholars have suggested that something revolutionary has taken place, the actual dynamics of this process have remained something of a mystery, which is perhaps why the more radical aspects of lower-caste politics have not adequately informed recent theorization of Indian democracy. This is all the more striking considering that prominent earlier work, such as Rajni Kothari's (1970) *Caste in Indian Politics* and the Rudolphs' (1967) *The Modernity of Tradition*, demonstrated the ways in which caste identities became the basis for new relationships between recently enfranchised voters and an independent, democratic Indian state that, particularly for Kothari, had clearly radical implications.

Throughout this book, I seek to demonstrate that democracy in Bihar operates according to dynamics that cannot be understood by focusing either on abstract identities (detached from structures of power) or the abstract interests of individual voters, politicians, or parties. Rather, I argue that we need to take account of processes of state formation that produced structures of power and identity (the two being linked) within which a caste-based politics made sense to most people. I show the ways in which colonial and then postcolonial strategies of governance resulted in the emergence of caste networks that continue to link state institutions with locally powerful groups, producing a state unable to impartially deliver services or enforce individual rights. This is the crucial context within which the instrumentality and corruption often associated with caste politics play out. But I also illustrate the ways in which lower-caste politics challenged this mode of governance, not by attempting to reform a corrupt "system," but by systematically weakening state institutions and development activities controlled by upper castes and, when possible, by openly and unapologetically using corrupt practices to turn the tables on upper castes that had long done the same more discreetly (disguised with the rhetoric of development). The result was a political movement positioned against development.

The next section briefly sketches my framework for understanding lower-caste politics and the implications that follow for understanding India's democracy.

Lower-Caste Politics and India's Postcolonial Democracy

The legacy of colonialism has shaped the contemporary experience of democracy in crucial ways, which is very clear in the case of the politics of caste.[22] A substantial body of literature has explored the ways in which colonial strategies of governance shaped caste identities. The Raj utilized caste to categorize, rank, criminalize, recruit, and divide—in short, to govern—colonial subjects (Cohn 1987a, Dirks 2001). Caste was, therefore, central to colonial "governmentality" (Foucault 1977) and to the government's increasing endeavors to survey, manage, and regulate the "population" under its control (a process that accelerated after the British government took formal control of India in the mid-nineteenth century). This history goes a long way in explaining why caste remains so central to political life in contemporary India, as we shall see in the next chapter. Notions of democratic rights took on specific meanings that reflect the ways in which power was structured. As Thomas Hansen (1999) puts it, "Because the paramount issue governing the political field in colonial India was (limited) representation of communities through elite representation, and because colonial governmentality had authorized community as the natural oriental form, the discourse of rights and equality was applied almost entirely to collectivities."[23]

Another body of historical research has shown the ways in which the Raj shaped agrarian relations through the introduction of systems of land tenure intended to prop up colonial rule and facilitate a cost-effective means of governance through the intermediation of a class of rural elites. Yang (1989), for example, describes colonial Bihar as a "limited Raj" wherein powerful *zamindars* (landlords) had almost complete control over the villages wherein they had the right to collect revenue. The vast majority of *zamindars* were upper castes, although a handful of middle castes were present as well.

Once these two aspects of colonial governance are considered together, the political implications of caste become clear. The Raj utilized caste as the glue to connect the two spheres of agrarian relations and governmental institutions—members of dominant castes were given not only effective control over their villages, but also privileged access to, and support from, governmental institutions (as long as they were perceived as being loyal allies to the Raj). Categorized groups were not passively manipulated, but actively forged new caste identities and networks in struggles to advance their relative positions within this new context, an endeavor in which dominant groups had clear advantages. The result was a distinct form of governance combining bureaucratic institutions with more direct forms of dominance in village contexts that perpetuated the control of powerful groups in the countryside, which has continued long after independence. Caste-based networks integrated state institutions with relations of dominance and subordination in local sites.

These networks, although of crucial importance to contemporary political practice, have received little scholarly attention. As we shall see, caste networks today are made up of politicians who operate within the sphere of institutional politics while simultaneously engaging in very different activities within their constituencies, corrupt bureaucrats, police officers and other government employees, "mafia" figures, and political brokers who have relationships with this cast of characters as well as with local elites (see Corbridge et al. 2005, 192–206).

I first realized the practical importance of caste networks while observing Akhilesh, my research assistant, use his Rajput caste network to locate a contact (often a distant relative or friend of a relative) in virtually every government department from which we needed access, as well as in many villages near Rajnagar, my primary research village. In part because Akhilesh's distinct caste network allied him with specific individuals and groups, I was compelled always to work alone within the politically charged context of the village. The pervasive influence of caste networks explains why in getting a job or a loan, interacting with the police, dealing with mafia figures, interacting with or negotiating a bribe with a government official, or even renting a flat or commercial space in the capital, caste mattered. It is no coincidence that government offices, apartment complexes, colleges, shopping complexes, and criminal networks in Bihar were often populated with people sharing similar caste backgrounds.

Although relationships between politicians and shadowy power brokers are, of course, a common characteristic of democracies everywhere, the distinctiveness here is that these networks are organized in relation to caste, and that they connect state institutions with local relations of dominance and subordination. The violence that accompanies elections in many parts of India, nowhere more so than Bihar during the period of this study, serves as a regular demonstration of the interpenetration of institutional politics and struggles over local dominance.[24]

On the one hand, then, politics involves the institutional politics that is the focus of most analysis and media attention, revolving around politicians who hold elected office, the leadership of political parties, the negotiations of larger political coalitions, and legislative proceedings. On the other hand, pervasive relations of dominance and subordination and routine acts of violence operate according to very different logics and are generally hidden from public view outside of the specific sites where dominance is exercised. Chatterjee (2004) captures such a distinction with his contrast between "political society" and "civil society" discussed above. Caste was central both to the colonial argument that a civil society based on liberal citizenship was impossible in India and to the emergence of a postcolonial political society that deviates from constitutional norms. As Dirks (2001, 16) points out, "Caste has moved from its place as a colonial substitute for civil society (or, in Chatterjee's terms, the colonial argument for why civil society could not grow in India) to a new position as a specifically postcolonial version of political society." In fact, these two domains only appear separate from the outside (where their relationship is viewed as deviation and corruption); for the vast majority of voters, the linkages between governmental institutions and local power are self-evident. "Corruption" is the rule, not the exception.[25] Examining the relationships between these two spheres in practice provides a key window into the dynamics of Indian democracy, not because this division corresponds to reality, but because demonstrating the interpenetration of institutional politics and local power destabilizes any pretence of the former's autonomy and renders visible modes of governance that stretch across this artificial divide, which, I suggest, is exactly how most people in India perceive things (for an elaboration on this point, see Witsoe 2011).[26] The interconnectedness of these two spheres has several important implications for democracy in Bihar, which I elaborate throughout this book and briefly sketch here.

First, state institutions that are autonomous from local power, as assumed by almost all democratic theorists, do not exist. Rather, postcolonial modes of governance interweave the operation of state institutions with the dominance of local groups. Such pervasively "blurred boundaries" (Gupta 1995) between "state" and "society" have been extensively ethnographically documented in India and many other postcolonial contexts.[27] This also explains the observed disjuncture between higher levels of the bureaucracy, such as the professional Indian Administrative Service, and lower levels, where effective implementation is often subverted (Kaviraj 1997, 52–53). Within such a context, democracy cannot simply be about electing leaders who represent their constituents by reflecting their interests in policy formulation and legislation. There is no impartial state apparatus capable of effectively implementing policy changes. Consequently, politics in India, and especially in Bihar, is rarely about "constructive" policy debates, but revolves instead around the naked exercise of power, and, contrary to the moralizing in English-language newspaper editorials, this is not primarily because of an uneducated citizenry who are fooled by self-serving, corrupt politicians, but because policy debates are meaningless without state institutions capable of delivering.

Furthermore, this interpenetration of institutional politics and local power changes the meanings and implications of elections and of democratic "representation." Because the practice of party politics is intertwined with relations of dominance and subordination in local sites, representation is not primarily about "representing" constituents' interests through legislation or policy formulation (which both assume institutions capable of effective implementation), but about determining the very contours of regional and local power. Elections are therefore not simply a matter of citizens choosing their leaders, as in Schumpeter's (1976) well-known model, but are also an important factor in determining which groups control village and regional territorial spaces, a dynamic highlighted by the prevalence of "mafia" politicians in Bihar.

The very character of Indian democracy is impacted as the rights at the heart of the "liberalism" of liberal democracy require not only a constitutional mandate, but also state institutions capable of enforcing this mandate. What happens, however, if state institutions lack the capacity, or the will, to enforce liberal rights in anything resembling an impartial manner, rendering rights relatively impotent? As Chatterjee (2004, 38) starkly puts it, "Most of the inhabitants of India are only tenuously, and only then ambiguously and contextually, rights-bearing citizens in the sense imagined by the constitution." Rights, such as freedom of speech, of assembly, and, of course, to vote, do constitute the basic institutional infrastructure that makes party politics possible (the *laathi* rally, for example, would have been impossible without such rights). These rights, however, largely exist outside of local contexts. In countless Bihar villages, many people did not enjoy freedom of speech, assembly, or even a free vote, especially before the 1990s.

Within such a context, any actualization of democratic aspirations required a transformation of power at the local level where rights are routinely violated. I suggest that, within such an environment, two very different political possibilities have emerged, neither of which approximates the liberal democratic vision of individual citizens voting on the basis of ideology or policy preferences. One response to the realities of postcolonial democracy is for an enlightened leadership to claim to transcend local political limitations and seek to transform society through top-down state intervention, often despite the corruption of their own parties. This project reached its pinnacle at the national level under Indira Gandhi, but it is increasingly playing out at the state level as well. Even when voters demand development—as they did in the 2005 and 2010 elections in Bihar—this does not involve a public debate of policy issues. Rather, voters judged whom they considered to be a better "Vikas Purush" (man of development), and they voted for state-directed development as embodied in an individual who promised to overcome political limitations by centralizing power at the top in an attempt to overcome the structures of dominance below.

The second possibility, and the one examined at length in this book, is for political leaders to attempt to transform oppressive power structures through actualizing the principle of popular sovereignty—to translate the electoral force of numbers into structures of governance that represent the interests of the lower-caste majority. Dipesh Chakrabarty (1999) observes that for most people inhabiting postcolonial India, liberal citizenship is perpetually deferred until they are "developed" into proper citizens. But he also notes another moment where the subaltern is always already a citizen and where citizenship is not endowed through individual rights but enacted through democratic performance, above all the act of voting. "The question is: how do we *think* the political at these moments when the peasant or the subaltern emerges in the modern sphere of politics, in his or her own right" (2000, 10). Although it can be asked whether the "subaltern can speak" (Spivak 1988) within dominant discourses, she can, and most certainly does, vote. This is why, as Mukulika Banerjee (2008) observes, voting in India takes on a festive, almost sacred ethos, a vivid demonstration of the privileging of the logic of popular sovereignty in Indian democracy.[28] It is the act of voting, then—or, more broadly, the entire constellation of practices, organizations, and actors related to party politics and the electoral process—wherein equal citizenship becomes a meaningful reality for most people. In Bihar, popular sovereignty has in practice meant the rule of caste groups, or alliances of caste groups, as determined through the electoral process. This responds to the structures of dominance discussed above, but adds what the democratic theorist Claude Lefort (1988) referred to as the "radical indeterminacy" of an often unpredictable democratic process and, therefore, corresponds to at least a partial displacement of hierarchy within public life in favor of new representations of caste as "discreet groups in competition" (Gupta 2000; see also Tanabe 2007).

Postcolonial Democracy and Hegemonic Practice

The "radical indeterminacy" (Lefort 1988) of democratic practice means that, while a focus on processes of colonial/postcolonial state formation

is essential for understanding the context within which postcolonial democracy operates, it is insufficient for understanding the ways in which
democratic practice transforms this context over time. In other words,
the colonial legacy shapes India's postcolonial democracy in ways that
should not be ignored, but it does not predetermine democratic outcomes.
I, therefore, find it useful to combine the focus on state formation detailed above with an emphasis on hegemonic practice (Laclau and Mouffe
1985). Antonio Gramsci's (1971) well-known concept of hegemony contains two related, but distinct meanings, which were meant to explain both
why revolution had not occurred in postwar Europe and also how a revolutionary party could further its aims within contemporary political systems. The first meaning of hegemony, originally drawn from Lenin, refers
to the structure of class alliances, the complex of interests and identities
that enable the "ruling classes" to avoid dissent by co-opting the privileged sections of other classes, as well as the potential counter-hegemony
of the proletariat, wherein the urban proletariat serves as the vanguard
for a movement including peasants and the urban poor. The second meaning of hegemony emphasizes the ability of the ruling classes to utilize the
state to co-opt popular culture for the culture of the ruling classes (see,
for instance, Hall 1986), thereby wining the subtle consent of the governed. This "cultural hegemony," while drawing its repertoire of symbols
and discourses from a larger cultural matrix, is actively reworked into a
buttress for established power (Comaroff and Comaroff 1991). Gramsci's
assertion was that subaltern classes should combat this process through
forging their own hegemony, again referring to both an alliance of groups,
interests, and identities, but also to a cultural practice that would coun-
teract dominant discourses and allow people to imagine alternatives to
an oppressive social order.[29] The concept of hegemony—especially as developed by Laclau and Mouffe, who stress the indeterminacy of social life
and, therefore, the constructed nature of political formations that cannot
be reduced to preexisting structures or classes—allows us to appreciate
how democratic movements, articulated in culturally specific forms, can
alter, or even displace, governing alliances, and how this relates to the articulation of new identities and discourses.

My framework combines examination of democracy as hegemonic
practice with an emphasis on the postcolonial, a combination that necessarily transforms both concepts. Such an approach alters our understanding of the colonial legacy, enabling recognition of processes of democratic
change that are significantly modifying colonially shaped structures of

power, identity, and discourse. An awareness of colonial processes of state formation, on the other hand, modifies the concept of hegemonic practice to emphasize the interconnections between identities and discourse, state institutions, and local power. For instance, Laclau and Mouffe's (1985) insistence on defining "hegemonic articulations" exclusively in terms of "discourse"—a useful approach for understanding "new social movements" in advanced-capitalist democracies—cannot capture the complex relationships between caste identities, state institutions, and local dominance—often backed by recourse to a very material violence—that is central to the practice of democracy in India.

It is useful here to consider Ranajit Guha's (1996) argument that colonialism entailed "dominance without hegemony," resulting in a sphere of popular politics with a logic other than that of hegemony—that of dominance and subordination. This is precisely the division underlying the Subaltern Studies project that Chatterjee (2004, 2011) takes into the postcolonial period with his distinction between an elite "civil society" and the "political society" of the majority discussed above. While I would suggest that processes of state formation in India have resulted in a fusing of these two spheres—a progressive interpenetration of local sites wherein territorial dominance is central and the institutions of the Indian state—the conceptual distinction remains important. Of course, Gramsci, like all Marxist theorists, stressed that hegemony coexists with very real and material forces of repression, that hegemony is "an outer ditch, behind which there stands a powerful system of fortresses and earthworks" (Gramsci 1971, 447), and that hegemonic practice represents a "war of position," that would eventually lead to the direct military frontal assaults of a "war of maneuver." Force and consent, violence and hegemony, are in this way bound together. But the "war of maneuver" in India is not just a separate phase of action, as undertaken, say, in the brazen attacks of Maoists, and violence and repression are not just foundational, embodied in the "violence of law" (Benjamin 1973) and the implicit repressive military forces of the state, but are part of the everyday practice of democratic politics. This is reflected in the open and competitive use of deadly violence during elections in Bihar, but also in the myriads of struggles over dominance and subordination that accompany everyday political practice.

Postcolonial hegemony, therefore, has to be taken as fluid, subject to political change, but also limited or, if you will, hybrid. The alliances and identities active in larger-level democratic practice only make sense when "plugged in" to local struggles that have their own logic. Likewise, ruling regimes may exercise hegemony through a dominant discourse, but this is only part of the story; within specific sites, power is rooted in relations of dominance and subordination backed by violence and the threat of violence. On one level, it is as if democracy were superimposed on colonial modes of governance, as if popular sovereignty were fused with a colonial sovereignty (Mbembe 2001) that is still operative within local sites. What I seek to show in this study, however, are the ways in which these very different political logics have transformed each other, resulting in what I refer to as postcolonial democracy.

But we must go further and guard against naturalizing a false dichotomy (O'Hanlon 1988), in the process failing to take account of multiple, overlapping structures of power resulting from long histories of state formation. As I argue in the next chapter, there have been very different uses of caste as a modality of governance in the colonial and postcolonial periods, and all of these forms of caste continue to shape political life. It is not just that state policy is frustrated by the realities of local power, then, but also by translocal caste identities and caste networks that reach the highest levels of government. An analysis of an election, a development project, or a popular movement will likely reveal a complex and contingent interweaving of all of these very different configurations of power and identity.

This argument implies that certain forms of knowledge may not be as hegemonic as often assumed. Take the "discourse" of development. Scholars such as James Ferguson (1990) and Arthuro Escobar (1995) assert that development is an almost universal concept, noting that even when development is challenged, it is usually done in the name of an "alternative" or "real" development. Escobar (1995, 5) writes, "Development had achieved the status of certainty in the social imaginary. Indeed, it seemed impossible to conceptualize social reality in other terms.... Reality, in sum, had been colonized by the development discourse." As Chatterjee (1993, 121) has noted, the ideology of planned development was central to the legitimization of the postcolonial state in India, justifying the expansion of the very administrative apparatus that the anticolonial struggle had been contesting. And Gupta (1998) argues that the internalization of development discourse is at the heart of the "postcolonial condition" in modern India.

In Bihar during RJD rule, however, the very concept of development was relegated to the sidelines, making Lalu Yadav's Bihar something of a spontaneous experiment in "post-development" (Escobar 1992). I often heard the question repeated in politicians'as speeches, "Development for whom and for what?" A popular slogan during the early years of RJD rule, *vikash nehi, sammaan chahie* (we need dignity, not development), expresses such a temperament, and Lalu Yadav himself is reported to have referred to development as a "foreign and polluted concept."[30] Lalu Yadav's democratic insurgency succeeded in simultaneously displacing not only upper-caste hegemony, but also the discourse of development. A similar story can be told about liberalism (regardless of India's vocally liberal national elites), and even the influence of print and televised media (which Lalu Yadav regarded as politically inconsequential and routinely antagonized).

The rise of "populist" lower-caste leaders in Bihar and other parts of India reflected the penetration of democracy that privileged a disruptive conception of popular sovereignty, wherein "the people" are contrasted with an elite minority. But the identity of "the people" is not a given; it must be politically articulated (Laclau 2005, 167; see also Paley 2008, 10). And this articulation will inevitably be influenced by the ways in which power is structured. Since the hegemony of an elite minority had long been predicated on caste as ideology (the Brahmanical "caste system" that gained increased salience during the colonial period), as caste-based patronage networks that emerged from the late colonial period, as castes conceived as homogenous, deterritorialized communities that emerged as central categories within colonial strategies of governance, and as dominant caste lineages whose localized power was consolidated by the colonial state's "limited Raj" (Yang 1989), it is not surprising that counter-hegemonic movements interpreted democracy to mean rule by the lower-caste majority. Since caste impacts the everyday experience of inequality, the politics of caste involves everything from issues of honor and dignity to relations of production, control of regional economic activity, and access to public employment and development resources. For most people in Bihar, therefore, democratic practice is not something reserved for professional politicians (although we shall see that they have important roles), nor just a matter of periodic voting; democracy relates to peoples' immediate social milieu, to the households nearby that have held power over them, their parents and grandparents, to issues that are simultaneously economic, political, and social.

Most theorization of radical democratic movements has emphasized their exteriority from party politics and the state (for example, Escobar 1992, Touraine 1981). Lower-caste politics, in contrast, mobilized almost

exclusively through political parties and pursued a one-pointed program
focused on capturing state power.[31] Considering the hybrid nature of postcolonial hegemony outlined above, this makes perfect sense: the everyday
practices of state institutions are a constituent part of the structuring of
local power that counter-hegemonic movements cannot ignore. Although
lower-caste politics did not approach the state as an external force, it did
wage an assault on state institutions seen as controlled by upper castes.
Lower-caste leaders democratically captured the state in order to systematically weaken it. Lalu Yadav, after becoming chief minister in 1990,
created a formidable coalition of lower-caste and Muslim supporters
who perceived themselves as struggling against an "upper-caste system,"
and his government sought to weaken the institutions of this "system" as
much as appropriate state resources. The result was not only a change in
the social backgrounds of those appropriating state resources, and the instability and breakdown of development-oriented governance that have
been so often commented on, but also a transformation of power relations within myriads of sites, including the rural economy. This is also why,
in addition to the collapse of development-oriented governance and "law
and order," lower-caste politics was a catalyst for democratic change that
is little understood, displacing upper-caste hegemony in myriads of contexts and transforming everyday life.

This does not, however, mean that demands for development ceased.
I shall suggest, rather, that political life in India can be usefully conceived
of as a creative tension between a "politics of the governed" (Chatterjee
2004) revolving around the project of state-directed development and a
populist politics of caste-based democratic empowerment.[32] The tension
between these two projects is not static or simply confrontational (as the
book's title could be incorrectly taken to imply), but, when viewed over
the long term, is part of a process of democratization that is a definitive
characteristic of India's postcolonial democracy.

Book Outline

The material presented is drawn entirely from the populous north Indian
state of Bihar, where lower-caste politics had arguably the most intense
impact. I have restricted my focus to one state because lower-caste politics, unlike Hindu nationalism or the long history of the Congress, did
not manifest as a national movement, but rather through regional parties

(such as the Rashtriya Janata Dal in Bihar and the Samajwadi Party and Bahujan Samaj Party in Uttar Pradesh) whose electoral successes have been almost entirely confined to a single state. Bihar is overwhelmingly rural (90 percent), with the lowest literacy rate (47 percent) among Indian states, the highest concentration of poverty, intense and brutal inequalities, and what is widely perceived to be rampant corruption. Although Bihar is in many ways an extreme case, many factors—the history of colonial exploitation, caste dominance, and an enormous rural hinterland—exist to various degrees across India, playing out in regionally specific ways where histories of colonial rule vary significantly, intersecting with other regionally specific factors to produce unique political worlds (Sivaramakrishnan and Agrawal 2003).[33] Bihar is also significant because of its sheer size (a population of more than one hundred million) and its similarities with its even more populous neighbor, Uttar Pradesh. The two states have a combined population of more than three hundred million and are home to one in four Indians. By examining how democracy has become so embedded in everyday life in Bihar, we will be able to gain important insights into the dynamics of Indian democracy.

In Chapter 1, I begin with a historical account of movements for caste empowerment that are crucial for understanding lower-caste politics in contemporary India, revealing why caste identities became so important to democratic practice. Chapter 2 turns to the political project of caste-based "social justice" that Lalu Yadav's and his wife's governments in Bihar pursued for fifteen years. This chapter examines what occurred when militant lower-caste leaders—who emerged from the "backward caste" movement described in the previous chapter—captured the reins of power. Chapter 3 examines the particular mode of governance that resulted as politicians clashed with bureaucrats and many state institutions were systematically weakened and replaced by shadowy political networks. Drawing from interviews I conducted with senior bureaucrats in Patna, and many hours that I spent in government offices, I explore the often tense relationship among members of different state institutions in Bihar. Chapter 4 explores the ways in which the larger political developments described in the first two chapters played out within sites of regional political practice. I examine the ways in which different caste identities were used within electoral practice and relate to local struggles over control of territory. Chapter 5 explores the crucial relationship between caste and grassroots support for political parties within the context of Rajnagar, a village where I lived. I explore the ways in which this relationship is grounded within the particular spatial context of the village and how this village context is crucial for an understanding of the ways in which democratic practice plays out in Bihar. Chapter 6 extends the analysis of the previous chapter to examine Yadav villagers in Rajnagar, a large group of people who represent themselves to outsiders as a homogenous community, especially during elections, but that are divided into three very different groups who have rather limited social interaction with one another in day-to-day life. I explore the ways in which political and economic changes of the last fifteen years have differentially affected different sections of Yadav villagers in Rajnagar, allowing an investigation of the class dimension of caste politics. Chapter 7 examines the remarkable changes that have occurred since the fall of Lalu Yadav's RJD government in 2005 and reflects on what lower-caste politics can teach us about the experience of democracy in India and what this means for understanding postcolonial democracy.

State Formation, Caste Formation, and the Emergence of a Lower-Caste Politics

In a penetrating analysis of the symbolism of the Imperial Assemblage of 1877 that was held to proclaim Queen Victoria empress of India, Bernard Cohn (1983) demonstrated that the ritual reflected two distinct "sociologies of colonial rule" that had emerged by the later part of the nineteenth century. An older theory, modeled on feudal Europe, saw India as "a feudal society consisting of lords, chiefs and peasants" with a "native aristocracy" that needed to be respected and, if necessary, even produced, in order to have allies through which to rule effectively (658). A second theory, emerging with force after the rebellion of 1857 and the direct incorporation of India into the empire, saw India as essentially consisting of communities of religions, regional ethnicities, tribal groups and, above all, castes. Such a theory necessitated both the production of knowledge about these communities—the notion being that a lack of knowledge about India was at least partly responsible for the rebellion—and the need to work through the "'representative men,' leaders who were thought to speak for, and who could shape responses from, their communities" (658). Both "representative men" and "native aristocrats" had been constructed by the imperatives of colonial rule, and both were present in the representational politics of the Imperial Assemblage.

These two sociologies of rule correspond to two different phases of colonial governance (roughly pre-1857 and post-1857) that coexisted rather uncomfortably in the late colonial period, but also to very different notions of caste that continued to shape India's political world after independence. Caste became increasingly imagined as translocal communities that could be democratically mobilized into "vote blocks" represented by caste-leader politicians, but most Indians also continued to experience caste as inseparable from the realities of local dominance by caste lineages who continued to see themselves, even if with increasing difficulty, as lords of the land. Colonialism, then, didn't just shape representations of caste; it also influenced the ways in which caste operated within the agrarian economy, where the "feudal" model of colonial rule still held sway in *zamindari*-settled areas until independence. In addition, emergent caste identities and caste networks played important roles within colonially constructed governmental institutions. I shall argue, therefore, that the colonial influence on caste must be situated in relation to overlapping, and often incongruous, processes of state formation that have had a lasting impact. The aim of the chapter is not to provide a comprehensive account of Bihar's modern political history—a task accomplished elsewhere—but to examine the ways in which the politics of caste documented in subsequent chapters reflects the contradictions of a specifically postcolonial democracy.

I draw here on Corrigan and Sayer's (1985) well-known study of state formation in England as cultural revolution. As they point out, processes of state formation do not just produce institutions and power relations but also identities and cultural forms. Such cultural transformation—playing out in India according to distinctly colonial strategies of rule—accompanied the governance of caste. And as Gilbert Joseph and Daniel Nugent (1994) emphasized in their theorization of the Mexican Revolution, processes of state formation are best thought of as being shaped by a dialectical interaction between the hegemonic culture and "cultures of resistance." While processes of colonial state formation shaped caste identities, processes of "caste formation" that occurred through a plethora of caste movements in the late colonial period profoundly shaped the functioning, if not the form, of the state. As a Yadav caste activist in 1914 saw it, "The world is full of change!" (quoted in Pinch 1996, 88). But this change was not revolutionary in a decisive way since colonialism ensured that earlier structures of power continued and the emergence of radical discourses have often masked underlying continuities.

The chapter then turns to the ways in which these processes of state/ caste formation continued in the postcolonial period. Independence added new sociologies of rule. India became a constitutional democracy with universal franchise, and Nehruvian planned development promised rapid socioeconomic transformation. But these "sociologies of rule" were superimposed over the colonial ones that Cohn identified and that continued to shape political life—caste as distinct communities with representatives, the realities of caste dominance within local sites, and caste as networks providing access to state institutions. The result was that neither planned development nor the legal provision of liberal rights resulted in decisive structural transformations.

This account builds on analysis of economic change in India as a "passive revolution" (Chatterjee 1986, Kaviraj 1988) that had to be painstakingly negotiated by elites with divergent interests and imposed from above through planned development. But I argue that the upper-caste control of state institutions—a legacy of long histories of state formation—and democratic mobilizations made such a project a practical impossibility. The green revolution occurred just as what became known as the "backward-caste" movement was taking off. Landlords were faced with increasingly politicized backward-caste tenants who could not be reduced to laborers, preventing landlord-driven development, while landlords used their control over state institutions to sabotage the growth of an alternate peasant-driven agriculture. Any passive revolution in Bihar, therefore, had to involve a restructuring of local power and the relationships between state institutions and local power. And the force of this gradual restructuring was caste-based democratization. I therefore argue that the project of state-directed development and democratic practice need to be analyzed as two distinct forces in a single process—a "passive revolution" of capital and a "silent" democratic revolution (Jaffrelot 2003). I will seek to show the ways in which there has been a back-and-forth process between efforts to utilize state-directed development in order to consolidate "historical blocs" from above and caste-based democratic mobilizations that have disrupted this project, utilizing democratic politics in an attempt to actualize transformations from below.

Caste, the State, and Local Control

Historical research demonstrating the changing forms of caste over time, and the crucial role of processes of state formation in these changes, discredits both the Orientalist conception of India as essentially religious in nature and the influential theory of the French anthropologist Louis Dumont (1980) who asserted that caste hierarchy was based on a Brahmanical opposition of purity and pollution, with the Brahman's "encompass-ing" of the king being the defining feature of the "caste system" (Bayly 1999, Cohn 1983, Dirks 2001). Nicholas Dirks (1987), for instance, dem-onstrates that in a "little kingdom" in southern India in the precolonial period, caste existed at the local level as lineages whose status (reflected, above all, in temple honors) was derived from proximity with the king. While Brahmans and temples were important for legitimizing kingship, it was the king who was always the first devotee of the deity, and "ritual and political forms were fundamentally the same" (4). Networks of proxim-ity with "the state"—even if, as Dirks points out, Western conceptions of the state cannot be applied here—were constitutive of what came to be known as "caste."

In north India, the Mughal Empire drew heavily from a Rajput tradi-tion of kingship in legitimating and spreading its rule—including strate-gic marriages with prominent Rajput families and the reliance on Rajput military recruits and officers—a process that facilitated the increasing im-portance of a *kshatriya* (kingly/warrior) ethic (Bayly 1999, 34–38). Such an ethic was of crucial importance at the village and regional level, where the lineages of castes that claimed a lordly *kshatriya* status were the local controllers and revenue collectors for the Mughals (Cohn 1983). "By the later seventeenth century, there were many areas of north and cen-tral India where the most fertile lands had become subject to lords based in mud-walled forts who used their bonds of marriage with fellow Raj-put, Maithil, Bhumihar or Kanyakubja to command a flow of resources and deference from non-elite tillers and dependent laborers" (Bayly 1999, 35–37).

The case of Rajnagar, the village that will be the subject of subsequent chapters, demonstrates how caste dominance worked during this period. It was within such a context of a Mughal/Rajput state that the *lohtamia* Rajputs migrated to Rajnagar and, later to surrounding villages (eight lin-eages claim descent from a common ancestor), in the seventeenth century, occupying an elevated fort (Rajnagar *garh*) surrounded by two moats, the remains of which are still visible today. As Cohn describes, the regional context was crucial since the lordly lineage not only had to maintain con-trol over its territory, but also had to unite in order to protect itself from would-be conquerors from outside and to maintain leverage vis-à-vis higher-level kings and emperors. The *lohtamia* Rajputs had to contend with other Rajput lineages—I was told by lineage elders that there was a history of territorial conflicts with the lineage of the legendary leader of the 1857 rebellion, Kuer Singh—with local kings (in this case the maharaja of Dumraon) and, of course, with Mughal revenue demands. But while the legacy of dominant caste lineages is the product of a history that stretches back more than three centuries, colonial rule altered the experience of local dominance in subtle but important ways.

In colonial Bengal, which included present day Bihar, land tenure was regulated through the legal framework of the permanent settlement, enacted by Cornwallis in 1793. Following a feudal "sociology of rule" (Cohn 1983), the permanent settlement was explicitly designed to "create a loyal elite based on landed property" (Dirks 2001, 111), a class of *zamindar* landlords who had the legal right—a right that could be bought and sold—of revenue collection, exercising a great deal of control over their tenants (Guha 1996, Mitra 1985). Most *zamindars* had been tax collectors for Mughal revenue extraction but now attained a significant degree of independence, a development that contemporary observers from the old regime fiercely criticized.[1] The desire of the East India Company in India to maximize profits discouraged the costly expansion of an internal security apparatus. Rather, *zamindars* were allowed to exercise a sufficient degree of control over their respective territories to extract the routine tax revenue from cultivators. *Zamindari* families also enjoyed privileged relations with the colonial state. From the mid-eighteenth century, the East India Company had encouraged recruitment of members of *zamindari* households into the Bengal Army, and "in the hope of keeping its soldiers loyal to their 'salt' . . . the Bengal Army had adopted elaborate techniques of selection and regimental ritual . . . designed to establish an explicitly high-caste identity for the army's regular regiments" (Bayly 1999, 202).

As the power and resources of the colonial state grew, *zamindars* and their rent-collecting agents (*thikadars*) not only retained, but also strengthened, their power at the local level. Anand Yang writes, "Endowed with political standing in their localities and by virtue of their positions as local allies of the colonial state, landholders thus enhanced their roles as local controllers" (1998, 68), resulting in what Yang (1989) refers to as a "limited Raj." "With the British leaning heavily on local allies and imperial considerations weighing decisively in favor of minimizing the economic costs of rule, a strong administrative machinery became less of a requisite for colonial government" (Yang 1989, 229). In fact, the only functioning bureaucracy at the local level was operated by the large *zamindars*, with the local police (*chaukidar*) and records keeper (*patwari*) effectively serving as servants of the *zamindar*, despite repeated attempts to integrate them into colonial administration.[2] At the local level, *zamindars* were the state.

The *zamindars*, who enjoyed legally sanctioned territorial control under British Raj, were from locally dominant lineages or, in the case of absentee *zamindars*, made their own alliances with these lineages. In Rajnagar, for instance, *lohtamia* Rajputs were given *zamindari* rights over the village with the Permanent Settlement. Over time, aided by what lineage elders described as a "close relationship" (*nazdik rishta*) with the British, *zamindari* rights were acquired over eight other revenue villages (usually comprising several residential villages) through auctions, with some located nearby but others located at considerable distance (with revenue collection farmed out to intermediaries).[3]

Caste divisions served to reinforce class relations within agrarian contexts, primarily through the distinctions between "twice-born" (*dwijas*) wearers of the sacred thread, peasant castes that did not don the sacred thread and had to settle for inferior tenancy arrangements and provide free or discounted labor and services, and "untouchable" castes whose ritual impurity perpetuated a class of landless and often bonded laborers.[4] These caste divisions underpinned the entire *zamindari* system. In addition, the steady expansion of population and of land area under cultivation, and the felling of forests, decreased the mobility of many groups, making flight and resistance more difficult in settled areas such as Shahabad. The East India Company largely succeeded in disarming previously armed groups and establishing a monopoly of the use of violence at the regional level (but not within villages).[5] This meant that armed conflict between landed lineages decreased precipitously, weakening the need to secure loyalty from subordinate groups. This concentrated power at the level of the village—with the possibility of expanding territory through conquest eliminated, and the fixed revenue demands of Permanent Settlement encouraging the realization of profits through coercive extraction (especially since *zamindari* rights had to be purchased).[6] "The chief consequence of these developments with regard to caste was a widespread hardening of boundaries between the superior landed groups and those deemed to be low and 'impure' in caste terms" (Bayly 1999, 203).

The Colonial Governance of Caste

After the 1857 rebellion and the direct integration of India into the empire, it became clear to many colonial officials that the feudal model of rule had become inadequate and, as part of a process of expanding the

state's presence, a sociology of rule based on "communities" gained influence (Cohn 1983). This emphasis on communities reflected a colonial version of civil society that, unlike the feudal mode, was conceived as having
the capacity to change over time (Cohn 1983, 633; Dirks 2001,16). Colonial governance increasingly supplemented limited rule with the system-
atic collection of ethnographic and statistical data on caste, and its use
within administration. In the process, formerly fluid and localized caste
lineages were categorized into homogenous ethnic identities that became central to the workings of colonial institutions. This was especially
the case in the judicial system and police force, where certain castes were
deemed "criminal" as "part of a larger discourse in which caste determined the occupational and social character of all its constituent members" (Dirks 2001, 181). In the Indian army, the old Mughal practice of
recruiting members of aristocratic families was replaced with a policy
of recruiting the "martial races" (Bayly 1999, 202–203; Dirks 2001, 177–
180). And, perhaps most influentially, the colonial census enumerated
broadly defined caste categories, "objectifying" caste as numerical data
that could be interpreted, compared, and politically utilized by both the
colonial state as well as various local actors (Appadurai 1996, 114–139;
Bayly 1999; Cohn 1987a; Dirks 2001, 198–228). The first Indian census was
held in 1872 and the decennial census began in 1881. The census became
the most visible project for systematically collecting information on caste.
The superintendent of census operations in 1921, wrote: "We pigeonholed
everyone by caste. . . . We deplore the caste system and its effects on social
and economic problems, but we are largely responsible for the system we
deplore. . . . Government's passion for labels and pigeonholes has led to a
crystallization of the caste system."[7]

Although the strategic use of caste titles and designations by rulers
can be traced to well before the colonial era, the colonial state's use of
caste categories served to regulate and "depoliticize" the actual fluidity
of caste identities and obfuscate their links with dominance in local sites
(Dirks 1987). This had novel effects. By enumerating castes using broad
categories that masked regional variation, the colonial state's caste representations were "deterritorialized," constructed without reference to
significant local variations, overlapping rights over land and relations of
dominance and subordination within villages that endowed caste with
its political vitality.[8] Colonially produced representations of caste were
so central to colonial rule that Dirks (2001) terms it an "ethnographic
state."

Caste Associations and the Forging of New Political Identities

The colonial use of caste as a master category of rule allowed the colonial regime to widen its base of support, created new cleavages to manipulate, and facilitated the promotion of a distinctly colonial version of modernity, with caste "communities" serving as a "native" version of civil society (Dirks 2001,16). But this was not just a top-down process. The attempt to classify and rank caste by social precedence during the 1901 census, in particular, was followed by a flow of petitions and intense lobbying from newly organized caste associations to influence their castes' ranking. The emergence of caste associations in this period is usually seen as the beginnings of the interaction between caste and modern politics in India.[9] But I suggest that these caste movements need to be analyzed as specifically colonial hegemonic projects that not only created new alliances and identities, but were part of processes of state formation that profoundly shaped Bihar's postcolonial political world.

There were two broad types of caste movements: those of economically well-positioned castes (that came to be categorized after independence as "forward" or "upper" castes) whose caste associations facilitated access to English education and public employment, and those of lower-caste associations that, although much less successful in providing access to public resources, sought to raise the caste status of their members and, therefore, represented a challenge to the established order in the countryside. The presence of these two very different types of caste movements points to a central contradiction in the colonial experience of caste: the homogenous caste representations enumerated by the colonial state served to obfuscate the relationship between caste and territoriality and had two opposite effects. On the one hand, the members of landed families who were the colonial regime's allies in the countryside could gain preferential access to public institutions and resources located outside of their areas of dominance. On the other hand, "deterritorialized" caste identities necessitated alliances between previously antagonistic groups (such as Rajput *zamindars* and Rajput tenants) and provided lower-caste activists with the means to establish a sense of identity and community transcending the narrow confines of village territorial subjugation.

As early as 1886, Kayasth *sabhas* (organizations) were formed across Bihar to advance the interests of Kayasths, a caste that had emerged as record keepers for the Mughals in an unusually direct example of the relationship between state formation and caste formation (Mishra and Pandey 1996, 42–50). The colonial census categorized Kayasths, who as scribes had taken part in Mughal court life with dietary practices that put their Hindu ritual status in question, as belonging to the *shudra varna*.[10] Prominent leaders of the Kayasth caste *sabha* spearheaded the movement to create a separate state of Bihar out of colonial Bengal, directly influencing the federal structure of colonial administration. This movement's success and the creation of a separate province for Bihar and Orissa in 1912, provided literate Kayasths with considerable advantage because a separate province reduced the dominance of educated Bengalis from Calcutta within government service and ensured the establishment of a university, a High Court and a state assembly in Patna. For the next decade, Kayasths had a virtual monopoly on educational capital and access to government employment (Mishra and Pandey 1996, 40).

Other castes soon followed the success of the Kayasths. In 1889, Bhumihar Brahman *sabhas* were formed to advance Bhumihar claims to Brahman status—culminating in the official title "Bhumihar Brahman"— after the colonial census also categorized them as *shudra*. This was an especially insulting categorization considering that so many *zamindars* and large tenants were Bhumihars. The Bhumihar Brahman movement, like the Kayasth movement, aimed at elevating Bhumihar caste status within the census and the colonial legal system. Rajput and Brahman movements soon followed. But, since the Bhumihar movement is perhaps the most important example of an initially conservative caste movement evolving in a radical direction, and thereby profoundly influencing processes of state formation, it is examined in some depth below.

The Bhumihar Brahman Sabha initially served the interests of large *zamindars*, represented by Sir Ganesh Dutt, "and could rightly be called 'the Bhumihar Landholders' Association'" (Mishra and Pandey 1996, 85). The aggressive promotion of caste associations by *zamindars* was a response to governmental use of caste categories that lumped them together with people who occupied subordinated positions within the agrarian economy and within regional status hierarchies in such a way that all of their status positions become interconnected. But many *zamindars* were also responding to increasing economic hardships, which intensified during the 1930s. Not only was the steady fragmentation of *zamindari* rights among heirs making them less economically viable in many cases, but agricultural prices declined precipitously during the Great Depression, and there was growing realization as the independence movement gained momentum that the *zamindari* system would eventually end, and some tenants even began refusing to pay rent (Das 1997, 53). "The decline in the prosperity of the *zamindars*, tenureholders and rich peasants (belonging mainly to the Bhumihar and, to some extent, the Rajput castes) as a result of subdivision and fragmentation of property drove them increasingly to English education as a means of improving their lot and securing a share or place in the power-structure" (Mishra and Pandey 1996, 39). Within this context, caste associations served as a vehicle to facilitate the supplementing of income from land with the pursuit of urban employment, especially in an expanding public sector that was dominated by Kayasths. Caste associations founded colleges and caste-based hostels and scholarships. In this way, agricultural surplus and rural power were channeled into urban pursuits, educational capital, and access to government, on the basis of emerging caste networks (Bayly 1999, 160–162, 264). The emergence of the Bhumihar caste movement was a reaction to changes in governmental practice and an economic and political context that necessitated an expansion of influence well beyond the localized boundaries of the *zamindari* system.

But caste movements that claimed wide membership could not remain under the control of a small number of *zamindars*, and these movements set in motion radical changes. By the 1920s a rival faction emerged within the Bhumihar Brahman Sabha led by Swami Sahajanand Saraswati, who represented the interests of tenants. (Sahajanand, in fact, came from a *zamindari* family that had been more or less reduced to tenant status through this process.) Sahajanand came to believe that "the rich used [caste associations] to strengthen their hold on the community in order to mobilize numerical support to realize their own ends" (Mishra and Pandey 1996, 161) and in order to "protect their landed and trading interests and to generally continue their supremacy" (cited in Das 1997, 77). The rivalry between Swami Sahajanand and Ganesh Dutt within the Bhumihar Brahman Sabha reflected the contradictions of a caste movement that, while representing *zamindari* interests, did so by broadening its base of support to such an extent that structures of power were altered and new elites emerged.

By 1929, Swami Sahajanand Saraswati's increasingly radical promotion of tenant interests inspired him to form the Kisan Sabha. The Kisan Sabha spearheaded one of the most important peasant movements in late colonial India and represented the most direct threat to the *zamindari* system in Bihar.[11] It is not insignificant that Swami Sahajanand began his political activities with the Bhumihar Brahman Sabha and that the Kisan Sabha (as well as the Communist Party of India in Bihar, which was heavily influenced by the Kisan Sabha) never shed its reputation as a "Bhumihar" organization.[12] In fact, this is perhaps the most important reason that, despite the legacy of the Kisan Sabha, an assertive peasant politics never emerged as a powerful force in Bihar after independence. The Kisan Sabha, however, was instrumental in the eventual abolition of the *zamindari* system, with legislation passed under S. K. Sinha, a Bhumihar chief minister who had also been a leader within the Bhumihar Brahman Sabha, becoming the general secretary of the Kisan Sabha and then joining the Congress Party (Mishra and Pandey 1996, 213). His career paralleled the Bhumihar movement, the focal point of which transitioned from caste *sabhas* to the Kisan Sabha to the Congress Party. In the process, the structure of the postcolonial state was transformed.

Movements for Caste Empowerment

The dominance of "twice-born" castes within an expanding public administration and professional class, as well as the role of caste divisions in underpinning class inequality in the agrarian economy, did not go unchallenged. The broad, homogenous caste identities that the colonial state employed and enumerated also underscored the numerical preponderance of the more populous peasant castes. These homogenous identities resulted in shared interests, and to some extent a shared sense of community, between the masses of small tenant cultivators and agricultural laborers on the one hand, and a much smaller but influential class of larger tenants, small *zamindars*, and educated professionals. From the perspective of many caste movement leaders, British Raj was an opportunity to break free from years of oppression. "Seen from the perspective of the *shudra* elite, British rule represented an historic opportunity to break out of the disabilities imposed by the Brahminical ideology of *varna* and *karma*" (Rao 1989, 10).[13] The often sympathetic attitude of the colonial authorities can also be interpreted as a tactic to counter the growing influence of upper-caste nationalists, especially Brahmans, whom many colonial officers perceived to be "the most formidable opponents of colonial rule" (Rao 1989, 10).[14] But in any case, these movements were reactions to the perceived opportunities and constraints resulting from the colonial governance of caste.

By the early twentieth century, numerous caste movements emerged that claimed *kshatriya* status for groups that were often seen locally as ritually inferior. While emerging in reaction to the colonial census like the upper-caste movements examined above, they were influenced by a longer history of Vaishnava religious reform. Lower-caste movements created new mytho-histories, new patterns of ritual and social behavior, and "reflected a particular kind of consciousness predicated on the creation, maintenance, and definition of community" (Pinch 1996, 148; see also Bayly 1999, 205–210; Michelutti 2008). Although pursued by many lower-caste groups, *kshatriya* movements were most prominent among populous castes that called themselves, and came to be referred to, as Yadav, Kurmi, and Kushwaha (or Koeri). The members of these groups claiming *kshatriya* status tended to be middle-sized cultivators with a few wealthy members, including a small number of *zamindar* landlords who were responding to similar economic pressures faced by high-caste *zamindars*. But for this small number of landed elites, the changes brought about by the colonial governance of caste must have been profoundly dismaying. While previously enjoying high status within their region of control based on *zamindari* title, patronage relationships and the honors associated with economic dominance, Yadav or Kurmi *zamindars* now found themselves consigned to an inferior caste categorization shared with the masses of sharecroppers and agricultural laborers.

Kurmi *sabhas*, consisting of castes largely employed in vegetable cultivation, formed in 1894 in reaction to the British policy declaring Kurmis as a "criminal tribe."[15] From 1909, Gopajatiya *sabhas* (literally "associations of the *gopa* caste") were founded across Bihar (in 1912 in Ara, near Rajnagar village in what was then Shahabad district), later developing into the All India Yadav Mahasabha. In reference to the caste identities that resulted from these movements, M. S. A. Rao describes "caste as a process of social formation. ... The Yadav category is a new social formation which resulted from politicization based on an ideology of challenging the legitimacy of hereditary privileges of 'twice born' *varna* categories. Hence reference to the Yadav just by the term caste is misleading because it does not capture the process by which a caste formation emerged with a shared identity across regional, sect, and sub-caste lines" (1989, 15). This "process of social formation" is at the heart of the political efficacy of contemporary caste identities. To forge new hegemonies, caste movements produced elaborate mytho-histories around the "empty" colonial-imposed caste categories, cultivated alliances between often diverse groups which now shared a common identity, and thereby attempted to influence the representational practices of the colonial regime. In doing so, these movements linked competition for influence within state institutions with struggles over dominance in the agrarian economy.

The members of the Yadav Mahasabha consisted of a range of groups, uniting *ahir*, *goala*, *gopa*, and other subcastes, and including cow and buffalo herders, cultivators, laborers, as well as a class of rich farmers emerging from the commercialization of agrarian production in some areas, united in claiming *kshatriya* status and descent from the mythic Yadava dynasty of Lord Krishna (Michelutti 2008).[16] Efforts were launched to increase social status through lobbying for changes in census categories as well as urging members to adopt more "Sanskritized" lifestyles and ritual practices such as vegetarianism, donning the sacred thread, and prohibiting widows to remarry.[17] In Rajnagar, for instance, there were a small number of Yadavs who claimed to have donned the sacred thread during this period—although they lived at some distance from the Rajput *zamindars*. The *zamindari* system of land tenure was organized around these practices. Twice-born wearers of the sacred thread, for instance, were given preferential leases (if they were tenants) and were not expected to perform unpaid labor (*begar*) or provide services or products (such as milk) at below-market rates. There was also an effort to redefine the labor of cultivation as compatible with *kshatriya* status, coming into direct conflict with a socioeconomic order built around the distinction between the servitude of those who worked with the plow and the high status of those who did not (Pinch 1996, 110–112). The cumulative effects of these caste movements were thus an attack on the use of caste distinctions within the *zamindari* system. "Kshatriya identities were coalescing in peasant society that would, ultimately, threaten to undermine the systemics (if not the principle of hierarchy by the middle of the twentieth century" (Pinch 1996, 88). Not surprisingly, these transgressions of boundaries resulted in numerous caste riots in the 1920s and, to a lesser extent, in the 1930s between lower-caste peasants affirming *kshatriya* status (especially Yadavs) and high-caste landlords (Das 1997, 70–74; Pinch 1996, 91–95, 121–131).

Lower-caste movements, however, did not pose a broad-based challenge to either the *zamindari* system or to the dominance of "twice-born" castes. Each individual caste simply sought to raise itself to twice-born status; the actual division between twice-born and *shudra* was left untouched. Little organization existed between individual caste movements, and while specific caste practices related to *zamindari* were challenged, these movements made no attempt to end the *zamindari* system itself. The most important alliance of lower-caste movements occurred in the 1930s with the formation of the Triveni Sangh, an alliance of Yadav, Kurmi, and Kushwaha candidates in elections to provincial bodies in Shahabad district (including present-day Bhojpur and headquartered in Ara). This alliance among the three most populous peasant castes, and the Triveni Sangh's demand that 60 percent of public employment be reserved for members of the "backward classes," was a precursor to the backward-caste movement of the 1960s (and has been often celebrated as such). But the Triveni Sangh had limited electoral success and by the 1940s was co-opted by the Congress.

One of the factors explaining why colonial caste movements were not more radicalized was that they included small but significant numbers of *zamindars* who were instrumental in providing funding and support for their respective caste associations. Another reason was the inability to counter the realities of the agrarian structure. Attempts to end the practice of forced labor and free services often ended in boycotts organized by high castes that usually succeeded. In one case, for instance, Yadav *zamindars* brought in Brahmans from their areas of control to break the boycott of priests, but "the inexorable economic laws acted and women are again selling cowdung cakes and milk" (colonial official cited in Pinch 1996,125). The defining limitation, then, was the continuation of the dominance of caste lineages, and the relationships of patronage and subordination that accompanied this dominance. This reflected the contradictions between the two colonial sociologies of rule that we have been examining—the apparently radical change made possible by a civil society based on caste communities was severely restricted by the continued presence of caste dominance reinforced by a "limited Raj" (Yang 1989).

After independence, the role of caste associations changed dramatically. Pinch writes, "For Kurmi, Yadav, and Kushwaha leaders, this [independence] would represent a sea change in Indian political culture, since a *kshatriya* identity only had meaning in the context of a colonial political system crafted around visions of martial grandeur" (1996, 143). Political parties assumed many of the claims of specific caste constituencies, but in times of political uncertainty and when popular support shifted to different parties, caste associations still emerged as important political platforms. The focus of lower-caste movements switched from assertions of *kshatriya* status to electoral mobilization based on a "backward-caste" identity, as I describe in the following section.

Although colonial caste movements were largely the product of relatively small groups of politicians, civil servants, intellectuals, and social activists, their impact has been considerable, especially because the collective identities that they labored to construct became central to electoral practice in the postindependence period. Even today in Bihar, many colleges founded by caste associations continue to enroll a majority of students from specific caste backgrounds. Most importantly, people continued to speak in terms of "Yadavs," "Kurmis," "Bhumihars," and so forth as natural categories of social and political life in Bihar, without necessarily realizing the extent to which these identities were the result of hegemonic projects that emerged in the late nineteenth and early twentieth century. Postindependence politics was to revolve around different sets of oppositions, yet caste identities and caste networks initially forged by these movements in the late colonial period continued to form a constituent part of the fabric of Bihar's political world.

Postcolonial "Sociologies of Rule"

Nehru and other Congress leaders believed that caste inequality would wither away as their version of socialism was progressively established in India through planned development. Instead of dismantling the institutions of the colonial state, as Gandhi had wanted, this project required the extension of state institutions into new areas of social life. This expansion occurred through the Community Development Project that created the development blocks, bringing state institutions closer to where most people lived. Since the basic structure of the state was left largely unreformed, and radical social change from below had been constrained in the name of national unity, state-directed development served increasingly as the glue of a new social contract that promised to be a catalyst for a broad and radical societal transformation from above (Chatterjee 1993, 121).

But development and democracy, the central discourses of the postcolonial state, were both put into practice through the structures of power and identity that had been forged through long histories of colonial state formation. Development was often conceived in terms of developing specific communities—Scheduled Castes, Scheduled Tribes, and the residual Other Backward Classes. The institutions of the developmental state were controlled through caste networks that first emerged in the late colonial period, and development resources flowed according to the long-established patronage channels of landed elites. As was described above, many of Bihar's educational institutions had been established by caste leaders or had become dominated by a particular caste. Upper castes' superior access to English education, as well as contacts within the administration, continued a profound caste bias within administrative recruitment at both the central and state level. Electoral practice was likewise largely articulated around the caste "communities" that emerged in the late colonial period, with politicians claiming to be "representatives" of their communities, while at the village level the delivery of votes played out according to long-standing patronage relationships dictated by landed groups and, if necessary, through the exercise of coercion and force. Even the Congress Party at the state level served as a nexus between landowning elites, politicians and bureaucrats, all of whom came largely from upper-caste backgrounds, serving to perpetuate a broad-based upper-caste hegemony despite the national leadership's radical rhetoric. In short, this absence of decisive structural transformation resulted in postcolonial processes of state formation being superimposed on colonial forms, and of postcolonial hegemonic projects being underwritten by older hegemonic projects that emerged in the colonial period. The outcome was a distinctively postcolonial democracy.

It is useful here to reflect on the seminal Gramscian concept of the "passive revolution of capital," which has been profitably utilized to understand India's distinct postcolonial political trajectory (Chatterjee 1986, Kaviraj 1988; see also Corbridge and Harriss 2000). "In situations where an emergent bourgeoisie lacks the social conditions for establishing complete hegemony over the new nation, it resorts to a 'passive revolution,' by attempting a 'molecular transformation' of the old dominant classes into partners in a new historical bloc and only a partial appropriation of the popular masses, in order to first create a state as the necessary precondition for the establishment of capitalism as the dominant mode of production" (Chatterjee 1986, 30). This analysis draws on Pranab Bardhan's (1984) influential analysis of an uneasy alliance between industrialists, rural elites, and bureaucrats wherein no group was hegemonic and their relative dominance shifted over time. Rather, at the state level rural elites tended to exercise more power, whereas industrialists exerted more influence at the national level. The developmental state became the agency through which these divergent class interests could be negotiated and through which capitalist development could take place, with change being imposed from above in the absence of revolutionary transformation from below. Thus while no single class was hegemonic, the discourse of development was, legitimizing the postcolonial state as the key agent of change.

But the case of Bihar does not easily conform to this model. The limitations of state-directed development had been clearly pointed out by theorists who argued for the characterization of Indian agriculture as "semifeudal" within the famous mode of production debate of the 1970s, wherein Bihar was probably the most important example.[18] Pradhan Prasad (1973), in an analysis of a survey of three districts in Bihar, observes that the economic behavior of landlords was "essentially directed towards preventing the strengthening of the economic condition of the direct producer rather than maximization of their rate of profit or rate of return. For example, in the context of the share-cropping system the landowners know that if the share-croppers are encouraged to take to intensive cultivation or to adopt new agricultural practices, etc, the rates of return from land, for both the parties, will be higher than before. But this would also strengthen the economic condition of the rural poor thereby ultimately freeing them from semi-feudal bondage." Therefore he concludes that, "unless the existing semi-feudal institutional set-up is replaced by a higher stage of 'production retaliations,' any attempt at 'investment planning' [the Congress strategy of planned development] will be an exercise in futility" (871–872). For my purposes, the most interesting version of this concept was that Indian agriculture was neither "feudal" nor "capitalist" but specifically colonial and, after independence, postcolonial (Alavi 1975, 1981, Banaji 1972). Colonialism both laid the foundations for capitalism—infrastructure for trade, a liberal legal system, and administrative framework—while making its actualization impossible because of the colonially shaped structuring of agrarian relations (and reliance on imperial centers of finance for the reproduction of capital).

An understanding of the specificities of postcolonial democracy modifies both the passive revolution and the semifeudal/colonial mode of production frameworks, providing a way out of the seemingly insurmountable conflict between them—in the former, capitalist development appears inevitable, in the later, nearly impossible. In considering Prasad's evidence of landlords forsaking potential profit in order to prevent an empowerment of tenants, for instance, what is striking is that landlords were so defensive. One might expect a process of forced proletarianization of tenants and family farms as landlords underwent a "molecular transformation" into agro-capitalists (see Chakravarti 2001 for a detailed description of such a process). But the spread of democratic politics, with a "backward-caste" movement representing tenants and small peasants serving as the main force of a growing opposition to the Congress, made such forced dispossession impossible. In addition, the long processes of state formation examined above, resulting in caste hegemonies that connected influence within state institutions with the dominance of landed elites, also prevented or sabotaged state interventions aimed at agricultural development that would benefit those who actually cultivated the land. The emergence of caste networks, their influence within state institutions, and their intersection with caste-based territorial dominance—all legacies of processes of colonial state formation—therefore produced a distinctively postcolonial political economy. But democratic practice has the potential to alter hegemonic formations and even displace them with new hegemonic projects (Laclau and Mouffe 1985). The key point is that the source of change had to be political. The passive revolution, therefore, could never be simply imposed from above in a democratic India—it had to be a democratic revolution as much as, and perhaps even more than, a state-directed imposition of capitalism.

Congress Dominance and Upper-Caste Hegemony

In the early years of independence, state politics was centered on Congress Party dominance, revolving around upper-caste factions; Rajput leaders, allied to Kayasth leaders on the one hand, and Bhumihar leaders on the other. While the primary arena for this factional contestation was the dominant Congress Party, opposition parties, including the Communists and Socialists, were minor arenas. Contemporary observers described the administration of Bihar's first chief minister, S. K. Sinha, who led the state government until his death in 1961, as "Bhumihar Raj" (Mishra and Pandey 1996) because of Bhumihar control of land, expanding presence within the bureaucracy, and dominance within both the Congress and opposition parties (especially the Communist Party of India). Sinha's main opponent within the Congress was the Rajput faction leader, A. N. Sinha. Although these two were widely considered to be leaders of rival Bhumihar and Rajput caste factions within the Bihar Congress Party, most analysts considered the state administration relatively stable during this period (Kohli 1990, 212). Despite their opposing politics, these upper-caste factions had a shared interest in maintaining upper-caste hegemony and generally represented the interests of the upper-caste commercial landlords who emerged after the abolition of the *zamindari* system.

Gradual changes set the stage for later political transformation in Bihar and other areas of north India. After independence, the abolition of the *zamindari* system of land tenure, which was not implemented until a decade or so later, weakened the position of large *zamindars*, although loopholes were exploited that still enabled very large landholdings to be maintained in many areas. Much of the land that former *zamindars* were forced to relinquish came into the hands of their former tenants, many of whom came from peasant caste backgrounds, including Yadav, Kurmi, and Koeri castes in Bihar. Competition between upper-caste factions within the Congress Party resulted in various upper-caste leaders seeking alliances with these politically ascendant castes.[19] In 1963, "chief minister Krishna Ballabh Sahay referred to a Scheduled Tribe MLA [member of the legislative assembly] as his 'right hand' and to Ram Lakhan Singh Yadav as his 'left hand'" (Frankel 1989, 87), and cut back the number of upper-caste members in his cabinet. Ram Lakhan Singh Yadav was elevated to the rank of minister, providing an emergent "Yadav" representation within the Congress. Nevertheless, the tangible influence that OBC leaders began to enjoy within the Bihar government was a result of their being co-opted by a Congress Party that continued to be upper-caste dominated.

Upper-caste hegemony in Bihar was little changed even after Indira Gandhi reorganized the Congress Party at the national level in 1969 by successfully challenging the regional "Congress bosses," split the Congress Party, and directly appealed to the rural poor (Frankel 1978). Her efforts aimed to centralize power and force change, an attempt to double down on the passive revolution model of state-directed development. Considering the ubiquitous presence of caste networks linking state institutions, the political system (including the Congress Party at all levels), and local power—a legacy of the processes of state formation during the colonial era—it is little surprise that these efforts failed.[20] Centralization of power coexisted with an increasing inability to wield power effectively at the local level (Kohli 1994).

But land transfers to former tenants in the wake of *zamindari* abolition (even though its implementation was partial), the progressive introduction of green-revolution technologies in some areas (even if their utilization was often uneven and the green revolution largely bypassed Bihar), and the scattered and the increasing political clout of an expanding class of OBC cultivators progressively weakened the patronage relationships binding small cultivators and bonded laborers to landlords. One impact of this was the radicalization of laborers with the spread of the Naxalite uprising, beginning in the late 1960s (precisely, we shall see, when lower-caste politics emerges as a powerful force) and intensifying by the late 1970s in waves of agrarian unrest.[21] Another was the rise of OBC politics, which Prasad (1980) considers to represent a weakening of "semifeudal" production relations. The expanding status of many backward-caste cultivators conflicted with their political marginalization within the Congress, especially since the patron-client ties that had allowed upper-caste landlords to control cultivators' votes were progressively weakening. With the ability of dominant castes to deliver votes weakening, the Congress Party increasingly relied on a combination of support from upper-caste landlords, Muslims, and Dalit laborers who were appealed to through Indira Gandhi's *garibi hatao* ("eliminate poverty") populism. This new class of expanding backward-caste cultivators, however, was neglected, and the socialist opposition successfully mobilized this neglected middle in a direct challenge to the hegemonic bloc underlying the passive revolution.

Lower-Caste Politics as Radical Democracy

Ram Manohar Lohia, perhaps more than anyone else, influenced the ideology of what came to be known as the "backward-caste movement" in north India. Lohia most forcibly articulated the relationship between the socialist political tradition and lower-caste movements, recognizing "the political potential of the horizontal mobilization of lower castes on issues of social justice and ritual discrimination" (Sheth 1996, 108).[22] Born in Bihar and a prominent figure in the independence movement, Lohia had a principal difference with other socialist ideologues: his emphasis on the role of caste as a defining characteristic of India's ruling classes. He rejected the claim commonly espoused by many Indian socialists—including Nehru—that caste inequality would automatically wither away once socialism was established (Lohia 1964). Since Lohia held that caste status along with English education and wealth were the three primary characteristics of India's "ruling classes," he believed that a purely class-based socialism could not unseat the ruling classes, even with full public ownership over what Nehru referred to as the "commanding heights" of the economy. He asserted, "A vested interest socialism talks of political and economic revolution alone. . . . Even in the Europe of changing classes, such a revolution would keep intact the distinction between manual workers and those with the brain. . . . Workers with the brain are a fixed

caste in India ... even after the completed economic and political revolution, they would continue to supply the managers of the state and of industry" (1964, 96–97). Lohia insisted that the socialist movement in India
had to adapt to Indian conditions and actively combat caste inequality, advocating intercaste dining and incentives for intercaste marriage
(even to the extent of proposing intercaste marriage as a prerequisite
for public employment), caste-based reservations in government service,
and lower-caste leadership within political parties. While the colonial-era
caste movements had sought to extend the boundaries of their particular
caste as far as possible, Lohia sought to forge a united "backward" identity. The backward-caste movement, according to Lohia, was an essentially counter-hegemonic democratic project centered on a new discourse
of lower-caste radicalism that sought to dismantle the entire system of
upper-caste hegemony.

The "backwardness" of "backward castes" appears at first glance to fit
with the project of development that became central to the legitimacy of
the Nehruvian state in postindependence India (Chatterjee 1993), yet the
history of its political usage could not be more different. As Gupta notes,
"If there is an enduring trope in developmental discourse, it is that which
equates 'development' with adulthood and 'underdevelopment' with in-
fancy and immaturity" (1998, 11). But defining "backward classes" in
terms of individual caste categories and the subtle switch to the popularly
used "backward castes" transformed the developmental trope. "Backward
castes" do not seek to become "forward castes" in the way that the colonial period caste movements sought a higher status in the colonial census.
On the contrary, these same organizations began to claim a "backward"
status for their members in order to take advantage of reservation opportunities. While this appears contradictory, it was simply a different tactic
to achieve the same ends—increased influence within state institutions.[23]

Instead of seeking higher status, the backward-caste movement sought
to highlight the continuance of pervasive caste inequalities in relation
to the formal equality of postcolonial citizenship. Interpreted in caste
terms—a framework that the colonial caste movements had already made
salient—formal equality was contradicted by a perceived continuance
of upper-caste hegemony in Indian public life, and the backward-caste
movement highlighted this contradiction. The contradictions of Indian democracy, and its destabilizing effects (examined in subsequent chapters),
are the result of the progressive extension of electoral democracy in the
absence of an institutional infrastructure capable of supporting the liberal

vision enshrined in India's constitution (and held by the national leadership in the decades after independence). This is why the Nehruvian "idea of India" (Khilnani 1997) ultimately failed—it was an idea grafted onto a colonially shaped political-administrative infrastructure unable to support it. Within this context, the backward-caste movement launched an assault on structures of hegemony that had long provided a minority of upper-caste elites with control over both state institutions and the agrarian economy.

The category "backward castes," like the *varna* categories that dominated politics in the colonial period, has a built-in ambiguity. It can refer to all groups that are not part of the upper/forward castes, or it can refer specifically to the "Other Backward Classes" (OBCs), a category including castes thought to inhabit socioeconomic positions falling between the Scheduled Castes and upper, or "forward," castes. Especially when used in its broader sense to refer to all non-upper-caste groups this administrative category has the potential to divide the Indian political landscape into a "forward-caste" versus "backward-caste" dichotomy. In stark contrast to the image of the postcolonial developmental state that legitimized a centralization of state power, backward-caste politics launched a political assault on the ruling elite and involved very different notions of what "the state" is and the aims of state power. Although state-directed development might have claimed to be eliminating the "backwardness" of "backward castes," the backward-caste movement has sought to make the government itself "backward," ruled by backward caste leaders in the interests of lower castes—a radicalization of caste through democratic mobilization.

Unlike the colonial period caste movements, then, the backward-caste movement was not seeking social reform and recognition of higher status by state authorities. The aims of leaders of the backward-caste movement were much broader. As R. L. Chandapuri, then head of the Bihar State Backward Classes Federation, wrote in 1949, "Whenever any revolution is to take place in India, it will be spearheaded only by the backward classes and downtrodden people. The landed aristocrats and forward class leaders who are in league with capitalism are blackmailers. They are only slogan mongers and their aim is to maintain status quo in Indian society."[24] Especially when used in its broad sense, to include all non-upper-caste groups, calls for the empowerment of backward castes amounted to a direct attack against the ruling elite in India. In this sense, Chandapuri called for a "second freedom struggle" to liberate the backward castes.[25]

In 1949, he wrote in the Hindi weekly *Pichada Varga*: "Only Shudra Raj in India can unite humanity and lead to the formation of one world government." This caste-based radical utopianism, along with a search for electoral support, led the socialists into an alliance with the backward-caste movement.

The Socialists and the Backward Castes

Francine Frankel writes that "by the 1960s, two new caste formations [forward versus backward castes] began to change the contour of Bihar's political life.... The emergence of these caste-based political categories led the state, by the late 1970s towards a politics of polarization" (1989, 47). The instigation of this polarization was the backward-caste movement, a loose association of leaders—many deeply influenced by Lohia—who operated both within the Congress and in opposition parties, sharing the goal of backward-caste empowerment. Although the movement lacked a clearly defined leadership and mass organizations—despite Lohia's efforts—its diverse leaders and activists found a common platform in the issue of reservations for the "Other Backward Classes" as well as demands for increased backward-caste representation within state and central cabinets.

In 1957, a faction of the All India Backward Classes Federation led by Chandapuri formed a short-lived political party and then merged with the Socialist Party after the Socialists passed a resolution supporting a 60 percent reservation for backward castes in political and government positions.[26] Many backward-caste leaders believed that Congress leaders, who favored an alliance of upper caste, Scheduled Castes, and Muslims, were neglecting their communities. The socialist opposition, spearheaded by Ram Manohar Lohia, exploited this gap, weakening the position of the Congress and leading to the emergence of non-Congress state governments during the late 1960s. The Socialist Party, whose decentralized Gandhian socialism differed from the socialism of Nehru's developmental state, was formed after the Congress Socialist Party (CSP) split from the Congress in 1948 (Dutt 1981). This relationship between backward-caste reservation politics and a political tradition of Gandhian socialism has been complex and often unsteady, reflecting the contradictions between a radical vision of caste-based democratic revolution and the particularistic interests of colonial-era caste identities.

With the prospect of defeating the Congress in 1967, the alliance between the Backward Classes Federation and the Socialist Party was revitalized. After the Congress defeat and the formation of the first non-Congress government in Bihar, opposition to the caste composition of the new cabinet resulted in senior members of the Backward Class Federation resigning from the Socialist Party to form the Shoshit Dal (Party of the Exploited). The Shoshit Dal then aligned itself with the Congress, toppled the new government, and elected B. P. Mandal the first backward-caste chief minister of Bihar (Frankel 1989). The next five years were marked by intense political instability, with nine different ministries and three periods of President's Rule. Much of this political crisis was caused by constant floor crossing in the assembly, with many MLAs shifting parties amid unstable alliances between various party and caste interests. During this period, OBC politicians actively emerged as powerful political players, and only two of the nine chief ministers in this period were from the once politically dominant upper castes. As Jaffrelot writes, "The mobilization of the backward castes on the quota issue in the 1960s contributed more than any other movement had previously done to the crystallization of a lower caste front in north India" (2003, 237). The backward-caste movement had come into direct conflict with the Congress regime, but was not strong enough to displace it. The result was political paralysis.

In Bihar, the most important socialist leader, and the figurehead for the growing anti-Congress movement, was Jayaprakash Narayan, a freedom fighter who was widely revered as a Gandhian figure popularly imagined as somehow above the perceived corruption of party politics (Chandra 2003, 95). In 1974, often violent, student-led protest movements emerged in Gujarat and then Bihar demanding the resignation of state Congress governments. In Bihar, Jayaprakash Narayan led this protest movement, known as the JP movement, which spread across north India, causing great disruption with massive rallies, strikes, and shutdowns. The movement eventually demanded the resignation of Prime Minister Indira Gandhi and threatened to *gherao* (surround) her house. Indira Gandhi responded with the imposition of emergency rule in June 1975 and the subsequent suspension of democracy in India for twenty-two months.

Jayaprakash Narayan (JP) considered his populist movement as the catalyst for what he termed a "total revolution" that would cleanse Indian public life of corruption and the authoritarian rule of the Congress Party and Indira Gandhi in particular.[27] The JP movement and the subsequent Emergency pitted two very different political projects in direct opposition—the interventionist state of the passive revolution and the Gandhian socialism of JP that emphasized democratic decentralization and a Rousseau-like conception of popular democracy as continual popular participation and agitation. The JP movement had a deep impact on political development in Bihar and other parts of India. Hindu nationalist organizations such as the Rashtriya Swayamsevak Sangh (RSS) became increasingly central to the JP movement, which was the basis of Indira Gandhi's and the Communist Party of India's (CPI) claim that the movement had a fascist potential, a claim that was meant to justify the imposition of emergency rule.[28] The JP movement also has had a profound influence on the regional parties claiming to represent lower-caste interests that emerged across north India in the 1990s and especially in Bihar where JP's influence was the strongest, although analysts of lower-caste politics have commented infrequently on this influence.[29] Almost every important contemporary politician in Bihar began his or her political career during the JP movement. In fact, it was within the JP movement that OBC politics first emerged as a mass, populist movement (see next chapter). This political background of oppositional agitation in part explains the hostility toward state-directed development among the lower-caste leaders who came to power in the 1990s in Bihar and the ensuing conflicts between politicians and other state institutions that are examined in Chapter 3.

During the Emergency, declared by Indira Gandhi in 1975 in the wake of the JP movement's attempt to dislodge her from power, she appointed Jagannath Mishra as Bihar chief minister, and many of the opposition leaders, including Jayaprakash Narayan, were jailed. Mishra was known as a "Sanjay man," referring to his proximity to Indira Gandhi's powerful son (Kohli 1990, 215–219). Kohli observed that by this time, "Power in states like Bihar had increasingly become a function of loyalty to Indira Gandhi. . . . As more and more officeholders were appointed from New Delhi, politics within the state took on a qualitatively new top-down characteristic" (1990, 216). This intensified a progressive weakening of the Congress Party as a grassroots organization in Bihar because "below Mishra was a highly fragmented and political elite and bureaucracy that did not readily respond to an appointed leader. One of the strategies adopted by Mishra and by nearly all subsequent state leaders was to consolidate control by appointing ministers, civil servants, and police officers who were loyal" (1990, 216). The Emergency regime was the most dramatic attempt to implement the Congress model of top-down planned development through the suspension of democracy, a desperate reaction to the contradictions inherent in this model. But since such an approach still required the use of colonially shaped state institutions for implementation, it was ultimately futile.

After the Emergency was lifted in 1977, the anti-Congress Janata Party came to power with Karpoori Thakur as chief minister in a sweeping repudiation of the Emergency regime. Karpoori Thakur, whose mentor was JP, was the most important backward-caste leader in Bihar until his death in 1989. Thakur was from the Nai (barber) caste, a small but geographically dispersed caste that is categorized in Bihar as Annexure One, or "backward" within the backward-caste category. This caste position was ideal for forging a backward-caste unity and contrasts with the positions of contemporary backward-caste leaders in Bihar who tend to belong to populous and relatively well-off groups within the backward castes (although I discuss the recent rise of nondominant castes in Chapter 7). In 1978, Karpoori Thakur implemented the 1971 Bihar Backward Classes Commission Report for state-level backward-caste reservations—known as the Mungeri Lal Commission—resulting in widespread rioting by forward-caste youths and the fall of Karpoori's government.

So although the socialist opposition relied on backward-caste support, divisions between upper-caste and lower-caste leaders within the coalition prevented the sustained merging of the socialist and backward-caste movements that Lohia had envisioned. Upper-caste socialist leaders resisted giving their backward-caste colleagues effective control of the state government, and backward-caste leaders, including Chandapuri, were willing to switch sides and join the Congress to achieve such control. As a result, both movements were weakened.

Thus in the longer view, the significant political challenges to Congress as well as to upper-caste dominance from the late 1960s forward were nonetheless unable to dislodge the supremacy of Congress and of the upper castes, and the Congress returned to power in Bihar—as in Delhi—for the subsequent decade. Rural development, conceived increasingly in terms of welfare provision for the poor, expanded significantly with the establishment of a system of village "fair-price" shops (by the 1980s India had become a food surplus country), and rural employment and housing schemes channeled increasing resources to the rural poor, reinforcing the Congress's political alliance of upper-caste brokers and Dalit laborers.

But although many people did benefit from the numerous welfare schemes that began during Indira Gandhi's long tenure as prime minister, at the local level, dominant landowning castes remained in control of the institutions charged with implementing these measures, and the poor received whatever development resources were not siphoned off on the way down. Congress rule during this period was replicated at the village level with one caste of dominant landlords usually mediating access to the state, and with development resources flowing according to long-established patron-client relations in the village (see Chapter 5). This political mediation allowed patron-client relations to persist despite the partial commercialization of agricultural labor markets in the wake of the green revolution that began in the late 1960s, expanding into many parts of Bihar by the 1980s.[30] Akhil Gupta (1998), for example, described a shift in the reproduction of caste dominance from a patronage that was based on control of land to a "brokerage" that was based on control over the distribution of development resources. And Paul Brass commented, "Local power cannot persist without control over or influence in government institutions" (1984, 334). Landowning castes maintained their dominance, not only despite Indira Gandhi's populism, but also through control of the very welfare schemes that were meant to end rural poverty. The Congress Party could contrast the continued dominance of landed elites within village contexts with the progressive intentions of a central leadership; the populist image of Indira Gandhi fighting vested interests on behalf of the poor majority was set against the "implementation failures" of planned development, attributed to the reactionary or corrupt tendencies of provincial-level government and party leaders (Kaviraj 1997, 52–53). In the process, of course, the Congress was also able to maintain its political hegemony, using a rhetoric of populist development to cement an alliance between upper castes and the rural poor that kept the status quo largely intact.

But the fact that the Naxalite movement and agrarian violence erupted with full force in the 1980s demonstrates the limitations of this strategy as the Congress alliance of upper castes and the rural poor was clearly breaking down in many places. The only trajectory of agricultural development that could be built on such a political alliance was landlord-driven agrarian capitalism. In the countryside, the concept of the passive revolution implied a "molecular transformation" of landed elites operating according to a feudal ethos into a class of agro-capitalists. This is what the green revolution was clearly intended to achieve and why there were concerns that it could turn from green to red (Frankel 1971). But while developing in some canal-irrigated areas of Bihar (see especially Chakravarti 2001),

this proved to be impossible as a path for the state as a whole because
of resistance from politically ascendant OBC tenant cultivators and the
emergence of armed resistance on the part of laborers in the places where
it did develop. This left peasant-driven agrarian capitalism as the only viable option.[31] And, as we have seen, there was intense resistance to such a
trajectory of development by upper-caste landed elites who were able to
leverage their influence within state institutions to prevent this from happening. The impasse, therefore, was essentially political—landlord-driven
development was blocked by the politicization of the peasantry while a
peasant-driven alternative was blocked by upper-caste control of state institutions. So the contradictions of development in Bihar, in fact, reflected
the specificities of postcolonial democracy—they resulted from an electoral democracy with universal franchise operating within institutional
contexts shaped by colonial processes of state formation.

By the late 1980s, the political strategies of co-opting OBC elites and
the containment of the poor through welfare schemes controlled by
upper castes had both reached their practical limits. The passive revolution model of state-directed development from above—unable to be effectively implemented in Bihar—was about to be overturned by a politics
of "social justice" seeking caste-based democratic empowerment.

Lalu Yadav's Bihar

An Incomplete Revolution

We examined in the last chapter how the tension between a "passive revolution" strategy of state-directed development that perpetuated upper-caste hegemony and a process of democratization that was progressively politicizing lower-caste peasants and laborers had reached an impasse. As a result, struggles expanded well outside the domain of democratic politics. There was a deepening agrarian conflict, a spreading Naxalite movement of armed laborers countered by a proliferation of caste-based militias (*sena*) of the landlords (Bhatia 2005, Das 1983, Louis 2002). The Congress-ruled state government, unable to contain growing unrest since it depended on upper castes to deliver votes and since state institutions remained under the influence of local elites, consistently sided with landlords in forcibly repressing challenges to their dominance. By the late 1980s, some analysts feared that Bihar was descending into chaos (Kohli 1990).

But the forces of democratization were soon to break this impasse, even if this did not mean the restoration of stability. This chapter examines what occurred when lower-caste leaders who emerged from the "backward-caste" movement captured the reins of power. This period began when Lalu Prasad Yadav became chief minister in 1990, with fifteen years of rule by him and, later, his wife Rabri Devi, thrusting Bihar into a very new political era. For his critics, Lalu represented everything that was wrong with Bihar, and even India. Bihar during this period came to be synonymous with bad governance, corruption, criminality, and what many considered to be a near total breakdown of law and order, public health, education, and development. For his supporters, Lalu came to embody a politics of lower-caste empowerment that overturned centuries of upper-caste hegemony, providing the dignity and influence generated by democratic participation to the oppressed masses. But Lalu Yadav's democratic revolution reflected the culmination of much longer political movements. The history of the backward-caste movement and the contradictions within the Congress-led "passive revolution" examined in the previous chapter explain how upper-caste political hegemony and the Congress regime were so quickly and dramatically displaced. This chapter examines the structure and dynamics of the new political formation that emerged—an exploration that will continue in subsequent chapters within specific sites—and the ways in which what Lalu Yadav termed the "upper-caste system" responded.

Since the "passive-revolution" political alliance was completely overturned and the discourse of development marginalized, we need an entirely different theoretical apparatus to make sense of Lalu Yadav's Bihar. In analyzing this tumultuous period in Bihar, I find it useful to draw from the political theorist Ernesto Laclau's (2005) theorization of what is often dismissively termed "populism" as actually reflecting a radically democratic political logic that is a central component of democratic politics in much of the world. I argue that the logic of Lalu Yadav's populism was fundamentally different from the Congress regime based on the project of state-directed development and poverty alleviation. The passive-revolution strategy was based on compromise, negotiation, and the co-option of the masses through promises to be delivered through state intervention. This is what Laclau terms a political "logic of difference" wherein demands are made based on particularistic categorizations (the rural poor, the illiterate, Scheduled Castes, widows, etc.), and resources distributed through an administrative apparatus. Indira Gandhi's *garibi hatao* (eliminate poverty) may have leant this strategy a populist dynamic at times by promising to bypass local elites in the name of the poor (see Gupta 1999), but the political logic remained that of meeting the demands of categories of people through a state machinery that remained effectively under elite control.

Such a political logic of difference is reflected in Chatterjee's (2004, 2011) conception of "political society" with categories of people making concrete demands of government (i.e., illegal electricity connections, subsidized grains) in order to navigate their often precarious life situations. Chatterjee (2008) argues this division reflects a new version of the passive revolution in the neoliberal era, with a civil society tied to corporate capital now acting as the agent of capitalist transformation, replacing the role of the developmental state. An increasingly bourgeois civil society, made up of an expanding urban middle class highly critical of democracy, exercises influence over national policy through technocratic interventions while political society reflects the sphere of popular democracy, functioning to counter the dislocations of capitalist transformation through the distribution of welfare resources. It should be noted that, as in the passive-revolution model, in this formulation democracy has an essentially reactionary role—corporate capital is the agent of change.[2] But in Lalu's Bihar, where a lower-caste dominated political society completely overwhelmed an upper-caste dominated civil society, the story could not have been more different.

Laclau's theorization of populism allows an analysis of the ways in which populist democracy can act as an agent of change.[3] He emphasizes a discursive division between "the people" and the elite, with the identity of "the people" articulated by combining diverse groups with various demands into a "chain of equivalence." Populism attempts to confront and transform "the system" through democratically mobilizing "the people." As we would expect, in India's postcolonial democratic context this played out in particular ways, reflecting the postcolonial character of political identities, state institutions, and the dynamics of local power. "The people"—the agent of popular sovereignty—was interpreted by the leaders of the socialist and backward-caste movements primarily in caste terms, as we saw in the previous chapter. The result was a discursive division between a "backward-caste" majority and a "forward-caste system." And the construction of this backward-caste identity involved a "chain of equivalence" composed of the individual caste identities of the late colonial period (Yadav, Koeri, Lohar, etc.), each of which was its own hegemonic project connected with specific caste networks and territorial interests, but which were tied together with the common aim of displacing a larger upper-caste hegemony.

The following sections examine the rise to power of Lalu Yadav, and the ways in which national political events provided Lalu with the opportunity to consolidate an alternate hegemonic alliance in Bihar, reducing the Congress to near irrelevance. I then turn to an analysis of Lalu's populist discourse of caste-based democratic empowerment, as well as its internal tensions with the narrower caste identities of the late colonial period, resulting in intensifying contradictions. This is followed by an examination of how the new, lower-caste hegemonic formation operated, particularly the democratic networks, centered on Lalu Yadav, through which power was exercised as state institutions were weakened. Finally, we turn to an examination of the unrelenting forces of opposition that Lalu's government faced, which, combined with internal contradictions within the new hegemonic alliance, resulted in a democratic revolution that ultimately remained incomplete, leading to the RJD's electoral defeat in 2005.

The Rise to Power of Lalu Yadav

Lalu Prasad Yadav was born into a family of marginal, near-landless cultivators in Phulwaria village in north Bihar, a background that was to become central to his populist appeal (Thakur 2000, 30). Nobody, including Lalu, knows the exact date of his birth—like many families living at the margins, such state-sanctioned markers of identity held little meaning.[4] Unlike most OBC leaders who came from landed families and represented the interests of a class of medium-to-large OBC farmers, Lalu's childhood experience of deprivation and upper-caste oppression resonated with the disenfranchised masses. As Shaibal Gupta put it, "Leaders like Karpoori Thakur represented a more Sanskritized section of the backwards, those with a certain level of education and economic power. It was a section that had achieved a certain economic empowerment and wanted to convert it into political empowerment through the socialist movement of the 1960s and 1970s. But with Lalu Yadav, we saw the emergence of the cockney backwards to the forefront, a non-Sanskritized, earthy, rustic section that spoke the local dialect and existed on the fringe of the market.... He, in a sense, reversed the process that leaders like Karpoori Thakur had begun. Under Laloo Yadav, electoral and political empowerment happened first, economic empowerment later."[5] This is a crucial point—Lalu's populism, rooted in his own humble background, is what would enable the backward-caste movement to expand its base of support well beyond the OBC elite in order to forge a radically different hegemonic formation.

As a boy Lalu moved to Patna, living with his uncle who was employed as a milkman at the Bihar Veterinary College. The often recounted story behind Lalu's move to Patna is that it was a response to harassment by upper-caste villagers who thought it improper that a Yadav cow-herder boy should be educated (Thakur 2000, 28). The small colony of simple one-room dwellings at the veterinary college, like Lalu's village roots, became central to his political identity. It is a surreal experience to visit the colony knowing that the man who ruled Bihar for fifteen years not only began his political career here, but continued to live in this urban slum for three months after becoming chief minister. As his uncle, clad in an old *lungi* and still living in his simple tenement, put it, "Everything began here."[6]

Lalu's long history of anti-Congress politics first began during his college days when he was elected the first OBC president of the Patna University Student Union. The start of Lalu's political career coincided with Jayaprakash Narayan's populist movement against Indira Gandhi in the 1970s (see previous chapter). Lalu emerged as the most prominent student leader of this movement in Bihar, leading agitations and being arrested along with other leaders. He earned a reputation for wit, humor, theatricality, and rustic oratory—delivering speeches in the regional dialect of Bhojpuri, instead of standard Hindi. While lacking a developed ideological foundation in the socialist and backward-caste movements, and not devoting much time to the nuts and bolts of political organizing, Lalu's oratory skills, charisma, and his background as a Yadav from a poor rural family made him an attractive leader for the socialist opposition (Thakur 2006, 54–65). As described in the previous chapter, the JP movement was the first time that backward-caste leaders engaged in a mass politics of agitation. Jayaprakash Narayan's enormous rallies in Gandhi Maidan at the center of Patna, with Lalu Yadav accompanying him onstage, were a prelude to the politics of populist agitation that would engulf the state in the 1990s (Thakur 2006, 65).

By the end of the 1980s, Lalu had already held offices as a member of the Bihar legislative assembly (MLA) and as a member of parliament (MP). In 1988, with the death of Karpoori Thakur, then the most important OBC leader in Bihar, Lalu Yadav became the leader of the opposition in the Bihar assembly. The 1989 national elections set the stage for the political transformations that occurred in the 1990s. At a national level, V. P. Singh's Janata Dal–led National Front defeated the Congress through the support of the BJP as well as the Left parties. It marked the end of one-party dominance in India and the beginning of the current era of coalition politics. This also marked the emergence of the BJP as a national political force. In Bihar, this was the first national election when OBC candidates, with twenty-two seats, won more seats than upper-caste candidates, who garnered only sixteen. In 1990, a Janata Dal–led coalition replicated this routing of the Congress in the Bihar assembly elections.

Thus began fifteen years of state governments formed by the Janata Dal, subsequently known as the Rashtriya Janata Dal (RJD), and centered on the personality of Lalu Prasad Yadav.

It was only after Lalu had become chief minister that he really began to consolidate his electoral base by mobilizing massive support in the villages. Lalu Yadav, in fact, narrowly managed to win the party vote in order to become chief minister. "The vote was divided on caste lines: the Harijans went for Ram Sundar Das [a Dalit and former chief minister], the upper castes for Raghunath Jha [a Brahman]. Lalu scraped through by a whisker, keeping most of the backward votes with him" (Thakur 2000, 62). But if Lalu Yadav becoming chief minister was the culmination of the merger of the anti-Congress and "backward-classes" movements in Bihar, it was also the point of departure for a new political project. Lalu quickly established a distinctive presence. Instead of holding his swearing-in ceremony in Raj Bhavan, the colonial-era governor's residence and the site of all previous ceremonies, Lalu selected the statue of Jayaprakash Narayan near Gandhi Maidan, the large public park in the center of Patna that had been a focal point of anti-Congress protest rallies during the JP movement. The ceremony marked the beginning of Lalu's populist tenure. "Thousands turned out. It was unlike any official ceremony; it was more a mass celebration, a boisterous *mela*" (Thakur 2000, 64).[7] Lalu promised, "Now there will be no atrocities, now there will be no excesses, now there will be no corruption, now there will be no dishonesty" (*ab koi atyachaar nahin hoga, ab koi zulm nahin hoga, ab koi bhrashtachaar nahin hoga, ab koi be-imani nahin hoga*, Thakur 2000, 69; my translation). This statement links the corruption and dishonesty related to misuse of state resources with the atrocities and excesses related to caste oppression in village contexts, simultaneously challenging upper-caste control of the state and territorial dominance. In retrospect many would see Lalu's emphasis on corruption as ironic, for charges of corruption related to what became known as the "fodder scam" were to become Lalu's largest political liability, as described below.

Initially, Lalu refused to move into the chief minister's official residence, continuing to share a small one-room apartment with his brother at the Bihar Veterinary College. He even held cabinet meetings on the grounds in front of the complex. After moving into the chief minister's official residence a few months later, he opened it to the public, drawing large crowds on the lawn outside the house. These gestures earned Lalu a reputation of being different from previous chief ministers; rather, he was a common man, connected to the masses, and who had now been raised to the highest office in the state.[8] As a prominent leader of the JP movement put it, "For the first time in the history of democratic India, the peoples' representative took oath on road. . . . We all thought that Gandhi, Jayaprakash and Lohia would have liked this very much, that the peoples' representatives left Raj Bhavan [the governor's house] and took their oath amongst the people . . . this was a turning point."[9]

Consolidation of a New Hegemonic Alliance

National political events were crucial for the consolidation of a new hegemonic alliance in Bihar. In 1990, V. P. Singh, prime minister under the National Front government that was elected in 1989—then only the second non-Congress government in Delhi since independence—decided to implement the recommendations of the Mandal Commission (headed by B. P. Mandal, who had been the first OBC chief minister of Bihar), reserving a portion of central government employment for OBCs. The aims of these reservations, comprising some twenty-five thousand jobs in a country of over one billion, went well beyond employment opportunities. Regarding the effects of Mandal, V. P. Singh wrote, "Now that every party is wooing the deprived castes, with every round of elections more and more representatives of the deprived sections will be elected. This will ultimately be reflected in the social composition of the local bodies, state governments, and central government. A silent transfer of power is taking place in social terms."[10] Mandal represented a direct assault on the social composition of government that had resulted from the long processes of state formation examined in the previous chapter, a direct assault on upper-caste hegemony. While this was a decision made in Delhi, it represented the coming to power of a socialist backward-caste alliance that had been forged primarily in Bihar and neighboring Uttar Pradesh, reflecting a complex intertwining of state and national political developments.

Lalu Yadav aggressively supported the Mandal Commission despite the widespread violence following Prime Minister V. P. Singh's earlier decision to implement these recommendations. This conflict was particularly intense in Bihar, where armed conflict broke out between upper-caste and OBC groups in rural areas across this state. Within this charged context, Lalu's militant campaigning for caste empowerment, just months after becoming chief minister, earned him a reputation as the foremost leader of

a "backward-caste" state government fighting against an upper-caste system, cementing his populist image. The effects of this were profound. The
socialist tradition of the Janata Dal became secondary to its status as a
backward-caste government embodied in the leadership of Lalu Yadav,
and upper-caste socialists who had been central to the Janata Dal coming
to power were marginalized. And under Lalu's leadership Mandal greatly
expanded the backward-caste movement's social base, moving beyond
the emerging elites of the lower castes who had previously been central to
the movement to develop a following among the mass of the rural poor,
many of whom had never even freely voted before. While this had been
the electoral strategy of the national Janata Dal crafted by V. P. Singh,
it was Lalu who successfully realized its potential in Bihar even as the
Janata Dal government in Delhi collapsed. As V. P. Singh put it, "The inexorable process of transfer of power to the deprived has begun. . . . Bihar
was my lab experiment of social justice. And under Lalu Yadav, it has
been a success."[11]

The 1990 election marked a critical turning point in the assembly—
for the first time the number of lower-caste MLAs exceeded the number
of upper-caste MLAs (Table 1). After Lalu Yadav became chief minister, there was also a clear increase in the number of lower-caste ministers
and a decrease in the number of upper-caste ministers in the cabinet, the
latter going from 62 percent in 1985 to 27 percent by 1994 (Jaffrelot 2003,
358). By 1995, the number of OBC MLAs had reached almost 50 percent of the assembly, up from 27.7 percent in 1985 and approaching the
52 percent that the Mandal Commission had estimated to be the national
population of OBC castes in India. The number of upper-caste MLAs declined to 17.3 percent from 36 percent in 1985. Although from 1972 the
trend had been gradually moving in this direction, in the space of just a
decade, from 1985 to 1995, the number of OBC candidates elected to the
assembly nearly doubled, while the number of upper-caste candidates was
more than halved. This dramatic transformation of political representation is what Jaffrelot (2003) means when he speaks of a "silent revolution"
in north India.

If Mandal laid the foundation for the emergence of a new hegemonic
formation in Bihar, another event consolidated it. In 1990, the BJP leader
L. K. Advani began his dramatic and highly controversial *rath yaatra*, a
"chariot procession" across north India aimed at stirring up popular support for building a temple at the site of a mosque in Ayodhya, which
Hindu nationalists believe was built over the birthplace of the Hindu god

TABLE I. **Caste Background of Members of the Bihar Assembly**[12]

	Upper Caste MLAs	%	OBC MLAs	%
1967	133	41.82	82	25.78
1969	122	38.36	94	29.55
1972	136	42.78	76	23.89
1977	124	38.27	92	28.39
1980	120	37.03	96	29.62
1985	118	36.41	90	27.77
1990	105	32.40	117	36.11
1995	56	17.28	161	49.69

Ram. When Advani reached Bihar, Chief Minister Lalu Yadav, in an un-expectedly defiant act that received national coverage, arrested him and impounded his elaborately equipped trucks, resulting in the outbreak of religious violence in Uttar Pradesh, Rajasthan, Gujarat, Madhya Pradesh, and Karnataka (Frankel 2005, 712).

In north Bihar, communal riots in 1989 in Bhagalpur, just before the Janata Dal had come to power, had already contributed to the declin-ing appeal of the Congress Party in the state, as many Muslims blamed the riots on Congress inaction. This was the latest manifestation of a long history of Hindu-Muslim tension in Bihar, going back to the cow protec-tion movements of the late ninetheenth century (Pandey 1990). Advani's arrest in 1990 enabled Lalu to gain the personal trust and electoral sup-port of Bihar's alienated Muslims, earning him a reputation as a force that could prevent the spread of the BJP and religious violence in Bihar. Two years later, this reputation was strengthened. It was a substantial accom-plishment that the Janata Dal government was able to prevent Hindu-Muslim conflict in Bihar at a time when riots broke out across many parts of north India, after Hindu nationalist activists demolished the mosque in Ayodhya. True to a populist logic, Lalu did not provide Muslims secu-rity through a well-functioning police force. Rather, wherever episodes of religious violence began to break out in Bihar, Lalu immediately trav-eled to the site and pressured local officials to contain the conflict, even camping there until peace was restored. One Muslim religious leader voiced the sentiments of many in asserting that, "For Muslims, Lalu has succeeded in creating an era of peace."[13] Lalu himself boasted, "I have made an alliance between those who worship the cow [Yadavs] and those who eat the cow."[14] In the larger national context of an ascendant Hindu nationalism, for Muslims peace and security took precedence over other issues. As one middle-class Muslim man explained to me his support for

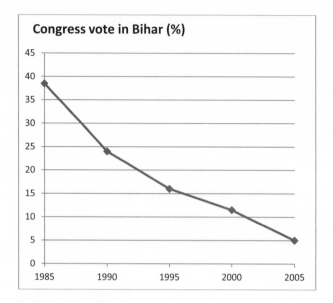

FIGURE 1. Congress vote in Bihar (%)

the RJD while traveling in a local train in 2003, "Sure, I would like to see more development, but the safety of my family is first."

The new electoral combination that Lalu forged based on support from Muslims and OBCs (particularly Yadavs) was popularly termed the "M-Y alliance." If Muslims are considered a single "caste" (as Lalu mistakenly assumed, contributing to his later downfall as we shall see below), then Muslims and Yadavs are the two most populous castes in Bihar, together comprising around 27 percent of the vote. In India's first-past-the-post parliamentary system with many candidates competing for any given constituency, as little as 35 percent of the popular vote can win a majority of seats. This combination, therefore, provided a very firm foundation.[15] By supplementing this core support with other OBC castes and Dalits, especially from the poor among these groups, the new hegemonic alliance that Lalu Yadav forged succeeded in reducing the once unassailable Congress to political irrelevance in the state (Figure 1).

The Discourse of Lower-Caste Empowerment

In April 2002, Lalu Yadav was sitting in the office of the speaker of the assembly in Patna, surrounded by fawning ministers. He had sent Rajan, a powerful Brahman member of the legislative assembly with a reputation as a feared "mafia don," to fetch me, probably foreshadowing what he wanted to say. After I sat down, Lalu dramatically declared in semi-fluent English, "The forward castes used to rule Bihar. I have finished them off." He pointed to various "forward-caste" leaders in the room, including Rajan, and named them by caste, "Brahman, Bhumihar, Rajput . . ." The implication was clear; they now served him. Raising a foot from his leather sandals, he said, "Look at my foot. See, I am missing a toenail. . . . *This is democracy.*" After a dramatic pause to let this bewildering statement sink in, he continued. "I lost this toenail when I was a poor boy living in my village. We barely had enough to eat and I used to herd buffaloes all day, sometimes so late that I would fall asleep on the back of a buffalo on my way home. One day, a buffalo that I was herding stepped on my foot and I lost the toenail. . . . Now look at what a tall chair I am sitting in [the chief minister's chair]! I have proven that ballot boxes are more powerful than machine guns. Votes can decide whether a man will be in the dust or riding in an airplane. I am a true Naxalite from birth, a democratic Naxalite."

Lalu invoked a very particular conception of democracy during this encounter that reveals a great deal about his political project. Democracy for Lalu meant, above all, a radical negation of upper-caste rule, embodied in his own position. While upper-caste mafia figures such as Rajan remained powerful, as did a largely upper-caste bureaucracy, they were now subordinated, at least publicly, to Lalu Yadav. This is how Lalu, the politician, was transformed into Lalu Yadav, the symbol, and why he constantly referred to himself in the third person. This explains why Lalu described his political project as metonymically actualized in his own person—his missing toenail—as someone moving from the position of a poor buffalo herder to become the most powerful man in Bihar through democratic means. He considered caste empowerment to be equivalent to what many people came to refer to as "Lalu Raj."

According to Laclau (2005), every populist movement needs an "empty signifier" to articulate the disparate, and often contradictory, demands into a unified movement. Lalu Yadav became such an empty signifier: a unified lower-caste struggle against upper-caste rule became embodied in his proudly rustic, combative and thoroughly antiestablishment persona. When I used to ask political observers in Bihar during this period who they considered to be the most important political leaders, a common response was some version of, "Lalu, Lalu, and Lalu, followed by Lalu" (and at this time it was actually Rabri Devi who was chief minister!). For fifteen years, Lalu, as symbol and as the apex of authority, was the pivot around which Bihar's political life revolved. Lalu came to be synonymous with the backward-caste movement in Bihar and—with a reputation of being an unwavering defender of secularism—he also articulated the alliance between this movement and Muslims opposed to the rise of Hindu nationalism. This is how such a radically different hegemonic formation was able to displace the "passive-revolution" alliance of the Congress era.

The political discourse of what many people came to refer to as "Lalu Raj" was drawn from the radical democratic vocabulary of "social justice" and popular rule of the socialists and Jayaprakash Narayan's populist movement, embodied in the figure of Lalu Yadav. By constantly mixing stories of his own rise to power from humble beginnings into his political rhetoric, Lalu sought to instill dignity and political ambition in people who had long been oppressed, and he succeeded in inspiring Bihar's lower-caste majority as no one before him had. Lalu built a mass base of support for himself in villages across Bihar, using a helicopter (which he called his "flying machine") to access remote villages, many of which had never been visited by a prominent politician. Instead of visiting the upper-caste sections of villages, where politicians in the past had been received, Lalu made a point of visiting poorer OBC and Scheduled Caste areas. And he told his lower-caste supporters that they had a right to access state institutions long controlled by upper castes. As a senior Janata leader put it, "Lalu's main aim was to uplift the poor. He told them about their rights. The poor didn't go to the block [local government offices] or the thana [police station]. Lalu taught them that going to the thana was their right . . . he gave them voice."[16]

He sought to mobilize supporters not primarily through policy initiatives, but by intimately identifying himself with the lower-caste poor. In response to a question about what policies the state government would adopt in order to protect Dalits after a massacre of Musahars (the poorest caste in Bihar, whose name literally means "rat eater"), for example, Lalu responded:

Listen, I know the pulse of the people. In the fields there is a species of rats known as kronsa. You catch it and burn a small hole in its belly, then pull out all the intestine, etc, stuff it with green chili and masala and then roast it. All the juices and hair get burnt out and when it is roasted properly you just peel off the skin and taste it. Our Musahars eat rats and I have also done it. That's why I know what they think, how they think.[17]

By identifying himself in such explicit terms with the poorest sections among the lower castes—here, even claiming to have eaten rats, a practice that many people, including people from his own caste, would consider to be extremely defiling—Lalu differentiated himself from other OBC leaders and expanded his base of support beyond his own caste. The fact that Lalu made these comments during an interview with an English-language newsmagazine with a predominantly urban, upper-caste readership reflected a lack of concern with what this segment thought of him. Such statements were a defiant challenge to the established order, an affirmation, at least in rhetoric, that the very lowest sections of society were now in power in Bihar.

One account paraphrases Lalu's rhetoric this way:

> He exhorted them to come out and claim what was theirs. "This government, this power, the state, this is all yours. You have been deprived of your share because those who ruled the state were not bothered about you. . . . But now your man has captured the establishment. . . . These people have oppressed and suffocated you for thousands of years, they have made you labor and they have kept the fruits for themselves. Tell them that they are not needed anymore, tell them their hour is over, tell them they are about to be cast in the dustbin, tell them you have assumed the reins, there has been a revolution in Bihar, the exploiters have been thrown out." (Thakur 2000, 82–85)[18]

The discourse of lower-caste politics was in many ways opposed to the project of development. A popular Janata Dal slogan was *vikaas nahiñ, samaan chahiye* (we need dignity, not development).[19] Another slogan, *bhurabal hatao*, meaning "wipe out the upper castes," used *bhurabal* as a Hindi acronym for the four upper-caste groups in Bihar: Bhumihars, Rajputs, Brahmans, and Lalas (Kayasths). *Bhurabal hatao* played on Indira Gandhi's famous slogan, *garibi hatao* (eliminate poverty), and indicates the ways in which the development discourse of antipoverty schemes and state planning had been replaced with appeals for caste struggle.

In an era of neoliberal reform, Lalu Yadav was also generally hostile to the corporate sector (seen as part of the "upper-caste system"), in stark contrast to other chief ministers who aggressively wooed corporate investment.[20] Lalu on occasion even questioned the benefits of India's much-touted "knowledge economy" for the majority of Indians, declaring, "IT-YT kya hota hai" (loosely translated as "IT; what the hell is this?").[21] But he also failed to even attempt the main alternative—a strengthening of the state as a bulwark against neoliberalism, as will be examined below. While the hegemonic alliance of the Congress era had been overturned by Lalu's M-Y backward alliance, the discourse of development was displaced with a radical discourse of caste-based popular sovereignty.

Underlying the symbolic unity of backward-caste empowerment, however, was the privileged position of the Yadav caste within Lalu's Bihar, which played out electorally with Yadavs' forming the loyal core of the Janata Dal's voter base. Laclau (2005) emphasizes that an "empty signifier" implies a part of a hegemonic project that, while having a particular social identity, comes to represent the movement as a whole. With Lalu Yadav emerging as the "empty signifier" of the project of backward-caste empowerment, many Yadavs saw their entire caste as taking on such a role, serving as a vanguard for the struggle against upper-caste hegemony. Yadav leaders justified an emergent Yadav hegemony within a purportedly "backward-caste" government by portraying their caste as the champions of the lower castes as a whole, the empowerment of the former automatically enabling the empowerment of the latter.

There is a longer history to this claim of Yadav leadership of the backward-caste movement. As early as 1966 at a Yadav caste *sabha*, "Ram Lakhan Singh Yadav—the Congress leader from Bihar—declared that the Yadavs 'were leading the 90 percent of the population which was backward,' and B. P. Mandal, who was then chief minister of Bihar, declared that the Yadavs should 'lead the revolution.' "[22] This assertion includes representations of Krishna, the mythological ancestor of the Yadavs—an identity that became dominant through the *kshatriya* movements examined in the previous chapter—as the protector of the backward castes and even as the first "democratic political leader." As Michelutti (2008) observes, Yadavs often refer to themselves as a "caste of politicians" (Michelutti 2008, 252).[23]

At a Yadav caste *sabha*, Lalu Yadav explained:

> Lord Krishna was a person who was determined to fight injustice. Lord Krishna fought for the cause of the Backward Classes, the farmers, the cowherders and the economically weaker sections of the society. He fought against powers based on injustice and malign intentions. The question at the time was to find warriors with the courage to fight injustice. He gathered the children of the milkmen along with Yadavs and cowherders to create an army to fight against all social evils. Lord Krishna was the person who was born in jail and who fought against social odds. (Lalu Prasad Yadav, AIYM Convention, Vaishali-New Delhi, December, 26, 1999)[24]

This explains why Yadavs enjoyed disproportionate influence, even with opposition from other lower-caste groups, leading to accusations of "Yadav Raj." This is reflected in the number of Yadav members of the assembly as well as Yadav ministers in the state government.[25] In fact, the bulk of the dramatic increase in OBC political representation in the 1990s (Jaffrelot's "silent revolution") was actually an increase in Yadav representation. Yadavs constituted no less than 27 percent of state assembly members after 1995. Moreover, 40 percent of the Janata Dal's assembly members were Yadavs, compared with only 17 percent from other OBCs. As the percentage of upper-caste representation declined, the Yadav caste benefited most disproportionally in the political arena.[26] And growing popular resentment against Yadav Raj was a crucial factor in the eventual weakening and defeat of Lalu Yadav's government.

Democratic Networks of Governance

The project of lower-caste empowerment did involve some policy interventions, even if the key policy intervention of this era, the recommendations of the Mandal Commission, were implemented by Delhi, not Patna. The Janata government increased quotas for what are popularly known as "Extremely Backward Castes" (EBCs, officially termed "Annexure One" castes within the system of reservations implemented by Karpoori Thakur, himself an EBC, in 1977) in government jobs from 10 percent to 14 percent, and eliminated government tree and toddy (an alcoholic beverage tapped from a coconut tree, typically done by lower-caste groups) tax, which primarily benefited EBC groups.[27] The minimum wage for agricultural laborers was also raised (although little enforced); slums were regularized, what were called *charvaha* schools were established in remote areas so that children could attend while tending cattle (primarily benefiting poorer Yadavs), and legislation was passed making violation of rules regarding caste-based employment quotas a punishable offense. In 1993, the Patna and Bihar University Bills were passed, which reserved 50 percent of seats in university decision-making bodies for OBCs, and the name of Bihar University was changed to B. R. Ambedkar University (Chaudhary 1999, 209). Yadav milkmen were allowed to freely establish cowsheds in cities and towns, with many residents of Patna complaining to me of an invasion of buffaloes (Thakur 2000, 86–87). And the Patna golf club was closed, becoming grazing land in a deliberately symbolic example of "civil society" being overrun in the state.

But beyond these measures during the early years, little in the way of serious policy initiatives was pursued and the few that were attempted, such as Lalu's idea of setting up *charvaha* schools, were not sustained. Why did Lalu and other lower-caste politicians not aggressively embrace constructive reforms in areas such as primary education and rural health services that would have benefited the majority of the lower-caste poor? We might have expected the Janata Dal government to pursue an agenda of redistributive policies that would have expanded the role of the state, but instead public institutions were allowed to deteriorate, and few pro-poor policy initiatives were even attempted. The problem was not that Lalu chose redistribution over growth, but that he did not systematically pursue any policies, redistributive or otherwise. And yet Lalu Yadav and his wife won three consecutive terms, the longest winning streak in Bihar's democratic history. Only when political developments are analyzed according to the specificities of a postcolonial populist movement can we comprehend Lalu's political project as more than mere anarchy or simply an opportunistic "looting" of the state, as many contemporary observers suggested.

While lower castes had displaced upper castes within the realm of political representation, this was not the case within the bureaucracy, as will be examined in detail in the next chapter. The enactment of redistributive policies requires organizational machinery capable of implementation. Since almost all public institutions in Bihar were effectively controlled by the same upper castes that Lalu Yadav was attempting to displace from power, relying on these institutions was not only precarious, but weakening upper-caste influence within public life in Bihar often meant weakening upper-caste-dominated public institutions.

But the absence of policies of radical redistribution also resulted from inherent contradictions within the backward-caste alliance. Lalu's populism in the wake of Mandal succeeded in solidifying a forward- versus backward-caste political divide that politicized the lower-caste poor for the first time. But this did not change the fact that the alliance also depended on a class of OBC middle-to-large farmers who had benefited from *zamindari* abolition and the green revolution. And it is from these OBC elites that political leadership was drawn. This is why the most obvious policy intervention for empowering lower castes was never seen through—substantial land reforms that had the potential to fundamentally transform relations of production in the countryside. Lalu, whose background and populist politics tied him to the poor among the lower castes, did consider such a historic intervention. In the state assembly he once even declared that police should not intervene if tenants forcibly occupied the land they were tilling. But since most of his own party's MLAs were landowners, many substantial landowners, it became clear that any attempt to implement a serious project of land reform would probably mean the fall of the Janata Dal government. As a senior RJD leader put it, "Lalu declared (*adesh diye*) in the assembly that those poor people who farmed the land of the rich, zamindari-type landlords, if it was a poor tenant, he would be given [land rights] (*usko ho* jayega).... [But] many MLAs have land. Lalu faced pressure from all sides and it was withdrawn."[28] On the other hand, the Janata Dal's support among the mass of lower-caste small tenants and laborers explains why pro-farmer policies that would have benefited OBC landowners were also not enacted (as they had been by the Karpoori Thakur government). So, in addition to endemic conflict with an upper-caste-dominated bureaucracy, the inclusion of a broad coalition of class interests within the Janata Dal's backward-caste alliance explains the lack of a coherent policy agenda. The "passive-revolution" policy agenda of the Congress era was overturned, but it was not replaced with anything, including the neoliberal policies adopted by other states during this period.

In the absence of a policy agenda, the project of lower-caste empowerment was pursued through three interventions. First, state institutions were systematically weakened (examined in-depth in the next chapter), made possible by the new Janata electoral alliance that provided formal executive control over the state government. Lalu's militant anti-upper-caste politics were directed against an upper-caste hegemony resulting from the long processes of colonial state formation examined in the previous chapter. Because upper-caste dominance depended on control over the state and state-directed development, systematically weakening state institutions and marginalizing development-oriented governance become a viable strategy of lower-caste empowerment. The project of backward-caste empowerment, then, was not primarily aimed at "capturing the state." Above all, it was a project to displace the dominance of upper castes within villages, even if the pervasiveness of caste networks linking state institutions with local power made capturing, or weakening, the state a necessary part of this project.

Second, many lower castes were politicized for the first time, particularly many marginalized groups that had never had an independent voice, through the discourse of caste empowerment in the wake of Mandal. This weakened patron-client ties at the village level and raised the stakes for landlords who attempted to put down insubordination through force. As described above, Lalu mobilized his supporters through frequent campaigning, and through massive political rallies in Patna, such as the *lathi* rally described in the introduction, attended by hundreds of thousands of people from villages across Bihar. During these rallies, tens of thousands of lower-caste village poor invaded the urban capital, demonstrating the strength of Lalu's personal support, and serving as a vivid representation of the empowerment that he claimed to have achieved.

Lastly, the Congress mode of governance was replaced by governance through democratic networks centered on Lalu Yadav. A political leadership whose stated goal was the realization of lower-caste empowerment could go a long way toward accomplishing this by transferring power from upper-caste recruited officials in the state bureaucracy and police force to lower-caste elected politicians. By the phrase "democratic networks of governance" I do not mean to imply a normative evaluation that these networks functioned in a "democratic" manner. They did not. Rather, by democratic network I refer to networks of influence based above all on electoral considerations—clout was directly dependent on the ability to deliver votes. The operation of these networks will be ethnographically explored in subsequent chapters. They included elected politicians (who had proven their ability to marshal votes), but also the entire range of party activists, political brokers, and musclemen who played key roles in the electoral process. Lalu Yadav accomplished this transfer of power from the bureaucracy to the political class by centralizing decision making in his own hands, through very frequent transfers of officials whose loyalty was in doubt (which included many, if not most, Indian Administrative Service officers) and by tolerating and even encouraging political interference in administration and policing at all levels.

The empowerment of the political class that was essential to the Janata Dal's politics of caste empowerment, therefore, was dependent on the centralization of governance around Lalu Yadav, in a similar way that the Congress regime had been centralized around Indira Gandhi (Kohli 1994). The difference was that whereas Indira governed through loyal bureaucrats, with politicians ensuring that the activities of state-directed development converged with the interests of the Congress's electoral alliance (the passive-revolution model), Lalu, unable to effectively control the bureaucracy, governed through networks of politicians. In this mode of governance, proximity to Lalu Yadav often defined one's power. But even opposition or independent politicians wielded a great deal of authority. Many received backing from politicians in Delhi (including control over the distribution of central government contracts), who were anxious to weaken Lalu Yadav's stranglehold on the state. Since it was always possible that any politician could switch sides—I know politicians who have literally belonged to every major party and who openly admit that they would readily switch again if it served their interests—even Lalu needed to heed their demands. And since state institutions were weakened, elected politicians who had links to criminal networks as well as strong sources of support within villages were able to fill the void. This explains why, despite the project of backward-caste empowerment, even upper-caste politicians (such as Rajan, introduced above) who managed to get elected to the state assembly or parliament enjoyed enormous power.

Lalu never labored to create a party organization, or a disciplined party cadre. Instead, he held his base together through his personal charisma and populist appeal. Very little activity, and no substantial decision making, took place at the RJD headquarters in Patna, which was either empty or sparsely populated with second and third-tier leaders on the numerous occasions when I visited—a demonstration of the extent to which decision making and authority delegation were not institutionalized. In stark contrast to the abandoned feel of the RJD headquarters, Lalu's house was the center of Bihar's political life. Whenever I would visit, there were always throngs of politicians and local leaders waiting in the courtyard for an audience with sahib. The central process of Janata Dal decision making consisted of informal meetings with Lalu, usually at the chief minister's residence. Within districts, Janata Dal offices were often empty or unimportant, and key Janata Dal leaders frequently held no official position within the party (see Chapter 4, where the activities of RJD-affiliated groups at the regional level are examined). Unlike the earlier period of Congress rule, when district and even village-level Congress Party elections were keenly contested, internal Janata Dal elections were largely cosmetic and bore little relation to the actual delegation of authority.

As we might expect considering the privileged role of Yadavs in the new hegemonic alliance, not all OBC leaders were enthusiastic about the centralization of governance around Lalu Yadav. A missing second tier of leadership fed internal dissent among party leaders who felt increasingly marginalized by Lalu's personal control. Partly out of frustration with an organizational structure that did not allow for multiple spheres of influence, important leaders joined the opposition, taking their political supporters with them. In 1994, the first split within the Bihar Janata Dal occurred as preparations were under way for the 1995 assembly elections. Nitish Kumar, the most prominent leader of another relatively large OBC caste, the Kurmis, and who, like Lalu, had also been involved in anti-Congress politics during the Jayaprakash Narayan movement (see Chapter 1), broke from the Janata Dal and formed his own Samata Party (along with George Fernandes). Such a move threatened to crack the backward-caste mobilization that Lalu Yadav's Janata Dal had been relying on for electoral survival. The split reflected frustration among many Kurmis who felt that Yadavs had gained disproportionately from Lalu Yadav's struggle for caste empowerment. This was a major development because the Kurmi and Koeri castes (Nitish Kumar also claiming to represent the latter) are the two most populous OBC castes in Bihar after the Yadav caste. As discussed in the last chapter, these were the three caste groups most active in movements for *kshatriya* status in the late colonial period. This episode demonstrates the ways in which the "backward classes" movement's attempts to forge a united OBC identity were superimposed over earlier caste identities that continued to exert influence. Later political developments would show that this first split within the Janata Dal's OBC base of support in Bihar was an early indication of growing contradictions within its social base.

"The System" Strikes Back

It needs to be kept in mind that Lalu Yadav's populist politics, while profoundly destabilizing, played out within a federal polity that limited his ability to control many key institutions. An upper-caste "civil society" composed of businessmen, the media, the higher levels of the bureaucracy, the judiciary, and a national government increasingly guided by neoliberal policies, even while marginalized within political life in Bihar, mounted a sustained counterattack from outside. But, following populist logic, Lalu utilized this resistance from what he termed the "upper-caste system" in order to mobilize supporters and maintain power despite sustained opposition.

Considering the threat that Lalu represented to so many entrenched interests, it is not surprising that he faced considerable opposition. The relationship between Lalu's government and the center was strained from the start. In 1990, Prime Minister Chandra Shekhar—from Lalu's own Janata Dal—demanded Lalu's removal and threatened President's Rule. Such an acrimonious relationship with the center continued with the subsequent Congress government of P. V. Narasimha Rao from 1991 onward. From 1990 until 1993, the Janata Dal in Bihar split between two factions: Lalu supported by V. P. Singh in Delhi, and Ram Sundar Das (whom Lalu had narrowly beaten to become chief minister) supported by V. P. Singh's rival Ajit Singh.

In order to counter such attacks, Lalu enacted the interventions described above, focusing not only on backward-caste empowerment, but also on the poor among the lower castes. This enabled him to consolidate his hold on the party by expanding his populist appeal to previously nonpoliticized groups. He expanded the cabinet to an unwieldy size and doled out chairmanships of key institutions to his supporters. These measures enabled Lalu to survive against strong opposition which accused him of financial mismanagement and of provoking violence as Bihar faced serious and growing problems. In the wake of the Mandal agitations, armed "mafia" groups, led by both upper-caste and OBC politicians, proliferated amid a general decline of law and order that would continue throughout his rule. The state's financial condition deteriorated to the point that, by the middle of 1991, government salaries were not being paid and development expenditure was completely halted in order to meet current expenditure demands. During this period the media frequently predicted the imminent fall of Lalu's government. That Lalu time and again proved these predictions wrong was the result of the strength of the hegemonic alliance that he had forged, and the effectiveness of a populist political logic that was able to frame opposition as anti-lower-caste.

In the election to the state assembly in 1995, for instance, the state government was beleaguered by the then-chairman of the Election Commission of India, T. N. Seshan, and his relentless quest for "free and fair" polls in a state renowned for political violence, "booth capturing," and other forms of electoral malpractice. Seshan deployed large numbers of paramilitary forces, postponing elections five times in what many people came to see as a personal standoff with the chief minister.[29] Lalu's forceful response to this opposition was to insist that "despite all efforts by the Brahminical forces, Chief Election Commissioner T. N. Seshan, the Congress and the BJP, to sabotage our chances, the Janata Dal is coming back with a two-thirds majority."[30] Although this was an exaggerated claim, the

Janata Dal did win an absolute majority of 164 out of 324 seats plus the support of the CPI and CPI(Marxist), who won a combined thirty-three seats. Nitish Kumar's Samata Party, hailed by the national media as a serious competitor to the Janata Dal, won only seven seats. Lalu Yadav became the second chief minister in Bihar's history, after S. K. Sinha, the first chief minister after independence, to last a full term in power and then be reelected. The election marked a consolidation of the changes under way since 1989: the emerging dominance of OBCs within Bihar's political world. There were clear changes in the caste backgrounds of ministers in the state government. The number of OBC ministers increased from 42 percent to 52 percent, while the number of upper-caste ministers declined from 30 percent to just 13 percent (Chaudhary 2001, 326; Jaffrelot 2003, 358). With the widespread support of Yadavs, Muslims, and many Scheduled Castes, groups which alone represent nearly 40 percent of the population in Bihar, as well as significant support from other OBC groups, Lalu's electoral base appeared insurmountable.

With thirty-two Janata Dal MPs from Bihar in the Indian parliament, Lalu Yadav also occupied a powerful position in Delhi, in 1996 becoming the national president of the Janata Dal and a possible contender for prime minister. And then what became known as the "fodder scam" erupted, a major scandal involving the illegal withdrawal of more than 9.5 billion rupees from the Bihar Animal Husbandry Department from 1989 to 1995, which surfaced in 1996. As one journalist put it, "Where politicians fail [to defeat Lalu], it may be the courts and the CBI [Central Bureau of Investigation] that may find success."[31] A source within the CBI also expressed his feelings at the time that, although Lalu could not be politically marginalized, he could be legally marginalized.[32]

Initially, the Bihar police pursued the investigation of the fodder scam on Lalu's orders. The leader of the opposition in Bihar, Sushil Kumar Modi of the BJP (who became deputy chief minister of the National Democratic Alliance state government in 2005), filed a Public Interest Litigation (PIL) with the Patna High Court seeking an inquiry by the Central Bureau of Investigation (CBI). Modi's PIL argued that such a transfer of jurisdiction was required to preserve "public confidence" in the investigation, considering that influential members of the state government were accused in the case. The PIL was heard by the Supreme Court, which ruled in favor of turning the investigation over to the CBI, further stipulating that powers of oversight be retained by the Patna High Court. This decision, which not only transferred the inquiry to the CBI, but elevated the role of the Patna High Court over that of the state government, ignored established processes in India under which state governments routinely handled charges of corruption at the state level. The judiciary's intervention occurred within the context of the rise of judicial activism in India during the 1990s, and the often hostile relationship between the judiciary and the Bihar government, which we examine in greater detail in the next chapter.

The investigation then was taken over by a Scheduled Caste CBI joint director, U. N. Biswas, whom one account describes as a man with "a reputation as a driven Lalu Yadav-baiter, a man who was out to get the chief minister, a man sometimes so zealous in his pursuit of the politicians behind the scandal that he attracted the charge of violating his brief, of acting in a manner that was politically motivated. He would make his findings public through the press. He would state that the CBI was close to nabbing Lalu Yadav, making it sound like he was waging a personal war with the chief minister, as though it were a duel. 'He is a very clever man, a very smart man, but we will get him in the end,' Biswas would say" (Thakur 2000, 127).

As the fodder scam investigation progressed, Lalu faced increased opposition from all sides. His arrest seemed imminent after the CBI chief, in an unusual Sunday press conference, declared his intention to "charge-sheet" the chief minister. The national leadership of the Janata Dal and its allies demanded Lalu's resignation as chief minister. This demand partly reflected a desire by many national politicians to distance themselves from Lalu's increasingly corrupt image within the national media. This opposition from within the Janata Dal, however, was also a reaction against Lalu's monopolization of power within the party as discussed above. Lalu, in true populist fashion, described his Janata Dal opponents as "scared by my mass appeal and rapport with the masses. They would not succeed in politics unless they finish a leader with a mass base like me."[33]

Two prominent Janata Dal politicians based in Bihar, Ram Vilas Paswan and Sharad Yadav, joined the anti-Lalu faction. Ram Vilas Paswan enjoyed significant support from Paswans, the largest Scheduled Caste in Bihar, and his split with Lalu began a steady decline in Lalu's support among Scheduled Castes. Sharad Yadav was a prominent Yadav politician, whose opposition threatened Lalu's core constituency.[34] Sharad Yadav prepared to defeat Lalu in party elections for the national presidency of the Janata Dal. Lalu responded to this challenge by splitting the Janata Dal, forming his own Rashtriya Janata Dal (RJD) and taking most Janata Dal MLAs and MPs in Bihar with him.

After the Bihar governor approved a warrant of arrest against Lalu, the CBI went to the extent of officially requesting the army to help with the arrest—a request that was approved in a controversial oral order by the Patna High Court—amid fears of rioting by Lalu Yadav's supporters. The personalized ferocity of the campaign by the CBI enabled Lalu to charge that these actions were a conspiratorial attack by the upper castes whom he had displaced from power, an assault aimed at robbing him of his democratic mandate launched by people who could not defeat him in elections. He stated, "The forces which could not remove me on the basis of votes want to do it with *chaturai* and *buddhi* (cunning) through the press which they control. These people are anti-Mandal, they do not want to see the rule of the poor. They want to send me to jail and have a BJP government."[35] Lalu insisted that it was a clear case of the "bureaucracy [CBI] trying to hijack the political process."[36]

As the opposition prepared to celebrate the fall of the RJD government that was expected after Lalu's arrest, Lalu surprised everyone. Just before voluntarily surrendering to the court, Lalu resigned as chief minister and called for an RJD party vote in which his wife Rabri Devi was elected chief minister. Despite his being the first chief minister in India to lose his office due to criminal charges and go to jail, Lalu managed to effectively run the Bihar government from his jail cell in what became popularly known as "Cell-phone Raj."

While managing to remain in power, all of this put the RJD government on the defensive. Even after being released on bail, Lalu was imprisoned on multiple occasions, serving a total of 356 days (although he had not been convicted of any crime). A significant amount of Lalu's time was consumed with court proceedings. Since he continued to exercise significant authority as de facto chief minister in a system centralized around him, this severely handicapped the functioning of the government. The extent of Lalu's guilt—theories ranging from Lalu as the mastermind of the entire operation to being a tool of shrewd operators around him—and the impartial role of the CBI and judiciary can be debated, yet the results were clear: Lalu Yadav was crippled, and an opportunity was created for the opposition to gain political ground in Bihar.

During this period, the opposition in Bihar had been steadily consolidating and strengthening its position. After Nitish Kumar's Samata Party won only seven seats in the 1995 state assembly elections, the Samata Party aligned with the BJP. The Janata Dal, led by Sharad Yadav (and including Ram Vilas Paswan) with whom Lalu had broken, joined this BJP-Samata alliance, which was renamed the Janata Dal-United (JD(U)).

This BJP- Samata-JD(U) alliance became part of the larger NDA that came to power in Delhi in 1998. NDA MPs from Bihar were given many of the most important cabinet positions in Delhi, providing leverage in their struggle against Lalu.[37] The NDA government in Delhi attempted to impose President's Rule in Bihar in 1998, claiming a constitutional breakdown, but K. R. Narayanan, India's first Scheduled Caste president, vetoed the order. Again in 1999, the NDA government at the center dismissed the Bihar government, claiming that under the RJD Bihar had become a "Jungle Raj." This time the president accepted the order, but after narrowly passing in the Lok Sabha, the bill was withdrawn because of lack of support in the Rajya Sabha (India's upper house of parliament).

After the fodder scam surfaced, the RJD experienced a steady electoral decline. The Janata Dal's number of MPs had declined to twenty-two in the 1996 national elections, of which eighteen remained with the RJD after Lalu split the party in 1997. This number decreased to seventeen in 1998, and then to only seven in 1999. In the 2000 assembly elections, the RJD returned as the single largest party winning 124 seats, higher than expected. This was, however, forty fewer than the number the Janata Dal had won in 1995 and short of the majority needed to form the government. Taken as a whole, the NDA won a few more seats than the RJD. The governor first invited Nitish Kumar to form the government in a controversial decision that passed over Lalu as the leader of the RJD and the largest single party. Nitish Kumar became chief minister for seven days but proved unable to demonstrate his majority in the assembly. Subsequently, the RJD, in a postelection alliance with the Congress and independents crafted a coalition that returned Rabri Devi as chief minister of an RJD-led state government.

Congress's support for the RJD was crucial in preventing the imposition of President's Rule, and although in Bihar many Congress leaders were opposed to the RJD, the Congress central leadership supported the RJD. By this time, the Congress had declined to a point where it was no longer a threat to the RJD in Bihar. With no prospect of forming another Congress government in Bihar in the foreseeable future, the central Congress leadership justified an alliance with the RJD as necessary in order to prevent the BJP and its key allies, the JD(U) and Samata Party (which merged into a single party before the 2004 parliamentary elections), from forming a government in the state. Similarly, the RJD needed the Congress to block the NDA's threats to impose President's Rule in Bihar.

The RJD was able to remain in power despite a strengthening opposition, a hostile NDA government at the center, and its leader periodically in jail, by framing opposition to Lalu as attacks against lower-caste empowerment and secularism. The RJD blamed the state's poor economic performance on a history of neglect by the central government, and the bias of current governments at the center. This claim is at least partially justified by the steep decline in per capita plan expenditure in Bihar, and the negligible support that the government of Bihar received from central financial institutions (Guruswamy and Kaul 2003). Lalu was successfully able to portray the fodder scam charges, threats by the BJP to impose President's Rule, and strict actions taken by the Election Commission, especially during the 1995 assembly elections, as reactionary strategies by the Hindu upper-caste establishment to reclaim power in Bihar at the expense of the RJD's lower-caste and Muslim supporters. According to a prominent RJD minister, "Lalu is being attacked in court of law because in court of public opinion he has succeeded in changing the power structure. So these cases are meant to discredit and destabilize him. As a result, he has to concentrate on these cases. When the head of a family is distracted by other concerns, then he can't attend to the family's well-being."[38]

Lalu argued that the entire "system" was against him. He explained, "You see, the system does not suffer a man who comes from the oppressed classes. The system is controlled by people from the upper castes. They are there in the media, they are the system. They will try and finish Lalu Yadav. You have been doing it—all you from the media. They call me a joker, a man of inferior intelligence. But do you think I care? The people of Bihar will see through this conspiracy."[39]

The alliance of some powerful OBC and Scheduled Caste leaders with the opposition in Bihar, however, complicated the campaign to preserve the RJD's image as a "backward-caste" government in opposition to a long history of upper-caste dominance. Nitish Kumar, Sharad Yadav, and Ram Vilas Paswan all came from lower-caste backgrounds, and officially supported secularism. The fact that these leaders were willing to join a national alliance led by the BJP in opposition to Lalu served to discredit Lalu's claim that he was the target of an upper-caste conspiracy. And although Lalu dramatically consolidated his electoral base through mobilization on a populist backward- versus forward-caste discourse, the privileged role of the Yadav caste was overtly evident (see above). Most striking was the lack of representation for what are popularly referred to as Extremely Backward Castes (EBCs).[40] Although an estimated 32 percent of the population, people from so-called Extremely Backward Castes made up less than 5 percent of the Bihar assembly. This unequal representation between different OBC groups made it increasingly difficult for the RJD to claim to represent all lower castes. RJD's Scheduled Caste support dropped by half from nearly 50 percent in 1995 to 22 percent by 2005, and support from non-Yadav OBCs also declined. This progressive chipping away of the RJD's Scheduled Caste and non-Yadav OBC support proved to be the decisive factor in the party's slow decline, with the NDA as the major beneficiary. Lalu was forced to fall back on his own caste for support, as well as even some sections of the upper castes, in order for the state government to maintain a thin majority in the assembly. All of this served to create popular resentment among many of the groups whose earlier support had provided Lalu with such a large mass base, resulting in a progressive fragmentation of his support base.

Yet despite this complicating factor, the RJD's response remained firm: a victory of the BJP-led NDA would usher in the return of Hindu upper-caste domination. In retrospect, the effectiveness of Lalu's claims that the many attacks against him were part of an "upper-caste conspiracy" was remarkable, frustrating the opposition's single-minded attempts to topple him for years. Voter surveys bear out this effectiveness. Most voters surveyed after the 2000 election said that development had declined or stayed the same; most thought that corruption had increased over the previous decade; and many people thought that security and social tension had worsened. Still, nearly 80 percent of people rated Lalu Yadav as a "good" or "very good" leader.[41] Survey data from the 2004 parliamentary election offer interesting contrasts. By then 64 percent of respondents thought that Lalu had encouraged criminals personally, and 56 percent believed that Lalu was corrupt (by disagreeing with assertions to the contrary). Still, 49 percent agreed that "Lalu is a true messiah of the poor," and 46 percent agreed that "there is no alternative to Lalu in Bihar."[42] Although people generally believed that development and law and order had deteriorated, and that corruption had increased—and that Lalu was implicated in both—many people continued to support him.

Lalu Raj and Indian Democracy

Lalu Raj represented an alternate hegemonic formation based on a populist logic of democratic empowerment. Lalu Yadav succeeded in mobilizing millions of lower-caste people through his populist rhetoric of "social justice," politicizing everyday social relations and creating the appearance for his supporters that, after centuries of upper-caste hegemony, the government was now theirs. He succeeded in making a radical, caste-based notion of popular sovereignty the center of political life in Bihar.

Just as the passive revolution was particular to India's postcolonial context (the lack of bourgeois hegemony), Lalu Yadav's alternative hegemonic formation was also shaped by specific histories of state formation. The backward-caste alliance was forged from the individual caste identities of the late colonial period. The RJD's populist antidevelopment rhetoric only makes sense when considering the role of development resources in reinforcing upper-caste dominance. And the use of democratic networks as a mode of governance was a reaction against upper-caste control of state institutions through their own caste networks. To provide space for lower-caste empowerment, the RJD systematically weakened upper-caste controlled state institutions and shifted power from upper-caste bureaucrats and police to lower-caste politicians and political networks.

But upper castes who could not be dislodged from many key institutions continued to wield significant influence. In addition, internal contractions within the RJD's support base, resulting from a backward-caste identity that was superimposed over the narrower caste identities of the late colonial period, stifled Lalu's revolution, which, in the end, remained partial and incomplete. Strengthening opposition and widening contradictions eventually ended the fifteen years of continuous rule by Lalu Yadav and Rabri Devi in 2005, signaling the emergence of new social forces in Bihar, the analysis of which I return to in the concluding chapter. In the next chapter, I examine the tense relationship between the RJD—a ruling party that claimed to be a "backward-caste" government—and other state institutions, the civil service and judiciary that have very different social compositions and functioning styles. Examining the institutional politics and conflicts of the Lalu period will be crucial for understanding the particular form of democracy that emerged and the ways in which people in regional and local sites experienced lower-caste politics, the subject of subsequent chapters.

Caste in the State

Division and Conflict within the
Bihar Government

D uring the many hours that I spent in the compound of the Bhojpur district secretariat in Ara, the center of district administration
containing offices of various government departments, I encountered
two distinct sites of governmental power. For day-to-day management,
the administrative center of the district headquarters was the office of
the district magistrate.[1] Commonly referred to as the "DM," the district
magistrate is a postcolonial successor of the colonial district collector
and is a member of the elite Indian Administrative Service (IAS), which
I examine below. The DM is in charge of the entire district administration, an area in Bihar with a population of approximately two million.[2]
This uniquely powerful administrative position was created in order to
enforce the top-down requirements of colonial revenue collection (hence
the title district collector) and the maintenance of law and order, a position described as "British rule incarnate" (Maheshwari 2005, 574). Even
as late as 1930, "the Indian Statutory Commission made the assertion that
the District Collector is 'in the eyes of most of its inhabitants the Government'" (Maheshwari 2005, 576). For most people living in rural Bihar, no
actor had embodied the state more than "DM sahib."

The office of the DM in the Bhojpur district headquarters embodied
this image. In contrast to the apparent disorder of the compound's other
cramped offices, filled with unwieldy stacks of decomposing files, the office of the DM was neat and modern, imbuing a sense of professionalism and authority within the often chaotic scenes of district bureaucratic

practice. This immediately set the DM apart from the rest of the district bureaucratic apparatus, a distinction increased by the presence of two uniformed guards blocking entry to the DM's office. Meeting the DM required submission of a written application to the DM's personal secretary, and usually a roomful of people was awaiting access. Whenever I met the DM, he was always clean-shaven, and well dressed. Unlike almost everyone else in the district headquarters, he spoke fluent English and was clearly from an urban background. When I asked a government employee who the most powerful man in Bhojpur is, he instantly stated, "The DM. The MP has to answer to the people and the party, but the DM has all power within himself. What he decides to do, he can do. He is the true king of Bhojpur."

But while the DM may have been popularly considered the king of Bhojpur in the past, this was no longer the case. The other site of governmental power in the district secretariat was the office of the chairman of the *zilla parishad*, the district council that is the highest tier of the *panchayat* system of local government, and the only elected office at the district level that occupies a position somewhat parallel to the district magistrate. Entering the office of the *zilla parishad* chairman—as I did whenever I visited the district headquarters—felt like moving to a completely different world. Whether or not the chairman was present, the office was almost always filled with khadi-clad politicians, often with armed bodyguards and supporters, receiving scores of villagers who would come with various problems and requests. Although the *zilla parishad*, like the entire *panchayati raj* system in Bihar, is supposed to be separate from party politics, the chairman as well as other politicians in the office readily identified themselves as members of the ruling RJD. In fact, the office functioned as the de facto RJD district headquarters.

During my first visit, I met Chairman Hakim Shah, a short, plump man speaking a rustic Bhojpuri, wearing kurta pajamas and sitting in a chair with a towel draped over it, resembling a throne. He sat in a relaxed, casual manner, appearing almost to melt into the chair. The chairman's secretary entered and whispered something into the chairman's ear, which caused him to give a look of acute interest and concern. A few minutes later, everyone abruptly stood up—including the chairman and, by reflex, me—as a very fat man wearing a white dhoti and kurta with thin wire-rimmed glasses and a conspicuous gold watch entered the room. I was introduced to the man as "Rai, a senior RJD activist." Although he held no official position within the government or the RJD, he was clearly the most powerful person in the room. A mid-level employee at the district headquarters later told me that Rai was "a Yadav businessman involved in the local wine mafia, *ganja* [marijuana] mafia, and construction mafia." He said that Rai was a "kingmaker" (in English) who had effectively "decided the *zilla parishad* chairman as well as the chairman of the Ara municipal council" by making deals behind the scenes. According to this man, and many other people with whom I spoke, Rai's status was the result of his "business" position within Bhojpur and his personal proximity to Lalu Yadav.

One of the reasons the *zilla parishad* office functioned as a de facto RJD office was because pressure could be exerted on the district administration—and the DM in particular—only through the RJD government in Patna. This explained the importance of Rai, known by everyone to have a direct relationship with Lalu Yadav.[3] Within the *zilla parishad* chairman's office, as in most other contexts, it was taken for granted by everyone that Lalu Yadav, not the DM, was the real king of Bhojpur, as well as every other district in Bihar.

At the time of my fieldwork, the *zilla parishad* in Bhojpur and other districts in Bihar exercised little direct influence on the administration even after elections to local bodies were held in 2001 under a new constitutional framework intended to provide more power to local bodies.[4] The influence of people like Rai and Hakim came not from their official positions within largely disfunctional institutions, but from their position within political society. The *zilla parishad* office staff complained to me that they had not been paid for more than sixty months. Hakim also complained that the *zilla parishad* had not received any funds, and he alleged that the bureaucracy was against *panchayati raj*. A local journalist described the situation as "democracy versus bureaucracy" (the phrase in English). A few months later in the same office, another member of the *zilla parishad* explained further, "The bureaucracy was started as part of the Raj. Now there is democracy, so conflict is inevitable."

This opposition of "bureaucracy versus democracy," underscores the tension between state institutions that were shaped by colonial strategies of governance and the destabilization caused by lower-caste politics. It highlights the tension between a top-down vision of development largely implemented by bureaucrats (in which the DM was a pivotal actor) and Lalu Yadav's populism that emphasized democratic change from below. And because most bureaucrats were from upper-caste backgrounds and most politicians were now lower castes, an often stark caste divide existed within and between state institutions. The conflict, therefore, was complex, multifaceted, and, while often involving lower-caste politicians in opposition to upper-caste bureaucrats, it could not always be reduced to caste divisions. The Bhojpur DM, for example, was always described to me as "backward caste"—although I could not find anyone who knew his specific caste background—as were the politicians for whom he openly expressed disdain. In fact, this DM was a good example of the types of appointments that the RJD government made. Not only was the DM from a lower-caste background, but he held a surprisingly sympathetic understanding of the caste oppression underlying the "Naxalite" communist movement that had begun in south Bhojpur district in the 1970s and continued to have a strong presence, pursuing a policy of constructive engagement in stark contrast to the opposition of many previous district officials who had tacitly supported upper-caste landlord militias.[5] But while the class/caste identities of individual bureaucrats were complex, the overall strategy of the RJD government was clear—to subordinate the bureaucracy to the democratic networks of governance examined in the previous chapter. In response, many bureaucrats more or less openly sided with the opposition, reinforcing Lalu Yadav's populist claim that it was an upper-caste institution. So while the identity of the bureaucracy as a distinct class did not disappear, it was seriously undermined.

Similar to the Bhojpur district secretariat described above, I encountered a stark division between elected bodies and bureaucratic administration in many sites in Bihar, from sites of local administration (examined in the next chapter) to the head offices of government departments in Patna. Drawing from interviews I conducted with senior bureaucrats in Patna, and many hours that I spent in government offices, in this chapter I explore this often tense relationship between members of different state institutions in Bihar. In contrast to subsequent chapters drawn from fieldwork in regional and village contexts, here I focus on the relationship between the highest levels of the bureaucracy, composed of the Bihar cadre of the Indian Administrative Service (IAS), and the RJD government.

This chapter also includes two case studies. The first—an examination of the politics surrounding quasi-state cooperative societies, which powerful upper-caste families continued to control even after fifteen years of RJD rule—documents the type of caste networks that have long reinforced upper-caste hegemony. The resilience of such caste networks—a legacy of colonial strategies of governance discussed in Chapter 1—ex-

plains why lower-caste politicians often have sought to weaken public institutions. The second case study examines a corruption scandal at the
Patna Municipal Corporation that pitted the elected mayor against unelected officials, showing not only how the divisions between lower-caste
politicians and upper-caste bureaucrats have played out at lower levels of
government, but also the complexity of these conflicts.

The story of the state in Bihar during RJD-rule was one of fragmentation and disjuncture resulting from democratic change and provides
a rather different perspective on the Indian state than much of the literature has portrayed. Typically, top-down, planned development and a
powerful administration are emphasized, even if it is widely acknowl-
edging that policy implementation has often been obstructed at lower
levels of administration (Kaviraj 1997, 52–53; Kohli 1994). This chapter, in contrast, highlights conflict between different state institutions at
higher-levels of state governance in the wake of the politics of lower-caste
empowerment. I begin by examining the ways in which the increasing representation of lower-caste groups within elected bodies resulted in conflict with other state institutions whose members were still largely drawn
from people with upper-caste, urban backgrounds.[6] These differences provide the underlying context for understanding intrastate conflicts in Bihar
and the ways in which the RJD government sought to bend an often hostile bureaucracy to its will.

A State Divided

The Bhojpur district magistrate introduced above was a member of the
elite Indian Administrative Service (IAS). The Bihar cadre of the IAS
consists of 244 officers who hold the most important administrative posts
in the state government, although many senior IAS officers are also periodically posted in central government departments in Delhi. Along with
the elite Indian Police Service (IPS), the IAS is an immensely important
component of Indian administration, often described as the "steel frame"
of the Indian state. The authority that IAS officers are given, the intensely
competitive recruitment exams (only around seventy-five officers are chosen annually from more than three hundred thousand examinees), rigor-
ous training in administration, an elite ethos and social autonomy that
they enjoy (IAS officers are provided plush houses, often colonial-era
mansions, complete with servants and bodyguards, and stay in special gov-

ernment guesthouses when traveling) set this institution apart, claiming
to be the most professional and autonomous part of Indian bureaucracy.
The distinct class identity of the bureaucracy that the "passive-revolution"
model asserted (Chatterjee 1986, Kaviraj 1988, see Chapter 1) is most obviously embodied in the IAS. The following examination, however, reveals endemic conflict between the IAS and the elected lower-caste leadership that seriously weakened its autonomy as the "passive-revolution"
regime was undone by Lalu Yadav's populist lower-caste politics.

Given the centrality of caste within Bihar's political world, especially
since the 1990s, an examination of the caste backgrounds of actors within
various state institutions is instructive.[7] In the Bihar cadre of the Indian
Administrative Service in 2002, among 224 officers that I was able to acquire information about (there were 244 officers in total), 133 officers
were reported to be from four upper-caste groups (Brahman, Kayasth,
Rajput, Bhumihar).[8] Among the Other Backward Class (OBC) officers, a
significant number entered through reservation, and most were from outside Bihar. The largest group after the Scheduled Castes, who, along with
the Scheduled Tribes, have had reservations since independence, were
officers identified as "Bania." In Bihar, the Bania caste category is considered a lower-caste group, although most officers thus identified came
from outside Bihar where it is considered a "forward caste."[9] Perhaps
most striking is the very small number of officers from the OBC groups
that have become politically dominant in Bihar. From the three largest
groups in the OBC category—Yadav, Kurmi, and Koeri—there were only
seven officers, three from Kurmi and four from Yadav backgrounds. In
fact, the situation had changed little from 1985, when there were only
three IAS officers from OBC groups (Goyal 1989, 425–433). In addition,
all four officers identified as Yadav had entered the IAS through promotion from the Bihar Administrative Service, an increasingly common practice. Promoted IAS officers are unlikely to occupy any rank above district
magistrate because promotion in the IAS is time-bound. Although terms
such as "Yadavization" (Gupta 1992) and "Yadav Raj" were frequently
invoked in Bihar and despite the fact that the Yadav caste is the most
populous in India, there was not, to my knowledge, a single directly recruited Yadav officer in the Bihar cadre of the IAS.

The number of IAS officers recruited under reservations for Scheduled Caste and Scheduled Tribe categories is substantial, but officers from
upper-caste backgrounds overwhelmingly staff the bureaucracy, especially
at the higher levels. As Kanshi Ram, the Dalit ideologue of the Bahujan

Samaj Party (in Uttar Pradesh) put it, "In this country, out of 450 District Magistrates more than 125 are from the SC/STs, but those from the OBCs are very few.... The number of OBC is 50 to 52 percent [of the population] but we don't see any of them as District Magistrate. The issue, which is special for us, is that reservation is not a question of our daily bread; reservation is not a question of our jobs; reservation is a matter of participation in the government and administration of this country. If 52 percent if the people cannot participate in the republic, then which is the system in which they can participate?"[10] Although caste-based reservations were slowly changing the social composition of the bureaucracy (Chaudhary 1999, 242–243), it remained overwhelmingly an upper-caste institution.

When the caste composition of the IAS is compared with the Bihar state assembly in Tables 2 and 3 below, stark differences emerge. I obtained the data for Table 2 from the office of the leader of the opposition in the Bihar assembly (a BJP politician). I was provided with a list of the caste of each individual MLA, organized by party. The very presence of such a list testifies to the importance of caste identities within assembly politics in Bihar.[11] The tables below, which use the same caste categories I found on the list, demonstrate remarkable differences in the caste backgrounds of actors within different state institutions. Although differences exist within the bureaucracy itself, the most dramatic contrast is between the legislature and the bureaucracy. The top levels of the bureaucracy (IAS and IPS), and even more so the judiciary, have remained composed

TABLE 2. **Caste in the Indian Administrative Service (Bihar Cadre)**[12]

Caste	Total	From Bihar	Other State
Kayasth	54	47	7
Brahman	60	38	22
Rajput	22	17	5
Bhumihar	7	6	1
Scheduled Castes	25	8	17
Scheduled Tribes	7	0	7
Bania	15	4	11
Muslim	10	9	1
Yadav	4	4	0
Kurmi	3	3	0
Christian	3	0	3
Sikh	2	0	2
Jain	2	0	2
"Backward"	9	4	5
Unidentified	21		
Total	244	140	83

TABLE 3. **Caste in the Bihar Assembly in 2002**[13]

Caste	RJD	BJP	JD(U)	Samata	LJP	Cong.	BSP	CPI	CPM	ML	CSP	Ind.	Total
Yadav	47	5	9	2	0	0	0	0	0	0	0	0	64
Kurmi	2	1	1	8	0	1	0	0	0	0	0	0	13
Koeri	10	1	0	5	0	0	1	0	2	2	0	1	23
Brahman	1	4	0	0	0	1	0	0	0	0	0	2	8
Rajput	6	5	0	6	4	0	1	0	0	0	0	4	22
Bhumihar	2	4	0	2	0	3	0	2	0	0	0	6	17
Kayasth	0	2	0	1	0	0	0	0	0	0	0	0	3
SC*	21	6	0	3	2	2	2	0	0	2	1	0	36
Bania	6	4	0	1	0	2	0	0	0	0	1	0	12
Muslim	16	0	0	2	0	5	1	0	0	1	0	0	25
Annexure One	4	3	2	0	0	0	0	0	0	0	0	2	11
Total	115	35	12	30	6	12	5	2	2	5	2	16	234

*almost exclusively composed of reserved seats

mostly of upper-caste, urban-based educated elites, while the legislature has changed dramatically since independence, with most MLAs now lower-caste and rural-based (see Table 3). A progressive increase in the number of OBC legislators is clear.

A "Backward-Caste" Government and a Hostile Bureaucracy

From the beginning of Lalu Yadav's tenure as chief minister in 1990, the relationships between his government and the higher levels of the state bureaucracy were fraught with tension and internal conflict. An inevitable conflict arose between Lalu's self-proclaimed "backward-caste" government and state institutions whose members were largely from upper-caste backgrounds. Thakur's (2000) journalistic account below describes the techniques that Lalu Yadav utilized in an attempt to neutralize the preponderance of upper-caste officers in the bureaucracy:

> No chief minister of Bihar had gone about undoing style and structure established by a succession of predecessors as drastically and determinedly as Lalu Yadav. . . . He was a storm blowing through, devastating norms and conventions, bending and breaking rules, slicing through red tape. . . . As a senior retired bureaucrat in Patna put it, "He was like an exotic animal on the rampage, you didn't know whether to keep staring at him in awe and admiration or to do something to stop him" (2000, 72–73). . . . And like he did with society, he created a divide in the bureaucracy, a very clear caste divide that favored the backwards and the pliant and flung the rest hither thither. At one time, nearly seventy percent of districts were headed by backwards or by Lalu Yadav's chosen favorites . . . . "He totally disrupted the bureaucracy with his style of functioning, playing havoc with the established order of things in the bureaucracy," one of Bihar's topmost serving officers told me. "For one thing, he totally demolished the hierarchy and created chaos. He would ring up block officers and *darogas* and give them orders on the phone. Having established direct contact with the chief minister, these officials never listened to their superiors in the services, they became part of Lalu Yadav's cadre. . . . He never let any official feel secure, he kept people on tenterhooks, he bypassed them, overruled them brusquely, insulted them publicly. His methods were totally unconventional and erroneous but he achieved what he wanted to." (2000, 190–92)

If Lalu Yadav created a "caste divide in the bureaucracy" by privileging officers from lower-caste backgrounds, this was because of the bureau-

cracy's overwhelming upper-caste composition and the fact that this was
the first government in Bihar that claimed to militantly represent lower-
caste interests. As discussed in the last chapter, this all took place in a
political environment shaped by V. P. Singh's decision to implement the
recommendations of the Mandal Commission—reserving a proportion
of central government jobs for the Other Backward Classes—and the
subsequent agitations that swept across north India, putting upper castes
and lower castes in antagonistic opposition. The resulting conflicts within,
and between, state institutions in Bihar must be understood within this
context.

The other way in which Lalu Yadav's RJD government exerted control over the bureaucracy was through the strategic use of transfers. The
practice of government transfers, formally requiring the chief secretary's
recommendation and the cabinet's approval, increasingly came under the
individual control of chief ministers (Sawshilya 2000, 161). Governments
(both at the national and state levels) do not have the power to dismiss
top-level bureaucrats in India and have limited disciplinary options; consequently, frequent transfers are often used as a means to control bureaucrats who are seen as hostile to the government in power. But while the
strategic use of transfers was nothing new, its scale and overall purpose
were very different when used by militant lower-caste leaders.[14] The Congress regime had long used the threat of transfers in order to enure that
bureaucrats did not undermine the interests of important Congress supporters, many of whom were upper-caste landed elites. While this type
of politically negotiated compromise was at the heart of the "passive-
revolution" alliance, the bureaucracy remained the core institution of
governance. During the Lalu era, in contrast, transfers were used in an
attempt to force the bureaucracy to submit to the project of lower-caste
empowerment. And since many bureaucrats refused to do so, transfers
were used to weaken the institution in order to shift power to democratic
networks.

Key administrative positions in the districts, especially the powerful
position of district magistrate, were given to OBC, Muslim, or Scheduled Caste officers. In 1993, the Lalu Yadav government replaced both
the chief secretary as well as the director general of police, both of whom
were Brahman, with lower-caste officers, overlooking two IAS and three
IPS upper-caste officers who were in line for the posts (Chaudhary 1999,
241). By 1995, twenty-six out of fifty district magistrates and thirty out of
fifty deputy divisional commissioners in Bihar were lower castes (Chaud-

hary 1999, 242), while officers from upper-caste backgrounds held 110 out of 113 positions in the state secretariat where higher-level administrative offices with little direct interaction with the public are located.[15] Although political leaders used transfers to punish noncompliant officers as well as to position loyal officers in strategic posts, few IAS officers in Bihar shared a similar political outlook as the RJD leadership. Within such a context, loyalty could be gained only at a price, and the RJD government's need to secure a loyal cohort of officers from a group that did not necessarily share the RJD's political commitments inevitably increased opportunities for corruption.

The differences between the caste backgrounds of the political and bureaucratic elite that emerged in the 1990s contrasted with the strong similarities among bureaucrats and Congress politicians before 1990, most of whom had been recruited from among upper castes. Following the implementation of the Mandal Commission's recommendations in 1990, establishing quotas for the recruitment of OBCs in the All India Services (the IAS and Indian Police Service, IPS), the divide between upper castes and OBC castes within Bihar's political world seeped into the bureaucracy. Inevitably, Lalu Yadav's politics, with a theme of caste empowerment and the stated intention of displacing the upper castes, created tension and lack of cooperation from a state administration that was dominated by upper-caste bureaucrats.

Transfers and preferential postings allowed the RJD government to bend the bureaucracy to its will, but transformation was not complete by any means. Many government departments and institutions in Bihar continued to be staffed almost entirely by upper-caste officers. Although recruitment for government jobs in Bihar is subject to extensive reservations, the effects of structural adjustment and neoliberal reform and the increasing precariousness of state finances seriously constrained the government's capacity to hire, even when more employees were greatly needed. These economic constraints significantly slowed the transformation of the social composition of the bureaucracy, resulting in a partial maintenance of the status quo.

In response to its inability to recruit lower-caste officers, the Lalu government often chose to leave positions vacant as part of a process that Santhosh Mathew (a Bihar cadre IAS officer who served during this time) and Mick Moore (2011) term "state incapacity by design." They note that "the positions of Engineer-in-Chief in the two principal engineering departments, the Road Construction Department and the Rural Organisation, both remained vacant for a long period of time, as did all 15 positions as Chief Engineer in the two departments, and 81 out of the 91 Superintendent Engineer positions" (Mathew and Moore 2011, 17). More than one third of postings for the key post of block development officer—the equivalent of the DM at the local level—were vacant, forcing most BDOs to simultaneously serve at two blocks (the next chapter focuses on the block level). "The Bihar Administrative Service cadre, from which Development Officers and Circle Officers and other senior officers up to the rank of Additional Secretary are drawn, had 633 vacancies against a sanctioned strength of 2248. The Bihar Public Service Commission, which is responsible for the recruitment to the Bihar Administrative Service and the posting of all class I and II officers, had only three members and the Chair position was vacant for a critically long period.... In the government health service, 90 per cent of doctors posts were vacant, as were 95 percent of posts for paramedical staff" (Mathew and Moore 2011, 17–18).

Although the crisis of state finances and a lack of qualified candidates were largely to blame, caste considerations were equally important (and the lack of qualified candidates partly reflected the flight of educated upper castes from the state). For instance, "between 1996 and 2006, only 30,000 new primary school teachers were recruited against the 90,000 that were required. The pupil teacher ratio, which was already 90:1 against the national norm of 40:1, worsened to 122:1. The government of India was willing to pay the salaries of these missing teachers under a Centrally Sponsored Scheme called Sarva Shiksha Abhiyan ('education for all'), and put increasing pressure on the Government of Bihar to undertake the recruitment. The state government appeared to concede, but exceeded its powers by changing the recruitment rules so that it would be better able to appoint teachers from within its own electoral base. This move was immediately struck down by the courts. The state government simply left the positions vacant" (Mathew and Moore 2011, 18). Rather than recruit upper castes, the Lalu government clearly preferred to allow governmental institutions to deteriorate.

As these examples make clear, the role of caste identities within governmental institutions had a profound impact on the popular experience of democracy. While theorists of the state have intensely debated the class character of the bureaucracy (for example, Poulantzas 2000), bureaucrats' caste identities are more readily apparent. Lower-caste politics highlighted the social character of the bureaucracy, undermining its already weak popular legitimacy and thereby challenging the myth of a neutral state apparatus that is a core assumption of constitutional liberalism and of the national project of development. A key part of Lalu Yadav's political project was to undermine the class interest of the bureaucracy that had been an essential feature of the earlier Congress regime and an upper-caste dominated "passive revolution" (Chatterjee 1986, Kaviraj 1988). Without the myth of an impartial, autonomous "state idea" (Abrams 1988), or even of a corrupt but potentially salvageable state (Gupta 1995), the idea of development was undermined, leading people to support a government that allowed many state institutions to more or less collapse. With state institutions publicly revealed as tools of upper-caste hegemony, it became inconceivable to many people that they could enforce rights or pursue development in anything resembling an impartial manner. Within such a context, the case was made that social justice could be achieved only through an aggressive and disruptive politics of agitation. This explains how the discourse of development was marginalized within Bihar's political world, replaced by a populist politics of lower-caste empowerment.

Administrative Centralization and Corruption

Long-standing practices of centralized decision making within the Bihar administration compounded the dysfunction of state institutions. The most obvious example was a twenty-five-year-old state regulation requiring approval for all development expenditures over 2.5 million rupees ($56,000) to go through a complex process involving a committee, the planning minister and planning secretary, the chief secretary, and finally the chief minister, who at that point could place it before the cabinet. The process, which had no parallel in any other state in India, took an average of four to six months[16] and became a vehicle to centralize more power in the chief minister's hands and to delay virtually all projects. Excessive centralization also existed at lower levels, with the approval of executive engineers required for expenditures over 100,000 rupees ($2,000). A chronic shortage of executive engineers to make such approvals diminished expenditure capacity in the districts.

The tense relationship between Bihar's political and bureaucratic elites further centralized interaction between the RJD government and the bureaucracy. Especially in the later years, Lalu Yadav's relationship with the bureaucracy became increasingly dependent on Mukund Prasad, a previous chief secretary (head of the state administration) who was serving

as the secretary of the chief minister's secretariat at the time of my research (Thakur 2000, 193–194). Mukund Prasad was widely believed to be
the most powerful bureaucrat in Bihar, and even when he retired as chief
secretary, his continued power eclipsed that of subsequent chief secretaries. Thakur (2000) explains Mukund Prasad's position as related to his
Bania caste status, the only OBC group with any substantial representation within the Bihar IAS (see Table 2). Mukund Prasad's position reportedly enabled the support of a significant number of Bania officers whom
Lalu supplemented with the privileged posting of Muslim and Scheduled
Caste officers, the latter consisting of a relatively high number from reservations. As can be imagined, running the government administration by
proxy through the use of intra-bureaucratic caste divisions does not lend
itself to bureaucratic efficiency.

Mukund Prasad became particularly important following the fodder
scam in 1996. He had a reputation for being reluctant to approve spending with the potential for misappropriation, which includes most development works. After the chief minister himself was imprisoned for corruption, many IAS officers commented to me that the bureaucracy effectively
froze, preferring inaction to the threat of legal action.[17] Fear of legal re-
percussions, and the bureaucratic style of Mukund Prasad in particular,
were often invoked as reasons for the disturbing fact that a state government with such a paucity of development funds consistently returned allocations from the central government because they went unspent (Thakur
2000, 188).

Conflict between the political leadership and the bureaucracy, therefore, undermined the Bihar government's expenditure performance.[18] According to the Supreme Court's Food Security Commission report, published in 2003, an estimated 10 billion rupees of central allocations were
forfeited every year in Bihar due to procedural inefficiencies. Part of the
problem was that the central government often released funds at the last
minute, making it nearly impossible for the Bihar government to spend
funds before they lapsed, and the administrative centralization described
above exacerbated this constraint. Bihar's own fiscal limitations proved
another impediment, especially with programs that required the state
government to contribute matching funds. The Food Security Commission, however, reported:

> Even when there is no requirement of state contribution ... one finds that
> Bihar's capacity for drawing these funds is as low as in other schemes. In fact,

where funds are transferred directly to the districts, Bihar does comparatively better. This implies that secretariat procedures of releasing funds need to be improved.[19]

The Food Security Commission concluded with an interesting assessment emphasizing intrastate conflict and the ways in which state institutions participated in wider power configurations:

> Although many civil servants hold the view that it is the nature of politics which largely determines the nature of the civil service and the ends to which it would be put ... causation is also in the opposite direction. The reasons for the decline in administrative capacity may be linked to politics, but administration has its own autonomy. Non-performing civil service leaves little choice to politicians but to resort to populist or caste rhetoric.... The problem in Bihar is not located with any single actor, but is structural. The present structure links the bureaucracy, politicians, and people in patronage relationships that are dysfunctional as far as growth and economic development are concerned.[20]

Lower-caste politics is often interpreted simply as irresponsible governance by self-interested politicians who use appeals to caste as a means of remaining in power and looting public resources. Such an analysis, however, fails to consider the "structural links" that made the pursuit of caste-based social justice through governmental policy all but impossible. The enactment of governmental policies, including redistributive policies, requires organizational machinery capable of implementation. Since almost all public institutions in Bihar were effectively controlled by the same upper castes that Lalu Yadav was attempting to displace from power, relying on these institutions was precarious, and weakening upper-caste influence within public life in Bihar often meant weakening upper-caste-dominated state institutions. Within this context, a political leadership whose stated goal was lower-caste empowerment could go a long way toward accomplishing this goal by transferring power from recruited officials in the state bureaucracy to elected politicians.

In the next section I examine the politics of cooperative societies in Bihar to demonstrate the continued influence of upper-caste networks within public institutions. The cooperatives are explicitly semi-state organizations with an elected board and chairman as well as a bureaucratic component. Power within the cooperative movement consists of relatively closed, caste-based networks of patronage and alliances that remained

dominated by upper-caste actors, even following the dramatic transformations in state politics during the Lalu period.

Caste and the "Cooperative Mafia"

The institutions of the cooperative movement comprise levels of organization ranging from the village to the state capital. In 2002, the state
government amended the Bihar Co-operative Societies Act (1935), and
elections were held in May 2003 after a gap of fifteen years, providing an
opportunity to investigate to what extent the dramatic political changes of
the last decade and a half had affected the cooperative institutions. I was
interested in whether the changes that had occurred in the distribution of
political power coincided with a new distribution of economic resources
within this key site of state-directed development. Although the cooperative movement is a small part of the economy, it had been a major component of planned agricultural development in postindependence India.

The state-level cooperative elections that I observed—limited to the
franchise of chairmen of forty district cooperatives, representatives of
state-level societies, and a few bureaucrats—were a largely private and
unexciting affair. In the elections for most of the big cooperative societies, the outcomes were more or less a certainty, as most of the candidates
stood uncontested. This does not mean, however, that there were not
competition and competing claims. Rather, almost all of the action seems
to have taken place behind the scenes, in preelection negotiations. By the
time that I had arrived, elections had already occurred for three of the
major cooperative apex societies—the Bihar State Cooperative Bank,[21]
the Bihar State Marketing Association (see below), and the Bihar State
Housing Federation[22]—but I was able to observe elections for the Bihar
State Land Development Bank. I will briefly examine events related to
this election to introduce the major players of the cooperative movement
in Bihar and to assess the ways in which lower-caste politics influenced
the cooperative elections.

My first encounters with major players in cooperative politics took
place during the nominations for the Land Development Bank elections.
Nominations for election candidature in Bihar are often ritually lavish
affairs, with prospective candidates parading to the election office with
throngs of supporters, often armed, in a show of strength. These were different elections, however, with a very restricted and specific electorate

compromising 274 board members of land development banks whose support was unlikely to be moved by such theatrical displays. The nomination process took place at the Land Development Bank headquarters in Patna. Supporters who were not cooperative members, or who could not pass as legitimate bodyguards, were stopped at the gate to the building by a substantial police presence (the guards granted me entry after lengthy persuasion). Even with such limited access, there was a chaotic scene of prospective candidates filing papers for the key position of chairman as well as positions on the board of directors.[23] By the time of nominations, however, three candidates had emerged as the central contenders for the key chairman post: Jagdish Sharma, Ajit Singh, and Kapil Singh.

Jagdish Sharma was a powerful MLA (independent) and chairman of the local cooperative bank in Gaya district, a district at the center of the violent agrarian conflict between various communist groups and upper-caste militias. As an independent MLA, Jagdish relied on muscle power and support from his Bhumihar caste supporters to forge an electoral base. He is an example of the self-styled caste-leader politicians whom I examine in the next chapter: he protects the interests of his supporters through his political status as a member of the state assembly and cooperative bank chairman, combined with his status as a "mafia don" who can directly employ armed force when required. Whenever I met Jagdish, armed guards/gunmen as well as numerous rural supporters always accompanied him.

Ajit Singh was the son of the late Tapeshwar Singh, who was a major player in the cooperative movement as well as the Congress Party, both at the state and the national level. Ajit Singh was chairman of the National Agricultural Cooperative Marketing Federation (NAFED), a powerful national body, and was considered the political heir of his father, a former vice president of the International Cooperative Society who had appointed a huge number of employees in all of the cooperative societies. His family's importance is demonstrated by the fact that Ajit was a relative of the recently elected chairmen of both of the other important cooperative apex bodies: the Bihar State Marketing Association and the Bihar State Cooperative Bank. As Ajoy Singh, Ajit's brother and himself a member of the Bihar Legislative Council put it, "We inherited our political positions."

Kapil Singh, a Rajput by caste, was a previous bank administrator. His main asset was the support of Sadhu Yadav, the feared brother-in-law of Lalu Yadav. Sadhu Yadav and his gunmen accompanied Kapil to file his nomination. After Sadhu arrived, both Ajit as well as Jagdish went to pay a respectful visit. In an empty office, they all met in an extremely tense closed-door meeting, which I was allowed to attend, as their heavily armed bodyguards nervously waited outside. After the meeting, which consisted of little more than polite small talk, I asked Sadhu rather bluntly why he was not supporting a Yadav or lower-caste candidate. He replied, "There will be no Yadav candidate in these elections."

I realized that Sadhu Yadav was exerting his influence on behalf of the RJD-led government when I accompanied Ajoy Singh to the speaker's chamber in the state assembly. In the presence of MLAs from various parties, the speaker of the assembly, Sadanand Singh, became visibly agitated with Ajoy because of his relative S. N. Singh's victory in the Bihar State Cooperative Bank chairman elections, elections in which the RJD, and Sadhu Yadav personally, had supported a Bhumihar candidate. The speaker angrily asked, "Are the cooperatives only for the Rajputs? Tapeshwar Babu at least gave some concessions to the Bhumihars."

This reference to caste was a recurring, if sometimes implicit, theme within cooperative practice. I was able to attend an informal meeting regarding the upcoming election that included Jagdish Sharma; the recently elected Bihar Housing Federation chairman, V. K. Mishra; and other cooperative leaders. They discussed the "Rajput domination" of the previous elections and in response were consciously attempting to create an alternate coalition. At one point during the meeting, a cooperative member read aloud the number of voters from each caste, underlying the theme that only a coalition of different caste factions could compete with the Rajput electorate. Caste was clearly the foundation of the alliance this meeting was attempting to forge and superseded party loyalties; members of the RJD, BJP, and Congress were all involved in the efforts. Although lower-caste members had very little independent political presence in the cooperatives, reservations in the 2002 amendments allowed a small but significant presence of lower-caste members on the board of directors. This attempted alliance cut across party lines and the backward/forward caste division in a way that would be impossible in other political contexts in Bihar (although this was common in previous decades). Such an alliance was possible only because of acknowledged upper-caste dominance within the cooperatives.

Even during the meeting, the participants appeared pessimistic. Jagdish Sharma said, "How can we compete with Ajit Singh? He is too powerful in Delhi." V. K. Mishra also later privately expressed his belief that Ajit

Singh would win. While sitting with the three relatives—Ajit Singh, BSCC chairman S. N. Singh, and Bihar State Marketing Association chairman S. K. Singh—at Ajit's house following the Land Development Bank nominations, I began to realize the tight grip that this family trio holds.

In the end, Ajit received 132 votes, winning by 56 votes. With such a small electorate, it had become more or less clear who would win much earlier, perhaps as early as the time of the nomination. Even with the support of Sadhu Yadav, Kalpdeo Singh received only 49 votes. Jagdish, knowing that he could not win, chose to contest anyway. At the time of the elections he reportedly said, "I just want them to know that we are still here." He received 76 votes. With Ajit becoming the Land Development Bank chairman, the family of Tapeshwar Singh, and Ajit Singh in particular—who was already on the board of directors of three apex societies, often holding multiple posts—enjoyed almost total control over the cooperative societies in Bihar.[24]

In every case, the winning candidate for the chairmanship of the state-level cooperative societies was an upper-caste individual with a historical connection to the Congress. Although the Congress as an organized party did not appear to be influencing the elections, the historical connection is important. As one cooperative leader said, "The cooperative movement has always been a training ground for the Congress." In this, family and regional connections were particularly salient. The family of the late Congress cooperative leader Tapeshwar Singh, in particular, managed an impressive hegemony. Three of the four societies' chairmen were from this family, and Ajit Singh held a number of director-level posts; with the exception of the Housing Federation, their presence seemed to be everywhere. The second important result in every case was the RJD government's attempt—and overall failure—to win, or at least influence, the election of the chairman.[25]

In most elections, the RJD-backed candidates lost. Compromises were made and the losing candidate was often elected to the board of directors, but the overall failure of the RJD, and of lower castes, is still noteworthy. Lalu was well aware of this fact. A cooperative official told me that, at his insistence, a college friend who was then a powerful politician had approached Lalu in 1991 to pursuade Lalu to increase investment to the cooperative societies as a medium of agricultural development. Lalu's reported answer was direct: "That is a thing of the Rajputs and Bhumihars; let it die" (*yeh rajput aur bhumihar ka chiz; marega*).

The elections revealed the continued existence of caste and family-based networks of control that have a long history in Bihar, a hegemony that the dramatic political changes of the previous decade and a half appear to have been—remarkably—unable to alter. As the managing director of a major cooperative society told me, "Their control is simply too strong. There was no chance of anyone else entering in." A member of one of the major Congress families who dominate the cooperatives described the inevitable outcomes this way: "Their attempt [RJD] to alter the bank elections was like the fuzz on the screen before the start of a movie."

Bureaucratic Management and Upper-Caste Hegemony

At a time when upper-caste interests in other sites were being challenged everywhere, upper-caste politicians maintained a stranglehold over the cooperatives. During a series of interviews that I conducted with the managing directors of a number of the cooperative societies, a man whom I will call Anil revealed a great deal about how this dominance was sustained. Anil explained that it was common practice for cooperative leaders to fill the societies with people from a similar caste background, often relatives from their native region, who in turn "manage" nomination procedures and the electoral process itself—this being possible because elections were handled in-house. Employees have a vested interest in having a chairman from their caste faction elected because doing so increases their probability of getting promotions and desirable transfers. When I asked a senior cooperative official about this caste "colonization" of the cooperative societies, he began to list which castes dominated the forty district cooperative banks. He listed almost all of these banks as dominated by either "Rajputs" or "Bhumihars," with a few "Brahman," a handful with a "mixed" dominance of these three groups, and a single bank that he listed as "Yadav."

A good example of this caste patronage is the Bihar State Marketing Association. Like the Bihar State Cooperative Bank, the Bihar State Marketing Association is the apex body of 224 block-level marketing societies. Although heavily in debt, it has significant fixed assets, including a fourteen-story tower at Gandhi Maidan, cold storage units, and godowns. Tapeshwar Singh was previously the chairman of the Bihar State Marketing Association from the late 1970s to the late 1980s. During this time, the number of employees rose from 1,100 to 2,700. When I asked employees about this expansion, I was told that almost all new recruits had been

Rajput by caste, mostly from Bhojpur district. Several cooperative officials told me that the Bihar State Marketing Association's economic decline was largely a result of this overstaffing that progressively consumed
ever larger proportions of the cooperative budget. Once economic decline began, it was very hard to reverse, not least because jobs given as
patronage are hard to vacate. When I asked one cooperative leader about
the future prospects of the Bihar State Marketing Association he replied,
"It is like an elephant that has been starved for years. How will it ever
get up?"

The effects of interactions between levels of administration on cooperative politics are also interesting to observe. Although regional control, especially of the district cooperative banks, was very important, Ajit
Singh's monopoly over the cooperatives at the national level was also a
decisive force. The ability of caste-based networks within the cooperatives
to make dynamic connections between these levels seems to be precisely
what allowed Tapeshwar Singh's family to secure domination.

The caste-based networks also allow control over the distribution of
resources—or the illegal misappropriation of resources popularly referred to as the "cooperative mafia"—and thereby, over the process of
adopting new members. It became clear to me that these caste-based networks extend from the chairmen of the apex societies in Patna down to
the cooperative extension officers and management of the primary societies. These networks' continuance, therefore, systematically prevents the
entrance of new actors into the cooperatives.

In Rajnagar village, only three members of the Land Development
Bank were living in the village at the time of my fieldwork, partly because
of the land requirement for membership in the cooperative banks. The
land requirement for receiving a loan from the Land Development Bank
was five acres, understandable since loans were for the explicit purpose of
improving land productivity through investment, especially in irrigation
works. But to become a member of the local cooperative bank, one had
to own two acres of land, a restriction that is much less logical, especially
when taking into account the patterns of economic practice examined in
later chapters. The land that is a required condition of receiving cooperative credit does not serve as collateral. In fact, the rate of collection
on these loans was well under 50 percent. In Rajnagar, Yadav and other
lower-caste petty cultivators who rent land from Rajput landowners perform most of the agricultural cultivation in the village. Since cooperative
credit was predicated on land ownership, most actual cultivators were ex-

cluded. Many villagers and even employees of the local cooperative bank told me that a large percentage of allocated cooperative credit was being used for nonagricultural, non-entrepreneurial purposes, such as marriage dowries. Most cooperative loans can be considered an unofficial government subsidy because they are not recovered. Instead of being used to expand cultivation, cooperative credit was being diverted as "rents" to upper-caste landowners.

The land ownership requirement for cooperative credit, however, was not the only barrier. In Chapter 6, I explore the economic dynamism and class heterogeneity of Yadav cultivators in Rajnagar. Still, very few of the increasing number of households that meet the land requirement are members of the cooperative societies. During a visit to the Bhojpur district cooperative bank in Ara, I asked a small group of employees about the lack of lower-caste members that I had observed. Their answers centered on bureaucratic "management" of the registration process: to be registered as a member of the cooperative societies, a form had to be filled out at the local office, which then had to be sent to the district headquarters for approval. I was told that undesirable forms were frequently "lost" or delayed. If registration forms managed to reach the district office, they could encounter barriers because the chairman and most of the board consisted of Rajput members who had a vested interest in registering members of their own caste and preventing the registration of others. And even for successful registrants, chairmen of the local cooperative societies, most of whom were Rajput landowners, decided the allocation of the bank's capital at the local level. There was, therefore, little incentive for lower-caste cultivators to become involved with the cooperative societies, or their upper-caste dominated bureaucracies and elected leadership.

Patna Municipal Corporation

The continued upper-caste influence over the cooperative societies contrasts starkly with many popular stories that I heard describing the subservience of the administration to Lalu Yadav. Many people told me that they had either seen or heard about the chief secretary of Bihar acting like a servant, holding a cup for Lalu to spit into while he chewed *paan* (beetle leaf), or serving him *kaini* (chewing tobacco) (Thakur 2000, 188). The widespread popular image was one of a bureaucracy in servitude to political power, and to Lalu Yadav in particular.

I was surprised, then, to hear senior IAS officers frequently comment on their increased power under the RJD government. The power they referred to was not explicit but resulted from superiority of administrative skills and knowledge of procedure, enabling behind-the-scenes tactics.[26] A particularly telling example of this was a case of corruption in the Patna Municipal Corporation (PMC). The case resulted in the transfer of the municipal commissioner of the corporation and a secretary of the Department of Urban Development following allegations that they had conspired to misappropriate funds intended to pay the salaries of lower-level employees, including street sweepers. As a consequence, the employees had not received their salaries for over a year, and held a series of strikes and protest marches. At one protest that I attended, angry employees surrounded the office of the municipal commissioner, and a strong police presence was required to prevent violence.

Among its elected representatives, the corporation had an overwhelming lower-caste composition. Among fifty-seven elected councilors, twenty-seven, including the mayor, identified themselves, or were identified by other councilors whom I interviewed, as "Yadav." These elected officials, however, had very little influence over the day-to-day operation of the corporation. As a report on municipal government states, "The municipal bodies have a dual system of governance. In this system there is a mayor, the head of the corporation, who is elected by the people and is accountable to the local populace but has little real power. On the other hand, there is a municipal commissioner (typically an IAS officer), the chief executive of the corporation, who is appointed by the state government and is vested with most of the power. The elected mayor and municipal councilors have no say in the selection of the municipal commissioner. Such a structure is a fatal flaw in the assignment of responsibilities related to provision of services" (Sadhu and Bharutwaj 2003, 242). Practical control of the corporation rested in the hands of the managing director, an upper-caste IAS officer.

The municipal corporation minister accused in the corruption case was a prominent Yadav leader, and the accused secretary of the overseeing department (the Department of Urban Development), was an upper-caste IAS officer. I asked a senior officer of the department whether the minister was also taking money. The officer responded, "I think that he also wanted to 'eat,' but he was too weak. How could he?" (*khana chahata tha lekin kaise, itna kamjor aadmi*). It is stunning that a cabinet minister, a prominent Yadav leader close to Lalu Yadav, was described as "weak" in comparison to his secretary. The "strength" of the latter clearly consisted of skill and knowledge of administrative procedure that in this case seem to have enabled effective practices of corruption.

This example should not be interpreted, however, simply as a case of corruption of upper-caste bureaucrats. Spending time with PMC representatives and employees, I repeatedly heard claims that Lalu Yadav knew about the scandal, and there were even accusations that he had indirectly received some of the funds, although this was impossible to substantiate. The context for this speculation was the failure of Munsa Devi, the wife of the chief minister's eldest brother, to get elected to the post of Patna's mayor, despite the presence of such a large number of Yadav councilors in the corporation (the mayor is indirectly elected by the councilors). Many councilors whom I spoke with interpreted Munsa Devi's candidacy as an attempt by outsiders to exert control over local power.[27] As one counselor put it, "Why a Gopalganj [home district of Munsa Devi, as well as Lalu and Rabri] Yadav? What, there are no Yadavs in Patna?" (*gopalganj ka yadav hi kyo mayor banega? patna me yadav nahi hai kya*). After the election results were declared, the victory slogan was "Long Live the Yadavs of Patna" (*patna ka yadav zindabad*). The mayor and his supporters believed that Lalu Yadav was taking revenge for the mayor's victory over Munsa Devi.[28]

The possibility that higher levels of the government were involved in this scandal, either through active complicity or intentional passivity, complicates the corporation scandal and demonstrates the complex interactions between different state institutions. Within caste categories, in this case the Yadav caste, there can be a great deal of internal conflict and heterogeneity, a theme that I discuss in subsequent chapters.

Judicial Activism

The conflict was resolved in the Patna High Court after the mayor of Patna filed litigation against the municipal commissioner and the government. The High Court directed the state government to pay corporation employees neglected salaries and ordered the transfer of the municipal commissioner and urban development secretary. The ruling stated:

> Self-governing institutions in Bihar have already been damaged by prolonged
> and continuous supersession. While Independence was sought to secure self-

governance by throwing out the colonial power, the administrators in democratic India worked for colonizing self-government institutions for themselves.
Superseding local self-government and putting administrators on them is a *sola
topi* approach with plumes and feathers suggesting the pattern of a *saheb* and a
native. There is no place for such a civil service under the Constitution of India.
That civil service was the guardian of the empire. It should have gone with the
raj. The chief executive officer in a municipality or a Corporation is subservient
to an elected body not parallel to it.[29]

This judgment explicitly associates the administration with the colonial
civil service, accusing the former of a continued colonial tendency—a remarkable recognition of the continued influence of colonial processes of
state formation on Indian democracy. The High Court was able to make
such a judgment because of the 74th Amendment to the constitution, enacted in 1993, which specified the power of elected municipal bodies. The
High Court, therefore, could present itself as the guardian of the constitution against the "colonizing" tendencies of state administration, whose
origins were as "the guardian of the empire."

The High Court's confrontation with the state administration in this
case is part of a larger context of increasing public-interest litigation since
the late 1980s, and what is often termed "judicial activism"—the tendency
since the 1990s for the judiciary to intervene in administration—which
has often positioned the judiciary against other state institutions (Dhavan 2000, Rudolph and Rudolph 2001, 132–40). In response to a perceived
breakdown of public administration in Bihar, the courts increasingly intervened in matters normally under executive authority. The role of the
judiciary in transferring the fodder-scam case to the Central Bureau of
Investigation with judicial oversight by the Patna High Court resulted
in Lalu's imprisonment, as was described in the previous chapter. In response to civil writ petitions and public-interest litigation, the High Court
in Patna frequently issued directives to the Bihar state government to pay
salaries, complete development works, improve city sanitation, or undertake other tasks normally under the purview of the state government. The
High Court went so far as to call departmental secretaries, the chief secretary, ministers, and even the chief minister to appear before the court
under threat of being held in contempt and jailed. Public-interest litigation also directly intervened in the political process, forcing the government to hold long-delayed elections to local *panchayat* bodies in 2001.

The state government's limited financial and legal resources, however, and the enormous number of petitions filed against it in the High Court resulted in many court orders being ignored. In 2005, more than 5,500 contempt applications sat pending against the Bihar government in the High Court.[30] Such litigation weakened the ability of the courts to efficiently handle other cases, further extending the already long delays that accompany the legal process in India. A vicious cycle resulted: administrative breakdown prompted excessive litigation against the government, which cost the government significant time and resources, further constraining administrative capacity.

Many politicians and bureaucrats with whom I spoke about the increasingly active role of the judiciary interpreted judicial activism as partisan interference. During numerous interviews, RJD politicians attributed the court's interference to an upper-caste conspiracy against the RJD government.[31] Many lower-caste politicians, in fact, demanded caste-based reservations in the judiciary; on the other hand, the bureaucrats usually complained that the judiciary was overstepping its boundaries and threatening the constitutional separation of judicial and executive branches of government.[32]

The judges themselves, however, defended their activism as a safeguarding of public interest in the face of an increasingly corrupt and ineffective administration that was threatening the principles of the constitution.[33] Instead of partisan interference, the judiciary described its role as that of an impartial, constitutional institution with a duty to correct other state institutions that had lost their impartiality.

On one occasion, for example, I was visiting the then–Bihar chief justice at his official residence, a huge colonial-era mansion. A Patna-based academic and two Dutch photographers accompanied me. The chief justice, openly expressing his disdain for Indian bureaucrats, stated, "In other countries [as opposed to India] you don't even notice the bureaucracy." The photographers asked the chief justice if they could take his photograph while seated in front of his desk in the High Court. Although he did eventually agree, the justice was reluctant, stating that judges should not be "personalized" and arguing that the impersonal attribute of justice underlies the judiciary's legitimate authority. He continued, "A judicial judgment should come from above, like the law received by Moses."

Through this metaphor of Judaic revelation, the chief justice alluded to a conception of sovereignty based on the transcendental stature of the constitution and the judiciary's privileged role as its interpreter and protector, a conception that allowed him to place the judiciary in opposition to other branches of the state. In practice, however, judicial activism overwhelmed an already dysfunctional government that in any case lacked the capacity to effectively enforce constitutional rights. And the fact that most judges came from upper-caste backgrounds reinforced a perception among many lower castes that the judiciary—far from being a guardian of liberalism—was actually part of the upper-caste "system" that had long oppressed them. Members of other state institutions, as we would expect, have their own self-perceptions and conceptions of legitimate authority. In the next section, I give two different accounts of the bureaucracy's conception of itself in relation to the state government.

Bureaucratic Perspectives

Mishra, a senior IAS officer, exemplifies the perspective of the upper-caste dominated bureaucracy in relation to the political changes following Lalu Yadav's rise to power. After being charged with corruption, Mishra was transferred to an undesirable post. A minister had taken over his office, so Mishra was forced to run a government department out of his home. When I met him, he had arranged a temporary office in an out-of-the-way room in a house that socialist leader Karpoori Thakur (see Chapter 2) had once occupied and that had been made into a museum after Thakur's death in 1989. The location was an ironic place for a Brahman IAS officer to take refuge since Lalu Yadav and his supporters claim to be the political heirs to Karpoori Thakur's tradition of "backward-caste" socialism.

When I asked Mishra about the impact of recent political change on the bureaucracy, he described the government's practice of frequent transfers "as a tool to demonstrate power." He accused the RJD government of "terrorizing the system," but affirmed, "You can't destroy the system. The system remains but you need the will to implement it." For Mishra, the autonomous "system" of the bureaucracy persists as an ideal, even when undermined in practice.[34] This response is a natural one from a civil servant who, like other IAS officers, had spent many years being trained in, and operating within, the complex procedures of Indian administration. Still, the corruption charges against him, whether or not warranted, pointed to the reason why many lower-caste people do not share his assessment of the impartiality and professionalism of the Bihar bureaucracy. As with the corruption scandal at the Patna Municipal Corporation, many upper-caste bureaucrats responded to the rise of lower-caste politics by engaging in even more corruption than they had in the past, taking advantage of the new generation of politicians' lack of knowledge of administrative procedure. Some also used this knowledge advantage to stealthily subvert and sabotage through bureaucratic foot-dragging the few constructive policy interventions that the RJD government attempted.

I encountered a great deal of hostility from civil servants toward politicians and members of elected bodies. On one occasion, I asked the Bhojpur district magistrate (DM), introduced at the beginning of the chapter, whom he thought would win the 2004 parliamentary elections in the Ara constituency. He quipped, "I don't know who will be the winner, but I do know that we will all be losers." His remark reflects a common perception that senior civil servants have of themselves being the key upholders of law and order and the agents of development in the face of increasing interference from politicians perceived to be incompetent to govern or act in the public interest.

In contrast, Vishwas, an IAS officer and secretary (administrative head) of the Public Relations Department during the time of my fieldwork, held a very different vision of the government's relationship with the bureaucracy. Vishwas, a self-affirming Dalit (Scheduled Caste) and someone I came to know quite well, was completely open about his contempt for the upper caste—especially what he called "Brahman"—domination of the bureaucracy. He constantly expressed disdain for upper-caste domination in social life and often commented, "For a Brahman India is heaven on earth, but for a Dalit it is a hell." In Vishwas's large, modern office in the state secretariat, the only picture on the wall behind his desk was of the Dalit leader, Ambedkar. During the many hours I spent in his office, many lower-ranking Dalit bureaucrats would visit Vishwas, and the discussion would inevitably turn to venting anger at the discrimination they suffered from perceived upper-caste interests within the bureaucracy. Vishwas commonly commented, "How many general secretaries and additional secretaries belong to the deprived communities (referring to high-level posts in the central administration in Delhi)?" Vishwas's office functioned as an informal rallying point for Dalit power within the bureaucracy.[35]

Although he lamented the RJD government's lack of emphasis on primary education, Vishwas generally supported the government and considered many of these failures the result of a hostile bureaucracy and political attacks by upper caste leaders. Since an independent Dalit politics like that of the BSP in Uttar Pradesh did not exist in Bihar, and, as discussed, Lalu relied heavily on Dalit bureaucrats to compensate for a lack of OBC officers, bureaucrats like Vishwas were integral to the RJD's project of lower-caste empowerment. As Vishwas put it, "they [Lalu Yadav and the RJD government] are sitting on a tiger. There is danger if they stay on; there is danger if they get off. Politics is constant warfare." His metaphor emphasized the hostile nature of the bureaucracy and other state institutions that the RJD was attempting to "tame." For Vishwas, the frequent criticism of the RJD and especially of Lalu Yadav in the media and elsewhere represented a reactionary tactic by upper caste interests afraid of losing power. For the upper castes, as he put it, "The mere thought of a rustic, unsophisticated man holding the reins of power brings revulsion." Although serving as the top bureaucrat in a government ministry, Vishwas himself conceived of the state in caste terms that implicitly subverted any claim to autonomy or impartiality. My time spent is his office taught me the extent to which caste-based conflict had penetrated the bureaucracy, even at the highest levels, emphasizing the ways in which the project of lower-caste empowerment displaced the discourse of development.

Lower-Caste Politics and State Institutions

As lower-caste politicians increasingly came to dominate electoral politics—and therefore the legislature as well as the political leadership of Bihar state government—inevitable conflict occurred with a bureaucracy still largely composed of officials from upper-caste backgrounds. The increasing conflict between and within state institutions reinforced popular perception of the state itself as a site of political struggle. To many within the bureaucracy and judiciary, the conflict represented an invasion of the state by corrupt and "casteist" forces, a viewpoint that assumes the idea of a constitutional and rule-bound legal and administrative system capable of impartially acting in the interests of citizens. Like Chatterjee's (2004) "civil society," however, such a constitutional ideal existed largely in theory, being rather limited in contexts where corruption tended to be the rule, not the exception. Many lower-caste people, in contrast, viewed state institutions from the perspective of "political society," wherein pervasive links between state power and local dominance were seen as an entrenched reality, and lower-caste leaders claimed that their struggles against an upper-caste bureaucracy simply reflected the state's inherently political character now revealed, a pulling back of the veil.

The result was—to repeat the quote from the beginning of the chapter—"democracy versus bureaucracy," which, should be noted, deviates extensively from the liberal democratic model. An impartial and effective bureaucracy and the establishment of the "rule of law" and "good governance" are usually seen as a crucial component of, or even a necessary precondition for, the consolidation of liberal democracy. In Bihar, however, the expansion of popular political participation and the democratic idea of popular sovereignty were accompanied by a weakening of many state institutions and a collapse of law and order and development-oriented governance. As we have seen, this conflict and destabilization were not the unintended results of increased demands "taxing the system." Rather, the weakening of state institutions was part of a political strategy intended to facilitate lower-caste empowerment.

But this strategy faced severe limitations. The RJD's inability to permanently reform state institutions or dislodge upper-caste influence within them, as the case of the cooperative societies demonstrates, highlights the incomplete nature of Lalu's revolution. This explains why, even after capturing state power though electoral democracy, the leaders of the "backward-caste" movement remained in conflict with many elements of what they termed "the system." At best, Lalu succeeded in temporarily placing relatively sympathetic officers in key posts and in weakening those institutions wherein upper-caste control could not be checked as a way to limit bureaucratic obstruction of his political agenda. Whatever change occurred in Bihar during this period, therefore, was not the result of state intervention but occurred through dispersed democratic practice within local sites. In the next chapter, I turn to Bhojpur district to examine the ways in which lower-caste politics played out within regional sites, and the shadowy political networks and sources of informal power that emerged as state institutions were destabilized.

CHAPTER FOUR

Caste, Regional Politics, and Territoriality

Fifteen years of rule by a self-avowed backward-caste government in Bihar opened new spaces of contestation, resulting in complex and often contradictory relationships between governmental institutions and local power. As we have examined, colonial processes of state formation resulted in the emergence of caste-based networks linking state institutions with landed elites, reinforcing a broad upper-caste hegemony that continued in the postcolonial period in the name of a national project of development. In response, the RJD dramatically increased politicians' influence and daily interference within state institutions—greatly empowering this political class that claimed to represent the lower-caste majority—in an attempt to democratize the state. This chapter examines the ways in which the RJD's project of lower-caste empowerment played out within a particular region. I examine Koilwar's political world, a semi-urbanized, block-level (one hundred villages) administrative headquarters in Bhojpur district, to determine what the RJD's emphasis on a caste-based notion of "social justice" actually meant in practice.

The actors I introduce constituted "political society" (Chatterjee 2004) in Koilwar, and examining its anatomy reveals a web of relationships entwining politicians, economic interests, struggles over territorial dominance, multiple levels of state administration, and the compulsions of electoral politics. This is a complex and contested world reflecting the fragmentation and struggles between and within state institutions as different groups struggle for access to public resources. It therefore documents the everyday negotiations and struggles for state resources that Chatterjee's theorization of political society emphasizes. But that was not the entire story. The emergence of a lower-caste political society and the shifting of power from administration to political networks worked to profoundly reshape Koilwar's political economy. Understanding the complexities of political society in Koilwar will be important for examining the ways in which lower-caste politics transformed village realities, the subject of subsequent chapters.

Koilwar's political life highlights two aspects of political society that are not sufficiently emphasized in Chatterjee's account—the crucial importance of territoriality and the complex, often contested relationships between state institutions. I explore how electoral politics and the politicians who claim to be self-styled caste leaders relate to the control of specific territorial spaces. This examination reveals the extent to which "political society" is grounded within struggles for territorial control, which I define as the ability of specific groups to control resources and the activities of others within specific spatial sites. These sites could be agricultural fields, roads, marketplaces, polling booths, and other places that have economic, political, or social importance.[1] As in the case of the cooperative societies, caste identities have served as a central reference point for relationships between state institutions and locally dominant groups, and the changing relationships between caste identities and territorial dominance are crucial for understanding political change resulting from lower-caste politics.[2] The prominence of caste-leader politicians reflects a mode of governance wherein state institutions were integrated with informal forms of power and territorial dominance. As has been stressed throughout the book, this is what subverted the enforcement of rights and why the logic of popular sovereignty became central to democratic practice.

"Territoriality" here is differentiated from the territoriality of the nation-state, and from the legally delineated units (the parliamentary constituency, municipal ward, etc.) that are electorally contested. In fact, struggles related to democratic practice can extend well beyond the boundaries of the official positions being contested—a battle for a single parliamentary seat is translated into myriads of micro-struggles for village and regional dominance. Elections, therefore, tend not to be about competing policy platforms or ideologies. Rather, for the dominant group, elections are about maintaining standing in the village, controlling labor, and ensuring continued access to state patronage. And for the subaltern, elections are about challenging the dominance of oppressive landlords (to whom one's parents and grandparents may have been bonded in subservience), demanding minimum wages (already legally mandated but not enforced), preventing indiscriminate violence by upper castes, and asserting the long-trampled honor of one's caste. Because democracy plays out in the context of relations of dominance and subordination that are underpinned by violence and the threat of violence, the electoral process takes on added intensity, but often results in a vicious cycle: groups who exercise territorial dominance are able to deliver votes, and the politicians thus elected reciprocate by protecting their supporters' territorial interests. Although the relationship between electoral politics and territorial dominance tends to perpetuate inequalities, I seek to show how democracy—precisely because electoral practice is embedded within everyday forms of dominance and resistance—also opens the possibility for social transformations, such as those occurring across north India during the last two decades.

Finally, an analysis of Koilwar's political society reveals the relationships between territorially grounded, localized castes and caste identities that are imagined to exist across much larger spaces. Although Srinivas's (1962) concept of the "dominant caste" is well established within both academic and popular sociology in India, this concept takes caste-based dominance as an analytic starting point, failing to address how caste dominance is produced in the first place and why power in Bihar, and other places in India, continues to be experienced and understood in caste terms.[3] The concept of the dominant caste was formulated within the context of the village studies of the 1950s and 1960s, and the concept suffered from a reification of the village as a natural spatial unit, thereby suppressing the critical examination of larger-level influences. An examination of the mutually reinforcing relationships between caste representations, trans-local caste networks, and caste-based territorial dominance is needed to explore how caste dominance is produced and reproduced, and how these processes change over time.

As in the concept of the dominant caste, caste can refer to specific groups of actors competing for dominance within particular sites. Time and again I heard locals refer to villages in Bihar as being "dominated" by a specific caste: "That is a Rajput dominated village" (*yeh rajput dominated gaon hai*), or more simply, "This is a Yadav village." Even when I left village contexts, I found this relationship between caste identities and dominance evident everywhere; at the regional and district levels people spoke of "caste belts"; a "Bhumihar belt," a "Kurmi belt." and so forth.

Caste can also refer to identities that are detached from particular sites

of practice: the caste that politicians invoke and that is present within official state language, identities that include "forward" versus "backward
castes," "Other Backward Classes" (OBCs), "Dalits," "Scheduled Castes,"
and more specific "deterritorialized" caste identifications that are defined
without reference to local territory (such as "Yadav," "Rajput," "Paswan,"
etc.). As discussed in Chapter 1, these latter identities emerged from colonial governmentality and were invigorated by caste movements in the
late nineteenth century; and the former emerged from the developmental
categories of the postcolonial state, transformed by the backward-caste
movement into a populist challenge to the status quo. An analysis of the
interaction between caste dominance within specific sites and these more
abstract, deterritorialized caste identities necessarily implies an examination of the relationships between local power and larger-level political
practice. And the interaction between these two forms of caste identification is at the heart of what is popularly termed "caste politics." To conduct
such an analysis entails observing how caste is utilized as political/state
discourse within localized sites of political practice: noting when categories such as "Yadav," "Rajput," "Backward," and "Scheduled Caste"
come into play, their respective political effects, and the ways in which
these categories relate to one another. My aim is to explore how caste
identities relate to specific territorial contexts, and what this reveals about
the popular experience of democracy.

In the following sections, I draw on ethnographic material from Koilwar, a semi-urbanized village and center of regional politics near Rajnagar, the village where I lived in 2002 and 2003. Koilwar is located on the
banks of the Sone River, fifty kilometers south of Patna and twenty kilometers north of Ara, the largest town and administrative headquarters of
Bhojpur district. The chapter concludes with an account of the 2004 parliamentary elections within Koilwar and Rajnagar village as a further example of the ways in which electoral practice relates to local territorial
contexts, and especially the crucial space of the polling booth.

The Democratization of Local Administration

At the local level, the most distinctive site of the developmental state is
the block office. Koilwar's block office is located in the semi-urban block
headquarters, a centrally located village ten kilometers from Rajnagar
(see next two chapters), on the road to Patna. The division of India's

districts into development blocks, each containing around one hundred villages, is the result of the bureaucratic expansion of the development state immediately following independence. The block office and the adjoining circle office (concerned with land records and land taxes) are a nexus for the different government departments that operate at the local level through the block's organizational structure. The most important local functionary of the development state and the overall manager of the block's activities is the block development officer (BDO). The BDO (along with the circle officer, in charge of land revenue) is admitted into the Bihar Administrative Service through competitive examinations.

Spending time at the block office, I constantly encountered numerous individuals whose livelihoods seemed to depend on block related activities but who did not hold any official post. Most of these people were easily identifiable by their distinctive white khadi kurta pajamas, a style of clothing made famous during the 1920s anticolonial movement and which subsequently became identified with the Congress Party and then with politicians generally (see Chakrabarty 2002). This clothing identifies these men as politically active, as local *netas*, local leaders, and they were central players within Koilwar's political society. When I asked these people questions about their occupation, they would usually describe themselves as *thikadars* or, in English as "contractors." Other people would sometimes refer to them as *netas* (leaders), as "media men," or would occasionally use the more derogatory term *dalal* (usually translated as "broker"). I soon found that every village had a number of *thikadars* and that almost all of these people were connected to the local member of the legislative assembly (MLA).

The *thikadar* is not a new phenomenon. Numerous ethnographic accounts describe what F. G. Bailey (1963) termed the "broker," a class of politically connected middlemen who mediate between the state and the village. Subsequent ethnographies described the development of this class of mediators and their importance in reproducing the local dominance of landowning castes (Gupta 1998, Jeffrey and Lerche 2001, Robinson 1988).[4] Ample ethnographic evidence depicts how dominant landowning castes were able to control and profit from green-revolution state interventions in India.[5] After independence and the formal abolition of the *zamindari* system, connections with bureaucrats and the police were crucial to the maintenance of caste dominance, either by having relatives working in government, or through the services of political "brokers."[6] Prior to the 1990s, brokers—usually only one or two from a village—were mostly members of the locally dominant landlord caste. Although from a single caste, they served as the broker for the entire village, reinforcing patronage links between landlords and their tenants and laborers. At the same time, these middle men were members of the Congress Party, a party that claimed to represent the nation and especially the lower-caste poor, even as its own political structure perpetuated the dominance of a small minority of upper-caste elites.

Koilwar is located in Bhojpur district, a district that has a long history of caste movements and agrarian struggle. From the Triveni Sangh and the Kisan Sabha in the 1930s to the formation of the Naxalite movement in Bihar in the 1970s (see Chapter 2), Bhojpur has been at the center of a great deal of agrarian struggle, although in many places attempts to empower backward castes have been met with ruthless resistance. At the time of my fieldwork, two paramilitary groups had a substantial presence in Bhojpur. One was the Communist Party of India (Marxist-Leninist) "Liberation" CPI(ML), a group whose activists mostly are drawn from Dalits and laborers from backward-caste backgrounds. In response to the CPI(ML), forward-caste landlords formed private caste militias (*senas*), and numerous massacres have been committed on both sides. The Ranvir Sena, a private militia of forward-caste landowners that was formed to fight the communists, was the only *sena* active at the time of my fieldwork. Its membership is almost exclusively drawn from the Bhumihar caste. Both the CPI(ML) and the Ranvir Sena have areas of control where they collect "taxes" and dispense privatized justice.[7]

Until recently, Rajput and Bhumihar families continued to dominate the economic life of Bhojpur, and the position of many of these families is still considerable. After the rise of Lalu Yadav and the RJD in the 1990s, however, there was a shift in the political economy of the district as a whole, and the emergence of rival centers of economic power, which was reflected in the double nature of many facets of political economy in Bhojpur. In the district headquarters of Ara were two high-end hotels, each with generator-powered electricity, one owned by Rajput businessmen and the other by a Bania family. I often heard one referred to as a "forward-caste" hotel and the other, built just a few years before my fieldwork, as "backward caste." (As discussed in Chapter 3, the Bania caste is considered a "backward" caste in Bihar.) I frequented both hotels and I also observed this backward/forward differentiation reflected in the clientele, especially wedding parties as well as candidates during elections, when the hotels functioned as de facto election offices. There were two big rice mills in Bhojpur, two big government contractors, and two important caste leaders known as *bahubali*, mafia musclemen, all spit between "upper"- and "backward"-caste owners.

Following this regional trend, a democratization of brokerage had occurred since the 1990s. Every village now had a small number of *thikadars* — there were five in Rajnagar—and dozens of smaller brokers representing the interests of caste communities from various areas of the village. Since most of these brokers typically demanded either illegal "commissions," and/or the future commitment of votes, corruption was the oil facilitating the everyday interaction of villagers with public institutions. These "commission" rates were widely known and officials were considered "corrupt" only when they took more than the going rate or performed the work only on paper.[8] In addition, *thikadars* often served as organizers and campaigners during elections, collecting relevant electoral information and brokering deals, thereby serving as a medium for the local distribution of development patronage and enabling the MLA/MP to make political gains. I also saw *thikadars* present in almost every police station that I visited, and a "representative" of Lalu Yadav was even present the few times that I met with the director general of police (head of police in Bihar) in his office. In these ways, the functioning of governmental institutions in Lalu's Bihar was subordinated to political interests. As such, the increase in the number of lower-caste *thikadars* resulted in many people feeling an increase of voice and participation in local administration. Politicians in Bihar sometimes referred to this as "corruption from below," the feeling of entitlement that a voter has to make concrete demands of the politicians that he or she helped to elect, even if these demands are extralegal or would result in an unfair distribution of resources. Yet, many lower-caste people felt, for the first time, their vote mattered. And while corruption became more visible as more people were participating, this was a reaction to much older forms of corruption that had long allowed dominant groups to disproportionately benefit from governmental institutions.

Much of local leaders' activities revolved around creating spectacle and appearance. Leaders needed to be seen at important political functions, in the company of higher-level politicians, and within the buildings of state institutions even if they were not actually doing anything, what could be called a "politics of proximity." The time that I spent with politicians at all levels frequently involved sitting around and telling stories, usually about the activities of more powerful politicians, the performative logic being to create the appearance of a relationship between the narrator and the subject of the story. A particularly dramatic example occurred while I was at the official house of Sunil, a young MLA, in Patna. He was sitting with another MLA and two other young politicians, all having a reputation for violence and criminal activities. Sunil started telling stories about his recent visit with a powerful member of parliament from Bihar. At the climax of his story, he declared, "He was casually ordering people to be killed without any hesitation. He is crazy!" The accuracy of the story is impossible to confirm, and is not important; but the performative role of this story was definite. Sunil in effect was implying that he had a relationship with a more powerful political figure who should be feared. The obvious implication was that we should also fear Sunil, increasing his own spectacle of power. Similarly, local politicians constantly recounted stories of the exploits of higher-level politicians to increase their own reputation through dramatically emphasizing the power of the politicians with whom they were connected. Their accounts created a chain of dramatic representations of power ascending to the most powerful political figures.

The most important relationship for local *thikadars* was with Lal Bihari, the local member of the state assembly (who is described in more detail below). Enjoying virtual control over the local block development officer (BDO), Lal Bihari ensured that his supporters were given contracts, in addition to the contracts that he was able to provide directly through his MLA fund. Bipin, who was previously an important *thikadar* in Rajnagar, frequently reminded me of Lal Bihari's importance in relation to the BDO. Bipin had been close to the MLA and managed much of the development works in the village, but he had fallen out of favor with Lal Bihari. Although he still had a close relationship with the BDO, he often complained to me that he could no longer get contracts; his political influence and finances were clearly diminished, and he complained that he could not even afford a motorcycle (a status symbol signifying success as a *thikadar*). He would often point to a gold watch on his wrist, saying, "This is from before, now I get nothing."

Equally significant was the implementation of democratic decentralization, known as *panchayati raj*, which occurred in Bihar after the 2001 elections to the local bodies. Although *panchayati raj* is an institution with a long and debated history in independent India, local bodies were given unprecedented powers with passage of the 73rd Amendment to the Indian Constitution in 1993, especially in the implementation of development works. The *panchayat*, consisting of seven thousand voters and usually including one to five villages, now receives a significant portion of development funds directly, bypassing the block. Most of this new power rests in the hands of the *mukhia*, the elected head of the village who receives funds directly into a bank account in his or her name. A new class of local leaders and contractors at the village level has emerged, taking over much of the initiative in implementing development works that previously had been in the hands of the BDO, local administration, and *thikadars*. As one disillusioned villager told me, "The *panchayat* members are mainly interested in contracts (*panchayat ke log thika lene ke liye*). Before it was the BDO and [government] engineers, now they [*panchayat* members] have become the BDO and engineers." This shift toward local control, combined with the proliferation of local politicians and the political subjugation of governmental institutions that occurred in the wake of lower-caste politics, represented a "democratization" of administration, albeit one that remained dependent on the mediation of a new political class; for most people, access to state institutions and public resources in Koilwar was mediated by political society, which is why it was such a contested sphere.

But regional electoral dynamics complicated this process of caste-based democratization, as the case of the Barahara constituency examined in the next section demonstrates.

"Caste Equations" in Koilwar

The Barahara assembly constituency consists of Koilwar and Barahara, two administrative "blocks" containing approximately one hundred villages each. (Koilwar is also the name of the semi-urbanized village where the block-level government offices are located.) During my fieldwork, people in Koilwar recognized the emerging influence of Yadavs, but they commonly described the Barahara block as a "Rajput belt." In the 2000 assembly elections, the candidates from all major parties were Rajputs. This dominance has a long history. Rajput *zamindars* held power over most of what is now Bhojpur district during the colonial period. Even after independence, Rajput villagers owned a significant portion of agricultural land; they generally enjoyed strong relationships with local administrators and police, exercising what could be termed a regional dominance. This dominance had been actively challenged, especially after Lalu Yadav and the RJD came to power.

Lal Bihari had been the member of the legislative assembly (MLA) of the Barahara constituency since 1989, and before this his father was also an MLA. He was one of a handful of upper-caste socialist leaders (from the old backward caste/socialist alliance) who chose to stay with Lalu Yadav after the Janata Party split and Lalu formed the Rashtriya Janata Dal in 1997. This decision gave Lal Bihari an important position within the government that led to his position as minister for sugar-cane development in the state government. The political dynamics of the Barahara constituency easily demonstrate the reason for Lal Bihari's success.

Even though Lal Bihari is a member of the RJD, he is widely perceived as a Rajput (a forward-caste) leader who represents Rajput interests, which, people explained to me, enables him to receive a certain percentage of "Rajput votes." I spoke with many Rajput villagers who were firm supporters of the rival BJP but who still spoke highly of Lal Bihari. People often told me that Lal Bihari would make a point of paying courtesy visits to prominent Rajput households, even if they were outspoken supporters of Lal Bihari's political opponents. This practice gave an impression that Lal Bihari put his caste above party considerations. When I asked Kamlesh, a Rajput farmer in Rajnagar about this practice, he said, "People change parties all the time, but one's caste is for life. That is why caste relations are more important than party." This underscores Lal Bihari's self-representation as a Rajput caste leader, an identity essential to his political viability.

Politicians like Lal Bihari who claimed to be protectors of their respective castes have a dual role, constantly shifting between two distinct spheres of activity. On the one hand, they are self-avowed caste leaders involved with the protection of specific territorial interests within local contexts; on the other, they are politicians wielding influence over state institutions and resources. Embedded within specific territorial contexts, they connect these contexts with the practice of party politics and state administration, thereby producing a space for alliances and extended support. I often heard Lal Bihari described as a "bold leader," and his appearance certainly fit this description. Whenever I met Lal Bihari, he was surrounded by supporters and maintained a strong aura of authority. He had a stern face with intense eyes, imparting the feel of someone accustomed to wielding power, someone who would not hesitate to make full use of that power when necessary. This bold image was essential because Lal Bihari, a minister of the RJD government, had to be seen as an independent leader who could use his position to protect his supporters, particularly those from his own caste who would not tolerate any indication of submission to backward-caste leaders.

This point was clearly demonstrated during a political function attended by Lalu Yadav in a village about forty kilometers from Koilwar. Lalu occupied the only chair on stage as all the other leaders sat on the ground. In a gesture of hospitality, Lalu called me onto the stage and had another chair brought up for me, putting me in the rather uncomfortable position of having a seat while the other political leaders did not. These were leaders with whom I was in the process of building rapport, many of whom occupied powerful positions within regional politics. Lal Bihari, however, did not sit on the ground. After giving his speech he quietly left the stage and sat with supporters on chairs that were set up behind the stage. When Lalu finished speaking, he began looking around the stage and, clearly irritated, asked, "Where is Lal Bihari?" Not only was Lal Bihari then offered my seat (to my relief), but Lalu also took him back to Patna in his helicopter, a journey that conveyed a sense of proximity and respect. People were clearly impressed by this episode, and I heard this story of Lal Bihari's refusal to sit on the ground repeatedly narrated for weeks by Rajput villagers in Rajnagar and nearby villages.

Most local politicians whom I asked estimated that Lal Bihari received between 10 and 20 percent of Rajput votes during previous assembly elections. These votes supplemented those he received as an RJD candidate, a party membership that was expected to provide him with the majority of Yadav and Muslim votes as well as a variable percentage of votes from other backward-caste groups (see previous chapter). Whatever Rajput votes Lal Bihari received were not just extra votes; they were considered votes directly taken from the rival JD(U)-BJP combination, votes with double efficacy. So even though Lal Bihari, as a Rajput caste leader, received only a minority of Rajput votes, this support produced a hegemonic alliance—popularly termed a "caste equation"—that was enough to ensure victory. No wonder Lalu Yadav valued him. Lal Bihari's electoral support, therefore, reflected a compromise between the lower-caste supporters of the RJD and Lal Bihari's personal constituency that was connected to his image as a Rajput leader. This was a hegemonic alliance that combined party support at an all-Bihar level (the famous "M-Y" alliance discussed in Chapter 2), with the more localized territorial caste interests that Lal Bihari protected.

Apart from agriculture, Koilwar block had very few industries, with the exception of sand mining from the banks of the Sone and approximately a dozen brick kilns. I discovered that a simple way to determine local dominance in many parts of Bihar was to investigate who owned the brick kilns that proliferated in clay-rich regions like Koilwar. As a friend in Koilwar remarked, "Muscle and money power are needed for running a brick kiln." Without adequate local connections and protection, a brick kiln owner, whose highly visible enterprise often is located in remote locations, would have been vulnerable to robbery.[9] The electoral compromise implicit within Lal Bihari's base of support allowed the continued regional investment of Rajput capital, reflected in the ownership of the region's brick kilns, petrol pumps, and transport businesses. This compromise was somewhat at odds with the rest of the district and, as we shall see, resulted in persistent internal conflicts within the RJD in Koilwar. The importance of Lal Bihari, therefore, reflected the increased importance of elected representatives—his Rajput supporters were forced to secure their dominance through elections, and to make significant compromises with the RJD's lower-caste supporters in the process. And in many villages, such as Rajnagar (see next two chapters), the RJD's coming to power facilitated an overturning of Rajput dominance, despite Lal Bihari's presence.

Lal Bihari was a paradoxical political figure—he represented the historical dominance of Rajput *zamindars* while also belonging to a party that sought to challenge this dominance. As such, he was a living contradiction, raising the question, *who* exactly did Lal Bihari represent? If, as I have argued, the "social justice" that the RJD claimed to pursue was built on a caste-based notion of popular sovereignty mediated by political representatives, the "caste equation" that Lal Bihari represented complicates this considerably, and reflects the incomplete nature, and limitations, of Lalu Yadav's democratic revolution. These limitations are also reflected in the distorting effects of "caste belts"—the so-called Rajput belt in Barahara and Yadav belt in Koilwar—where in both of these cases, neither Rajputs nor Yadavs form even close to an absolute majority. Popular conceptions of "caste belts," therefore, demonstrate the ways in which caste dominance leads to an exaggerated sense of numerical preponderance since dominant castes are able to manipulate the voting process in their favor, as examined below. The concept of "caste belts" and the ability of dominant castes to manipulate the vote process, therefore, distorted even the strength of numbers at the basis of influence within institutions of democratic representation. At the same time, change was occurring, including changing popular perceptions of which caste was dominant according to changes in local power. The emergence of a "Yadav belt" in Koilwar reflects such change—earlier, this certainly would have been considered a Rajput dominated region. Caste-leader politicians such as Lal Bihari, therefore, did not simply "represent" their supporters within political institutions such as the state assembly, but also intervened directly in territorial struggles, actively structuring the contours of power.

A rival center of power had emerged in Koilwar, but it existed within the RJD and, therefore, was fraught with contradictions, based on the changes that occurred in Bhojpur district—changes very much linked to the ruling government in Patna—and the politics of Koilwar. As we have seen, in Koilwar, support for Lal Bihari as a Rajput caste leader was combined with support for the RJD at an all-Bihar level by quite different groups—a compromise between Rajput regional dominance and the RJD's larger political project. In other ways, however, the state leadership of the RJD encouraged the emergence of a new center of power in Koilwar opposed to Lal Bihari, as the case of the "*baloo* mafia" below will clarify.

The "*Baloo* Mafia": The Political Economy of Sand

Koilwar's most important economic activity is undoubtedly sand mining along the banks of the Sone River where hundreds of workers labor in the sweltering heat, shoveling sand into waiting trucks. An endless parade of trucks transports this high-quality sand, used in construction, to Patna, Varanasi, and other cities across northern India. Politics in Koilwar is intimately connected with control of this mining operation. Before 1988, the district administration controlled sand mining in Koilwar. Contracts were given to local contractors who managed the day-to-day operations. Much of the land along the river was owned by the owners of Kulharia estate, one of the most important Rajput families in the region, which allowed this family to control operations in a continuation of the *zamindari* system of control.[10]

In 1988, a system of auctioning rights to sand-mining sites was started. The group of men who won these auctions became popularly known as the "*baloo* mafia" or "the syndicate" (their self-designation), referring not only to their criminal connections but also to a collusion that artificially reduced the bid since few people outside of the group would even consider bidding against them. Most of the members of the syndicate were Rajputs, with some of the most prominent being associated with the powerful "coal mafia" in Dhanbad (what was then south Bihar and is today Jharkhand).

The story told to me by people associated with the sand mafia—I interviewed around a dozen people—was that, in 1992, Lalu Yadav was passing through Bhojpur when he was approached by Baby Yadav, the son of Ram Lakhan Singh Yadav, the most prominent Yadav leader prior to Lalu (see Chapter 1) who was from Bhojpur. Baby told Lalu that Rajputs controlled sand mining (*rajput log kabja kiye hue hai*) and asked him to intervene (*aap kuchh kijiye*). Lalu responded by effectively nationalizing sand mining, giving control of mining the Sone River to the Bihar Mining Development Corporation headquartered in Ranchi. But once Bihar and Jharkhand were bifurcated in 2000 (with Ranchi the new capital of Jharkhand), this arrangement was abruptly ended. So in 2002, auctions were held again. But this time the outcome was very different because of the control that the RJD was able to exert over the mining department— mining department officials told me of intense interference in the bidding process—and the political change that had occurred in the region, particularly the emergence of OBC contractors and criminals who had acquired enough capital to participate in the bidding. As a result, the new "syndicate" was entirely OBC without even a single Rajput member. The increasing importance of members of the "*baloo* mafia" was one of the changes that had occurred in Bhojpur district politics. It is important to note that the patronage of the RJD government in Patna, or at least some members of the government, made the rise of this group possible.

As when the district administration had controlled sand mining, the largest financial contributors of the group that purchased the mining rights were not themselves involved in day-to-day operations. Operational management, as well as the ability to extract various "commissions" or rents from truck drivers who had to pass over privately owned land, fell to a network of around three hundred local players through semiformal and informal arrangements. The banks of the river bordering Koilwar, and access to roads leading to the mining, were strictly divided into territories managed by specific groups. There were two principal controllers of sand mining operations in Koilwar town on a day-to-day basis: Mohan Yadav, a local contractor, and Lal Bihari, the powerful MLA of Koilwar's constituency and sugar-cane minister in the state government, introduced above. While Mohan Yadav had connections with the syndicate, Lal Bihari was given control over an illegal mining site adjacent to the Sone

Bridge—activity that eventually threatened its structural integrity—as part of the electoral compromise described above. While being excluded from the actual syndicate whose members were all OBCs, Lal Bihari was given a piece of the action in order to keep him loyal to the RJD and to avoid any challenges to the sand mafia's operations. While the syndicate collected payment from each truck for the sand, Mohan Yadav, Lal Bihari, and other men at other sites made sure that access roads were maintained, that operations went smoothly, and, in return, collected a separate "toll tax" from each truck.

The dividing line between the mining territories of Lal Bihari and Mohan Yadav on the banks of the Sone River marked more than just the most important economic division in Koilwar. Much of the political drama that I watched unfold in Koilwar was fueled by a rivalry between these two men. Their rivalry combined territorial struggles related to sand mining with political competition. When people living in villages in Koilwar block needed to access state resources, influence the police, or even get a loan, they likely did so through someone affiliated with either of these two.

The Social Justice Pariwar

Mohan Yadav was relatively unimportant in the political life of Koilwar until just a few years before my fieldwork. His increasing importance was a direct result of the changes in sand mining. Mohan Yadav's elder brother was a long-standing Congress politician who was the secretary of Baliram Bhagat, a Congress MP who had a very strong position within Ara for many years after independence. Another brother of Mohan Yadav was a contractor working with various departments in the district headquarters. Mohan Yadav's political position within Koilwar was very much related to his growing managerial control over sand-mining operations. Unlike Lal Bihari, Mohan Yadav was a resident of Koilwar village, and his political base reflects this more locally rooted position. Lal Bihari was not from Koilwar, or even Barahara, although his father was also an MLA from this constituency. Lal Bihari's house was in Ara, the district headquarters, and as an MLA and a minister he also spent considerable time in Patna. His control over sand mining was a result of his political importance in spheres outside of Koilwar; without Lal Bihari's support and active involvement, it would have been hard to keep the sand-mining operations running in a smooth manner, and everyone involved would have lost profits. His involvement in sand mining, therefore, was a necessity imposed from above. Lal Bihari's periodic visits to Koilwar were precisely that, visits, and he was necessarily removed from much day-to-day politics.

Mohan Yadav, on the other hand, was a permanent fixture within Koilwar's intimate social scene. In recent years, members of the newly elected *panchayats* and the Koilwar *panchayat* committee (*sammiti*)[11] became frequent customers of a tea stall near the block administrative headquarters, so much so that the owner referred to his shop as the *panchayat chai dukan* (the *panchayat* tea stall). This tea stall was an important center of public political life in Koilwar because of the contractors, petty politicians, and *panchayat* members gathered there. Mohan Yadav spent a few hours of the afternoon—when he was not supervising mining activity—at the tea stall on an almost daily basis, and it is here that he developed his political base.

I also made it a habit to spend time at the *panchayat* tea stall, and I got to know Mohan Yadav and his circle quite well. Unlike Lal Bihari, Mohan Yadav did not give the impression of being a "bold leader." His political style relied much more on his daily presence in Koilwar. He was not a talkative man and would spend most of his time at the *panchayat* tea stall sitting quietly and listening to the political discussions around him. When he did speak, however, it was with a reserve and well-thought purpose such that everyone, including myself, would always pay close attention. Mohan Yadav, although not a vehement speaker, clearly was at the center of the political group at the *panchayat* tea stall: he was always offered the best-placed chair even if this required other people to surrender their seat, and he always picked up the tab for all of the tea and snacks. At the *panchayat* tea stall, I first came into contact with the Social Justice Pariwar (literally "family").

Mohan Yadav's active political career began during the period leading up to the 2000 assembly elections. At that time, he established the Social Justice Pariwar, an organization agitating for increased backward-caste power within regional politics. "Social justice" (*samajic nyay*) is a term drawn from political discourse that in Bihar is associated with backward-caste struggle, and is a term the RJD, and Lalu Yadav in particular, used extensively. Mohan Yadav's Social Justice Pariwar, however, was very much a local organization responding to Koilwar's particular political context. Although the Social Justice Pariwar was a relatively small organization with activities confined to the area of the Barahara constituency (including Koilwar and Barahara blocks, about two hundred villages), I became interested in it because an analysis of its activities allows an exploration of how political discourse associated with state-level politics, a discourse central to contemporary political developments in Bihar, was utilized within a specific site of political practice.

Mohan Yadav and a small group of approximately a hundred supporters formed the Social Justice Pariwar as a loosely defined grassroots political organization with the primary aim of agitating against Lal Bihari. The organization conducted meetings in a building that Mohan Yadav had built for the purpose. In particular, the Social Justice Pariwar opposed the fact that, in Mohan Yadav's words, "backward-caste votes elect a Rajput MLA"—an explicit opposition to the "caste equation" within Lal Bihari's base of support, which represented an unacceptable compromise with Rajput interests. From the perspective of the Social Justice Pariwar, the RJD, a party identified as representing backward-caste interests, managed to win elections only by compromising with Rajput interests, thereby perpetuating Rajput regional dominance. Although the Social Justice Pariwar supported Lalu Yadav and the RJD government in Bihar, they opposed Lal Bihari. This reflected not only the fact that Lalu's democratic revolution remained incomplete, but also that lower-caste politics was an ongoing, conflicted, and complex process of democratization involving shifting constellations of territorial interests and caste alliances.

During the 2000 assembly elections, the Social Justice Pariwar supported an independent candidate from a Yadav caste background. She lost the election but did manage to receive twenty thousand votes, enough to be noticed and to create a visible threat to Lal Bihari and his backward-caste support. The Social Justice Pariwar's next important success was during elections to the state legislative council in June 2003. For the first time, a proportion of seats on the Bihar legislative council were to be elected by members of the *panchayats*, the political space that Mohan Yadav had spent so much time cultivating. He told me at one point, for example, that at least 80 percent of *panchayat* members in Koilwar block were members of the Social Justice Pariwar, and he listed approximately four hundred people who were registered members. On the day of the elections, supporters of different candidates were all sitting outside the grounds of the block headquarters where voting was taking place. Most politically active people from surrounding villages were present, and the atmosphere was that of a political festival. By far the most organized group was the

Social Justice Pariwar, with Mohan Yadav at the center of attention. The Pariwar had chosen to support Rai, the Yadav "businessman" from Ara introduced in the last chapter who had close ties to Lalu Yadav. Rai won the election with a large margin, which served to boost the reputation of Mohan Yadav and the Social Justice Pariwar.

The next big political test involved the *panchayat* committee (*sammiti*), the elected organization of the *panchayat* system at the block administrative level representing seventeen *panchayats* that included sixty-eight villages. A controversy arose within the *panchayat* committee between a large number of members and the *pramukh*, the elected committee chairman. The *pramukh* was a local Yadav villager who I was told was elected after being chosen as the candidate of the Social Justice Pariwar. After assuming office, problems began when the *pramukh* forged a close relationship with the BDO. Members of the *panchayat* committee complained that the *pramukh*, because of his close relationship with the BDO (who in turn was considered close to Lal Bihari), was favoring Rajput contractors and that he was forging the signatures of some backward-caste members. As a local contractor friend put it, "the BDO likes the *pramukh* because he is cheap," meaning that by giving relatively small "commissions" to the *pramukh*, the BDO could more or less control the *panchayat* committee's development funds. Any BDO in Koilwar block was inevitably close to Lal Bihari because his position as a minister in the state government meant that he could easily exert pressure to appoint and transfer civil servants posted within his constituency. Within this context, contractors close to the BDO were also necessarily close to Lal Bihari. Contractors who worked for the BDO were almost all Lal Bihari's men, petty politicians who supported Lal Bihari.

Obviously the Social Justice Pariwar had a problem, as the person they had chosen as *pramukh* had effectively gone over to the other side. Complicating matters a bit more, a large group of *panchayat* committee members, along with the local district council (*zilla parishad*, a higher level of the *panchayat* system) member, had written and signed a letter demanding a no confidence vote against the *pramukh*, and this letter had been formally presented to the BDO. Most of these members were from backward-caste backgrounds, and while presenting the letter in the BDO's office, the district council member turned to me and exclaimed "Dalit *virodh*!" (Dalit resistance!).

The problem for Mohan Yadav was that this was all done without his awareness and without the involvement of the Social Justice Pariwar.

The Social Justice Pariwar was Mohan Yadav's attempt to forge a new political base in Koilwar and to challenge Lal Bihari's dominance, and any other independent political activity in Koilwar organized around the theme of social justice could threaten this political project. Taking these events very seriously, Mohan Yadav called an emergency meeting of the Social Justice Pariwar to discuss these developments, which I was able to attend. About fifty people attended the meeting, including Mohan Yadav and his elder brother. To my surprise, the meeting began with one of the members who had signed the letter standing up and apologizing for acting independently of the Social Justice Pariwar and vowing to act in consultation with the Pariwar in all subsequent political pursuits. Similar apologies and affirmations from other members followed. In truly dramatic fashion, Mohan Yadav's brother then led all of these *panchayat* committee members to the nearby Durga temple, where they were asked to swear these affirmations in front of the Goddess, invoking her wrath if they were ever to break the vow. Finally, a select number of important Pariwar members, excluding the erring *panchayat* committee members, held a closed meeting (I was not allowed to attend) where they deliberated on how to proceed. They emerged declaring that they had decided to support the erring members and to press for a no confidence vote in opposition to the *pramukh* (who it was noted was still in possession of a motorcycle lent by Mohan Yadav himself). To counter the BDO's cunning, Mohan Yadav's brother suggested employing the services of an advocate in Ara. This turned out to be the key move that forced the BDO to accept the no confidence vote, and the *pramukh* was voted out.

The election for the new *pramukh* occurred a few months later and was an equally dramatic affair. By this time, Lal Bihari was actively involved, and the *panchayat* committee members had divided into opposing groups. All of the Yadav and Muslim *panchayat* committee members with whom I spoke claimed to support the Social Justice Pariwar's Muslim candidate, while all of the Rajput *panchayat* committee members claimed to support Lal Bihari's chosen Rajput candidate. The remaining Dalit and other backward-caste members were divided: many supported the Social Justice Pariwar's candidate, but a few supported Lal Bihari's and three, who were members of the CPI(ML), fielded their own candidate. By the election it was clear that voting would be close but that the Social Justice Pariwar's candidate would win by a few votes. In a shrewd last-minute negotiation, Lal Bihari directed his supporters to vote for the CPI(ML) candidate, which was just enough to ensure the defeat of the Social Justice Pariwar's candidate. This election revealed how tense the conflict was between Mohan Yadav and Lal Bihari. Lal Bihari was willing to elect a *pramukh* affiliated with another party to defeat a candidate who was a strong supporter of the RJD. In this case, internal contradictions within the regional RJD proved stronger than interparty rivalry, and territorial struggle proved more central than party loyalty.

Mohan Yadav was, on the one hand, a local actor whose sand-mining operation required control over a specific territory that supported his political activities. On the other hand, his political project embodied in the Social Justice Pariwar, drew on the language of the RJD that operated at an all-Bihar level. To gain support for his project and to counter Lal Bihari's influence over the block offices and related *thikadars*, Mohan skillfully recruited people from the elected *panchayats*, young politicians very much grounded within their respective village contexts. This project required the skillful interweaving of local, regional, and all-Bihar levels of political representation and practice. Underpinning this project was Mohan Yadav's territorial importance within Koilwar and especially within Koilwar's biggest industry, sand mining, which provided economic incentives to participate in his project and gave the project a concrete territorial basis within regional political economy. The Social Justice Pariwar, in a very real sense, was anchored in sand. It was also an extension of the OBC-dominated sand mafia that RJD rule enabled.

Many people with whom I spoke, in fact, criticized the Social Justice Pariwar as being the personal tool for Mohan Yadav's struggle against Lal Bihari, a struggle that involved clear economic interests. By 2005, many previously active members of the Social Justice Pariwar had withdrawn from the organization, complaining that Mohan Yadav, in the words of one former member, "treated the Social Justice Pariwar as his own organization." I also heard frequent criticism that the Social Justice Pariwar was not a "backward-caste" organization, but in reality a "Yadav" organization. This statement mirrored common criticism by the media and opposition parties in Bihar that Lalu Yadav, and the RJD government in general, was a "Yadav Raj." It is interesting, therefore, that the Social Justice Pariwar came into direct conflict with a minister in the RJD government.

I have examined the struggle between Mohan Yadav and Lal Bihari in some detail in order to highlight the internal contradictions within the RJD's regional hegemony, and the ways in which this hegemony was territorially grounded. Lal Bihari, as a minister in the state government, was able to utilize his influence within the state government and over the block office to patronize his supporters, thereby reinforcing his dominance, dominance dependent on his role as a Rajput caste leader and disproportionately benefiting Rajput supporters. This was the underlying context of the *pramukh* dispute. On the other hand, an actor like Mohan Yadav was able to emerge in the first place only because of the changes in sand mining that resulted from the RJD's control of state administration (in this case the department of minerals and mining). Mohan combined his connections with the sand mafia with influence among elected *panchayat* members, and connections with politicians such as Rai (who had a direct link to Lalu Yadav) to challenge Rajput dominance in the name of a caste-based "social justice." And the RJD tolerated Mohan Yadav and his Social Justice Pariwar despite the fact that he proved to be a liability for the election of an RJD MLA. In fact, Mohan Yadav's position depended on the RJD-affiliated sand mafia. So while the contradictions and complexities of Koilwar's political society resulted from an uneasy electoral alliance, the RJD's project of lower-caste empowerment remained a driving force.

The struggle between Lal Bihari and Mohan Yadav also reveals the extent to which Koilwar's political society revolved around conflicts over the control of territory. The power and influence of actors within political society extend well beyond the boundaries of governmental institutions, embodying a mode of governance wherein state institutions are integrated with informal forms of power and territorial dominance, and wherein political "representation" actively shapes the contours of power. There were actually two interrelated conflicts: one involved a conflict of territorial interests between Mohan Yadav and Lal Bihari (and their supporters), and the other a regional caste-based political conflict. While Mohan Yadav fit into the "sand mafia" that controlled sand mining in Koilwar and could claim a territorial right based on residence and local influence, both Lal Bihari's caste background and his imposition from above could be challenged. This was articulated as a challenge to Lal Bihari's base of political support and the caste compromise that it entailed. "What good is an RJD MLA," Mohan Yadav asserted, "if this does not translate into advantage for backward-caste people (*pichhare jaati log*)?" Of course, the emergence of actors like Mohan Yadav demonstrates that important changes had occurred, even if they involved compromise. This rivalry highlighted both the incomplete nature of Lalu Yadav's political revolution, as well as a continuing challenge to established power in the name of lower-caste politics and "social justice." But although the previously unrivaled Rajput dominance in the region had been seriously compromised, territorial dominance itself had not. Lower-caste politics did not end caste-based territorial dominance, but rather partially "democratized" it by facilitating the entrance of people from lower-caste backgrounds into political society.

To explore the ways in which relationships between caste identities, territoriality, and democratic practice intersected with national politics, I next examine the 2004 Indian parliamentary elections which I observed play out in Bhojpur district, specifically from the vantage point of Koilwar. This was the last national election held with the Lalu-Rabri government still in power.

2004 Parliamentary Elections

The results of the 2004 national elections for the Indian Parliament came as a shock to almost everyone. Just weeks before the elections began, the questions the media were asking were how much the then-ruling National Democratic Alliance (NDA) coalition government would increase their seat share and what the chances were that the Bharatiya Janata Party (BJP), the largest party in this coalition, could become the second party ever to gain an absolute majority in parliament.[12] To the NDA it seemed that India was "shining," and their campaign, enjoying a record amount of finance, centered on the slogan "India Shining" and the "feel-good factor," a campaign theme developed by an advertising firm.[13]

The results came as a political earthquake. Some commentators likening it to the Pokhran nuclear blasts that the BJP-led government conducted on May 11 and 13, 1998, the latter the same date as the election results six years later. The entire NDA did not even get a majority: every party in the NDA lost ground, some were wiped out, and the BJP was reduced to a lower seat share than the Congress.[14]

In retrospect, some politicians were much closer to the pulse of the Indian electorate. As one newspaper reported:

> Bihar's strongman Lalu Prasad Yadav is appearing all over as a bare bodied, hungry man in a publicity campaign aimed at taking some of the gleam away from the Bharatiya Janata Party's (BJP) "India shining" promotions. Posters with the ruling Rashtriya Janata Dal (RJD) chief as a common man in distress

due to the BJP-led National Democratic Alliance (NDA) rule at the Centre have already appeared in Patna.... "In the posters, Yadav is the bare bodied, hungry man carrying a stick in his hand to send the message that India may be shining and the feel-good factor might be working for the BJP but it is all missing in Bihar," insisted the RJD's spokesperson.[15]

In election speeches, often delivered in remote villages, Lalu attacked the NDA as being out of touch with rural India. At a rally that I attended in a village in Bhojpur district, Lalu made a series of jokes concerning the uselessness of mobile phones, which he used as a symbol of what he claimed was the NDA's emphasis on an economic policy that primarily benefited India's urban, "high-tech" middle class at the expense of the rural majority. He demonstrated that mobile phones never work when you need them—especially when in a remote village—joked at how stupid people look when using them, and even alleged that mobile phone use results in brain damage. Holding up an attendant's mobile phone he shouted, "This is what [then–deputy prime minister] Advani calls development. This is not the water that our villages need" (*yeh hamare gaon ka paani nahi hai*).

The effective campaign of leaders like Lalu Yadav—the RJD increased its seats in parliament from four to twenty-six and managed to acquire four ministry seats including the coveted Railways Ministry for Lalu himself—emphasized the continued importance of the backward-caste, populist leaders of regional parties who had emerged across much of north India (also in stark contrast to the 2005 state election in Bihar). Many commentators explained the results by arguing that in 2004, national elections turned out to be a series of local elections, with local issues and local political configurations dominating the results.[16] The secret of the continued electoral success of the RJD was popularly explained in relation to "caste equations," and it is true, as we have seen, that in Bihar local issues and local power were very much related to caste identities. As a typical local headline read, "It's the Stamp of Caste in Bihar; Despite NDA's Attempt to Take On Lalu Yadav with Its Development Agenda, Caste Will Be Key to the Poll Outcome in Bihar."[17]

Elections for members of parliament in India take place in large constituencies that usually include five or six assembly constituencies. Koilwar falls within the Ara parliamentary constituency (and the Barahara assembly constituency, as discussed above), and the electoral contest was essentially between four candidates. The RJD's candidate was Kanti

Singh, a former Union minister close to Lalu Yadav, and the only woman given a ticket by the RJD. The Ara parliamentary seat was previously held by another RJD candidate who many people told me had become unpopular because he did not spend enough time in the constituency. The story that I heard often repeated was that Kanti Singh was in a similar situation in a nearby constituency and that the two swapped constituencies in order to avoid "anti-incumbency" sentiments. An electoral alliance between the BJP and the JD(U) assigned the Ara seat to the JD(U) candidate Ashok Verma. In addition, the CPI(ML) fielded Ram Naresh Ram, an MLA from south Bhojpur who had been an active communist leader since revolutionary activity began in Bhojpur in the late 1970s. Making things even more complicated and tense, the founding leader of the Ranvir Sena, a landowners' militia connected with the Bhumihar caste, was contesting the election from Ara jail. Although the CPI(ML) as well as the Ranvir Sena candidates were leaders of very territorially grounded organizations that they had helped to build from the village up, both Kanti Singh and Ashok Verma were politicians who were not from Bhojpur, coming from other constituencies for the first time.

The following *Times of India* article concerning the Ara constituency is an example of popular political discourse that circulated about the election, reflecting the language used to discuss electoral strategy:

> The upper caste voters, who are expected to rally behind the JD-U [Janata Dal United] candidate, chief rival of Kanti Singh (the RJD candidate), stand deeply fragmented. While 1.25 lakh [125,000] Bhumihars have consolidated themselves behind Brahmeshwar Singh, a section of Rajputs, nearly three lakhs [300,000], have decided to root for Narendra Kumar Singh, 9th grade dropout and a moneybag from Mumbai who runs a successful security agency for Bollywood stars. N. K. Singh's spending power has enthralled the unemployed youth of the community who are campaigning in far off places. . . . On the other hand, the strong Yadav electorate of more than three lakh [300,000] has taken upon itself to protect the honor of lady of the community [Kanti Singh] and would not mind if development gets damned in the process. A kind of medieval farman [order] has been issued by Yadav leaders of nearly 100 villages, invoking all to vote for her.[18]

What are we to make of the caste language in this article? The journalist has numerically calculated the caste strength of various candidates although we are given no idea of the source of these numbers. Different explanations are given concerning the nature of candidates' caste support. It is apparently self-evident that forward-caste voters "are expected to rally behind the JD-U," and no reasons are given for why "1.25 lakh [125,000] Bhumihars have consolidated themselves behind Brahmeshwar Singh." Although N. K Singh's support is associated with his status as a "moneybag" (N. K. Singh's role was overestimated here, as he ended up receiving only a few thousand votes), Kanti Singh's support is attributed to the assertion that "the strong Yadav electorate of more than three lakh [300,000] has taken upon itself to protect the honor of lady of the community."

Comparing this article's language to my own experience within the Ara constituency in the days prior to the election is informative. During this time, this political contest dominated conversations, especially at tea shops where men would gather and discuss politics for hours. I found it surprising that with all of this political debate, comparatively little time was spent discussing election issues. Rather, in a similar way to the article, discussion focused around strategic issues related to caste arithmetic, what Chandra (2004) terms "ethnic head counting." The estimated caste support base of each candidate was commented upon in detail and numerically added up. Calculation of this type that I heard usually ended with an assessment that the numbers favored Kanti Singh not only because of Kanti Singh's own numerical support, but even more because of other candidates' splitting the support in the opposition's upper-caste base. The author of the newspaper article quoted above clearly gained his information in the same way as I did, reporting the numerical estimations of caste support that were circulating in tea-stall conversations all over the constituency. The author augmented the account with biases typical of India's upper-caste media, that the imagined "Yadav electorate ... would not mind if development gets damned in the process." More striking is the claim that "a medieval *farman* (order) has been issued by Yadav leaders of over a thousand villages." I certainly encountered no such *farman*, and it would be hard to make sense of why the Yadav electorate's support in particular should be characterized as medieval when it was clearly asserted in the article that all of the candidates had a numerically defined caste support.

As was the case for the concept of "caste belts" examined above, we must recognize that these numbers are exaggerated based on perceptions of dominance. For instance, this newspaper article—like the many discussions that I listened to—does not even mention the dozens of castes that collectively made up the overwhelming majority of the electorate. Rather, it was assumed that competition between the long-dominant Bhumihars and Rajputs and newly dominant Yadavs would determine the outcome. Public political discourse systemically obscured the ways in which territorial dominance, and not the pure strength of numbers, structured political practice.[19] Whatever their accuracy, these assessments were important because of people within Koilwar's political society whose economic livelihoods depended on having good relations with those in power. These people wanted above all to be on the winning side.

Even with all of this caste calculation, people usually conceded that the numbers could always change unexpectedly, reflecting a popular perception of the "radical indeterminacy" (Lefort 1988) of electoral outcomes. I often heard politics described as existing "in the wind" (*hawa me*). When I asked one local politician who he thought would win, for instance, he simply stated, "I am watching the wind." In another discussion, the brother of Mohan Yadav offered a similar caste analysis to that given by the journalist quoted above. He then offered an important qualification, "This is how things stand now, but I won't be able to say for sure until the last day. The wind could change at the last moment." This volatility, he explained, was possible because of the importance of local caste leaders who could change allegiance at the last moment. Because a large group of people want to be on the winning side, if rumors begin to predict a change in the numbers, a whole mass of voters could change course at the last minute.

The importance of local caste leaders within this national election became clear to me while I was accompanying Kanti Singh during her campaigning, especially within Koilwar. As Kanti Singh was essentially an outsider, her reputation depended on her perceived proximity with Lalu Yadav as well as her previous status as a union minister. This meant that she strongly invoked the representations of the RJD at an all-Bihar level, but had no real territorial links within Bhojpur—a position in stark contrast with Lal Bihari's. Kanti Singh had to rely heavily on a whole range of local caste leaders to effectively connect with her constituency. While campaigning, these leaders always accompanied her, and they were given prominence while in public view. Campaigning entailed moving through an area with a parade of cars and motorcycles, stopping at key locations. Sometimes these stops were at the houses or business sites of important local leaders whom Kanti Singh could not afford to neglect, and with whom she wanted to appear to be connected. Sometimes stops were for large groups of supporters who often arranged refreshments and elaborate receptions, including marching bands, elephants, and that always included shouting of slogans: "Kanti Singh zindabad" (long live Kanti Singh!), "Lalu Yadav zindabad," and "hamara MP kaisa ho, Kanti Singh jaisa ho" (What is our MP like? Our MP is like Kanti Singh!). At other times stops were for prearranged "functions" in villages where some sort of makeshift stage was set up and speeches were given. These speeches always began with the speaker slowly and deliberately paying homage to all of the important leaders present, including MLA's like Lal Bihari as well as village leaders like the village *mukhia*. In this way, whoever was present on stage, even if they did not give a speech, was explicitly associated with the campaign and helped to territorially ground Kanti Singh's political image.

The importance of local leaders in territorially grounding Kanti Singh's political image cannot be overemphasized. Even the the presentational arrangement of campaign posters reflected this importance. Photos of Kanti Singh and Lalu Yadav were always accompanied by photos of more local leaders like Lal Bihari and Rai. At times the importance of these local leaders was explicitly acknowledged. On one occasion, for example, Kanti Singh's campaign stopped at a local politician's house where there was no reception offered. Kanti Singh, along with Lal Bihari, left their vehicles in order to approach this leader. The man, who was sitting casually on his veranda, stood up to greet the two politicians. Staring intensely at Kanti Singh, he said, "I don't support you, but I will vote for the RJD only because of Lal Bihari." While it was obvious that this man would not actively participate in the campaign, this conditional acquiescence meant that he also would not oppose it.

I could easily see the relative importance of various local leaders as the campaign entered specific villages. For example, when the campaign entered a village next to Rajnagar which people commonly referred to as "Rajput dominated," the role of Lal Bihari was crucial, and he was given even more respect than Kanti Singh. As he arrived, a Rajput youth shouted, "Bir Raghvendra zindabad" (long live the brave Raghvendra [another name for Lal Bihari]), demonstrating the importance of Lal Bihari as a Rajput caste leader. In contrast, when the campaign reached Rajnagar, most of the huge crowd of supporters, including scores of delighted children, consisted of Yadav villagers who focused all their attention on Kanti Singh. Sitting in the yard of the village primary school that had been converted into a political stage for the occasion, and surrounded by hundreds of villagers, she gave a very simple speech that emphasized above all her kinship-like-connection with the audience. "I am your daughter, your sister. If you look after me, I will look after you." The fact that the overwhelming majority of her audience in Rajnagar was composed of local Yadav villagers made this kinship language effective.

But the campaign did not simply reflect pre-existing structures of power. Rather, the uncertain outcome, and consequent alliances, negotiations, and maneuvering by all sides had the potential to shift power relations in many contexts. Kanti Singh's election campaign, therefore, entered villages with a great deal of commotion and intensity, and I saw villagers mixing in ways that I had never seen before, ways that would be inconceivable in other contexts. In some villages, Rajput and Yadav men together with Musahar women were all sitting together on the ground listening to the speeches. Even if these various groups were to occupy the same space in other contexts, they would surely not sit on the ground together. This disruptive, "anti-structural" (Turner 1969) force of the democratic process allowed for alliances that cut across many of the everyday boundaries encountered in village life. At least temporarily, the campaign ritual restructured village social relations, because the outcomes of elections themselves structure relations of power. A campaign, particularly where the outcome is uncertain, therefore, represents a "luminal" phase that temporarily unsettles power relations.

As we might predict, this need to connect with local leaders was bound to lead to problems when it came to Mohan Yadav and the Social Justice Pariwar. When Kanti Singh campaigned through Koilwar, Mohan Yadav sat unassumingly at his usual spot at the *panchayat* tea stall. Obviously, he had no intention of actively receiving Kanti Singh as long as Lal Bihari accompanied her, but he was available if she decided to make a point of stopping to meet him. That did not happen, and afterwards, he organized a series of meetings of the Social Justice Pariwar to decide how to respond. The group decided to organize their own campaign through the villages around Koilwar, to invite Kanti Singh, and to make posters in the name of the Social Justice Pariwar that would include all of the normal photos with the conspicuous exception of Lal Bihari's.

This prospective campaign created a great deal of commotion in Koilwar and even in other parts of the district. While I was sitting with Lal Bihari and his entourage on the veranda of his house in Ara, someone asked him about the Social Justice Pariwar. Visibly angry, he replied, "These fools don't understand. If the RJD falls, Yadavs will be back in the fields with their buffaloes." In this way he emphasized his identity as an important RJD politician—and the widely perceived Yadav support for the RJD across Bihar—as opposed to the Social Justice Pariwar's local opposition within Koilwar. When the day came for the campaign, a number of problems had emerged, probably due to opposition from the RJD leadership, including from Kanti Singh herself. Even though about fifty people had gathered at the *panchayat* tea stall and a painted campaign vehicle had been constructed, the posters had not been printed and Mohan Yadav was nowhere to be found. The people gathered still seemed ready to begin the campaign until a phone call came from Lalu Yadav's house in Patna directing them to wait until Lalu returned the next day to decide on the matter. In the end, the campaign went ahead, but it was a rather small affair, without Kanti Singh, and with the words "Social Justice Pariwar" (*samajic nyay pariwar*) that were painted on the side of the campaign vehicle changed to "Long Live Social Justice" (*samajic nyay zindabad*). The purpose of this last concession was obvious; "Pariwar" was erased to remove the impression of a separate group with its own political project. The words "social justice," a key slogan of the RJD, were entirely acceptable as long as they had no connotation of opposition to the RJD's MLA in Koilwar.

On the election day, the importance of local leaders and caste-based territorial dominance was further underscored. In Rajnagar, for example, I observed that two of the three polling booths were occupied by local caste-leaders who were able to "manage" the polling booths. Voter turnout in these polling booths was 90 percent as opposed to the 50 to 55 percent average. The two polling booths near Mohan Yadav's house also had a 90 percent voter turnout. As I observed in some detail, the difference was the result of what is referred to in Bihar as "bogus votes," votes cast for people who were not present. In addition, inside the polling booths these leaders often managed to stand near the voting machines and to direct voters to vote for a specified candidate. Villagers referred to these as "managed polling booths," and it often required courage to vote for a candidate other than the one that the polling booth "managers" were supporting. While I was observing voting in a polling booth in Rajnagar, for example, a young Koeri villager voted for the JD(U) candidate and then defiantly clenched his fists while a crowd of RJD supporters yelled insults at him and threatened to beat him.

The ability to "manage" these polling booths in Rajnagar was a direct result of Yadav territorial strength and local leaders' decisive presence. Polling booths were located in specific residential sections of villages, usually in schools or *panchayat* buildings, overlapping inevitably with other relations of village spatiality and territorial dominance. Politicians often spoke in terms of "friendly" and "enemy" polling booths. There were great strategic differences, for example, if polling booths demographically dominated by various competing groups were in the same place or spread out. The presence or absence of police was also very important because of the prevalence in Bihar of what is referred to in India as "booth-capturing," a constant electoral threat. Booth-capturing may occur "peacefully," with a dominant caste group simply preventing other people from voting, "managing" the police and voting agents (see the next chapter), or fraudulently voting for absent villagers, or it may occur violently.

Violent booth capturing also takes numerous forms. Armed gunmen may take an enemy polling booth hostage and then artificially stamp the ballots (if nobody reports it the results hold; if they do, there is sure to be a smaller turnout in the re-poll); they can "loot" the polling booth and steal the ballot box; or they may use bombs and gunfire to cause panic and abandonment of an opponent's polling booth, stopping voting for a few crucial hours. I have witnessed all of these tactics employed in various elections to various degrees in Bihar.[20] "Booth capturing" in the 1990s became widespread during state and national elections, and it was generally understood that every party engaged in these activities, resulting in a competitive contest (although the ruling party enjoyed obvious advantages because of influence over police and election officials, even if the Election Commission tried to minimize this influence).

The act of controlling polling booths served to publicly demonstrate territorial dominance and provided local leaders with significant political capital since they could then claim to have contributed a few hundred votes each to their party. The relationship between electoral practice, caste identities, and territoriality is powerfully grounded in the spatiality of the electoral process itself, with the location of voting booths intersecting with the territorial divisions of the village, divisions that—as will be examined in the next chapter—are based largely on caste.

Although "free and fair" elections are considered to be a basic requirement for even minimalist definitions of democracy, here, even the right to vote was problematic. The increase in vote violence in Bihar coincided with an increase in popular participation (the "second democratic upsurge"). Many lower-caste people commented to me that before the 1990s they had never seen the inside of a voting booth—upper-caste landlords simply voted for them. In many cases, access to "muscle" was a precondition for voting at all, and this set the stage for relationships between criminals who could supply this muscle and politicians (with elected politicians themselves often being feared "mafia dons"), leading to competitive booth looting. In practice, the right to vote often had to be secured through violence, which raises an interesting question: was it more "democratic" when lower castes were simply excluded from voting without violence? Despite the fact that India's independent and generally respected Election Commission does attempt to minimize election violence through staggering elections—an election in Bihar occurs in six phases, and takes a few months to complete—and the deployment of police and paramilitary to "sensitive" booths, it is impossible to check "silent" booth capturing, especially when retribution for voting against dominant interests may occur well after the election takes place. Highly visible instances of "booth looting" and electoral violence, therefore, were a reaction to the practical absence of the right to vote for many lower-caste people in the past. The rise of "booth looting" actually reflected the lower-caste majority's increased political participation—a "democratization" of vote fraud—resulting in much more intense electoral contestation. If the right to vote had been universally actualized in practice, of course, profound transfers of power would surely have occurred decades earlier. But the realities of caste dominance rendered such an outcome impossible, and consequently, electoral violence was a necessary component of democratization.

The elections demonstrated the links between territoriality and electoral practice. In the last analysis, the most important territorial site for electoral practice is the polling booth, and control of this territorial space is very much connected to caste dominance within village contexts. In the end, Kanti Singh won by a huge margin of 150,000 votes. The surprise was that Ashok Verma, the JD(U) candidate, came in fourth, after the CPI(ML) and the Ranvir Sena candidates (this was the only constituency in Bihar where the JD(U)-BJP alliance did not even make third place).

In the following chapters I extend the analysis of this chapter to explore political life in Rajnagar, a village within the Koilwar administrative block. As at the regional level, relationships between caste, territoriality, and state institutions are central to understanding political practice within village contexts in Bihar. I explore the multiple ways in which democracy is experienced, engaged with, and imagined within Rajnagar, and the ways in which lower-caste politics transformed the village.

A Multiple Village

Caste Divisions, Democratic Practice, and Territorialities

In the last chapter, I explored the political world of Koilwar; in this chapter we examine how lower-caste politics transformed Rajnagar, a village within Koilwar block where I lived between 2002 and 2003 (returning for shorter periods in 2004, 2007, and 2010). Rajnagar is a large village with a population of 5,086 (according to the 2001 Indian census) located a few kilometers from the block headquarters.

The village perceptive is important because some 90 percent of voters in Bihar live in villages, and villagers actually vote more than their urban counterparts—a trend that exists across India. More important, village realities mediate peoples' experience of democracy. As we shall see, local considerations—especially the ways in which party politics intersects with local power—largely drive support for political parties. And this relationship became even more pronounced as political parties became explicitly associated with specific caste alliances during the 1990s. In this sense, it could be said that all politics is local. Rajnagar, therefore, can be seen as a prism through which to interpret larger-level political change. It certainly became such for me. But this is also true for everyone else—most Indian people also view larger-level politics through the prism of their respective villages. Even those in urban areas often have one foot in their ancestral village (which remains the nexus for their social networks), and this inevitably influences their politics.

Of course, every village is distinct, and my interpretation of politics in Bihar would have been somewhat different had I lived in another village. But since I was examining the intersection of larger political forces and village realities, I believe that the changes that I observed would have been evident almost anywhere, although to various degrees, playing out in different ways according to the specific histories, demographics, and political dynamics found in any village. The dynamics of political change in Rajnagar needs to be examined in relation to the material presented in preceding chapters, in relation to"interlocking multiple social-political sites and locations" (Ferguson and Gupta 1997, 37). This was, therefore, inherently multisited ethnography (Marcus 1998)—my experiences in the village provided insights for research in other political contexts (in Patna, Ara, and Koilwar) and vice versa. Although I spent a fair amount of time in surrounding villages and also visited villages in other regions of Bihar, it was only by spending an extended period of time in one place that I began to get a handle on how larger-level politics intersect with the complex dynamics of the village and how this shaped people's political subjectivities. And if, as I suggest, Indian democracy, and especially the politics of caste, is rooted in village realities, and if these realities mediate people's experience of democracy (and, thereby, their voting behavior as well), then there is no substitute for such a "bottom-up" analysis.

Recent ethnographic studies of north Indian villages have generally told the story of the continued domination of village life by mostly upper-caste groups. The means by which this dominance has been maintained, however, has changed significantly, from ownership of land to control of state resources and development funds. The position of these dominant groups is sometimes thought to be in decline (Wadley 1994).[1] In Rajnagar, however, a more complete transformation of village power relations has taken place.

People from surrounding villages often said that Rajnagar is economically and socially "backward"—although not very poor relative to many villages in Bihar, Rajnagar was visibly poorer than many surrounding villages—yet they also often described it is a "politically forward" village (*raajniti me aage hai*), being the native village of a number of past and present politicians. The old center of power, a residential area with a history going back to the Rajput *zamindars* of the colonial period, had been effectively displaced. By the time of my fieldwork, a multiplicity of power centers had emerged, overlapping with divisions of the village into caste *tolas*, residential communities largely populated by a single caste group,[2] although these multiple power centers were not equally situated. In this chapter, I explore the party support within these different *tolas*. A new dominance by Yadav villagers had emerged in Rajnagar that supported, and was indirectly supported by, the RJD's regional hegemony examined in the previous chapter.[3]

The importance of caste identities within political practice in Bihar is grounded in specific caste groups' territorial control over the village, or parts of the village. An understanding of the practice of democracy at the grassroots level therefore requires an examination of the crucial relationship between caste and territoriality within village contexts. I explore the divergent experiences of people situated in very different positions within the sociopolitical geography of the village, providing a sense of the ways in which different people interpreted the democratic changes that were occurring around them.

The Decline of Rajnagar's Zamindars

In the colonial past and well into the postindependence period, Rajput *zamindars* dominated life in Rajnagar, with Rajput Tola occupying the political, social, and ritual center of the village. Villagers claimed that Rajnagar *garh* (literally "fort"), a relatively wide hill about a hundred feet high, was man-made and, at one time, was considerably larger. Around Rajnagar *garh*, the remains of a sizable moat were still visible, and some Rajput villagers told me that a second moat had once surrounded the perimeter of the village. As described in Chapter 1, Rajnagar had been the site of a Rajput chiefdom with Rajnagar *garh* as its military center. The earlier presence of a visible military establishment within the heart of the village emphasizes the historical use of direct force to capture and maintain territorial caste dominance. During the colonial period, Rajput *zamindars* enjoyed revenue collection rights in most of Rajnagar as well as sizable areas of nearby villages. Former Rajput *zamindars* told me that *zamindars* had brought the service castes, as well as many of the laborers and tenants, to the village. Clearly, the history of Rajput power in Rajnagar was a long one, making the present decline of Rajput dominance in Rajnagar quite dramatic.

The Rajputs of Rajnagar and surrounding villages, referred to as *lohtamia* Rajputs, narrate an ancestral myth about four brothers who arrived around five hundred years ago from Rajasthan. They and their offspring founded five "legitimate" Rajput villages in the region, while some villages were said to have been founded by "bastards"—the storyteller always employing the English word—of the legitimate ancestors and their "kepts" (again using the corrupted English), or mistresses from other castes. Of course, the Rajputs of so-called bastard villages contest this myth, and consequently, I encountered a number of different versions. People told me that a handful of older Rajputs still refuse to accept water from Rajputs from "bastard" villages, a practice that was widespread in previous generations. Still, most Rajput villagers with whom I spoke gave little attention to these distinctions, emphasizing the need for Rajput unity. Even the factionalism between two offshoots of the orginal lineage—once the most important fault line within village politics—had vanished from the public life of the village (even if still evident at weddings and other household rituals). As one Rajput villager put it, "The problem with the Rajput race is their divisions. If we could unite, we could rule not only India but the entire world." In fact, many younger Rajput villagers appeared uninterested in their families' past history. When I asked a younger Rajput villager serving in the military about Rajnagar's *zamindari* history, for example, he said that he did not know or care to know. "That history is not important anymore. Now we are interested in national history."

Villagers from every caste, including Brahmans, usually did not describe the decline of the "Brahmanical tradition" as the major force of social change in the village. Villagers did not place Brahmans at the center of an imagined "caste system." When discussing the pre-independence period, villagers emphasized the supremacy of the Rajput *zamindars*, and time and again I heard invoked the decline of the *zamindars* and the consequent and continuing rise of backward castes, particularly Yadavs. Even when an inevitably older and religiously bent upper-caste interlocutor invoked the decline of "Sanskritic tradition," this discourse always revolved around the implicit role of the *zamindars* as the protectors and primary beneficiaries of the old order. For example, an older Brahman priest, while expressing his acute discontent with contemporary life (expressed in the broadest sense) reminisced, "The *zamindars* brought us to this village because they grew powerful and wanted priests. They gave us everything—land, food, even clothes—so that we could concentrate solely on worshipping God." Political change in Rajnagar is a story of the decline of Rajput territorial dominance.

The families with the largest landholdings in Rajnagar built two enormous pillared houses positioned to overlook the contiguous agricultural fields. These houses were both almost empty, the younger generation hav-

ing left the village to find employment in urban centers. The older generation did not consider this to be a positive development, even though their
children's remittances had become a key source of income. Sitting on the
veranda of his large house, Dharam Singh reminisced about the power
that his family had enjoyed in the past. Referring to the Yadav villagers,
now politically dominant in Rajnagar, he said, "They used to be our servants! Our position here has now become very bad." He explained that
his ancestors had considered landholding and the control of cultivation,
performed by others of course, to be the source of Rajput status. Dharam
Singh said almost all of the Rajput landlords had given up direct cultivation following widespread "theft" of crops by laborers in the early 1990s
and agitations for increased wages. "We all decided to give up farming; it
had become too difficult." I asked how the laborers had been mobilized,
and he referred to the politics of caste empowerment associated with Lalu
Yadav's rise to power as Bihar's chief minister in 1990: "Everyone thinks
that they are Lalu. . . . Control of the village has slipped from our hands."

The Multiple Village

When I first arrived in Rajnagar and attempted to find suitable accommodation, it was difficult to avoid living with the Rajput former *zamindars* even though I thought that this would impede and possibly bias my
work. Because I was interested in the political changes associated with the
political empowerment of backward castes and transfers in local power,
I had decided from the outset not to stay in an upper-caste house. I initially approached the father of the Yadav *mukhia* and asked if he could
arrange accommodation. There was a problem, he said, because "no
Yadav house would be comfortable for you." I suspect that another issue
was that most Yadav houses in Rajnagar are very much lived in. Although
Yadav households are improving their economic condition, there are also
visible signs of an increased seclusion of women (see next chapter). This
means that these houses would be very sensitive to an outsider male staying for such an extended period.

The Rajput villagers I met, on the other hand, were more than wel-
coming. "You must stay here; we will not let you leave now. Go, get your
things; you can stay for free." I sensed a feeling that there was a matter of honor involved in these repeated offers. In the past, if an outsider
came to the village, there would have been no question where he would

have stayed. A number of Rajput families with *zamindari* pasts have huge houses, now mostly empty, which made these offers all the more attractive. When I refused all of these requests, I sensed hurt pride. Not only had the Rajputs in Rajnagar lost effective control of the village, but now the anthropologist stays with other castes, having a great deal of interaction with the very people who have displaced them from power. I sometimes felt as if I was rubbing salt in their wounds.

I ended up arranging to stay as a paying guest in the small "guest room" off the veranda of a Muslim household that most villagers held in high regard. (Gender segregation prevented me from access to the inside of the house; in fact, I never once saw the women of the house even though they prepared my meals every day. My great luxury, however, was the use of a nearby outhouse.) This had been a landlord family in the colonial period and, although they had lost almost all of their land and fallen into harder economic times, a legacy of cordial relations with the Rajput ex-*zamindars* remained. My host, for instance, would always be invited to Rajput weddings and funerals and given due respect. The family also enjoyed very good relations with lower-caste villagers because Muslims formed a core support base of the RJD, and my host Jafar was a self-declared RJD activist. Jafar's house proved to be an ideal base for my work, providing access to the entire village.

Since caste identity is central to the organization of village political activity, a brief sketch of Rajnagar's caste groupings is necessary. Rajnagar, like other Indian villages, was spatially organized around caste groupings. Residential areas of the village were referred to as *tolas*. There were three Yadav Tolas, a Koeri Tola, what was often referred to as the "Harijan Tola" (what I refer to as Dalit Tola[4]), two Musahar Tolas, and a Rajput Tola.[5] The largest numbers of houses were located in the three Yadav Tolas that border the agricultural fields and extend along the main road. These *tolas* largely consisted of households engaged in petty cultivation and dairy production, although there was significant variation that I will examine in some length in the next chapter. The Yadav Tolas were the most economically dynamic areas of the village and the spatial expansion of these *tolas* over the last decade is striking. The Yadav caste is classified by the government as an Other Backward Caste (OBC) or in the Bihar government's classification as Annexure Two, a backward caste but considered relatively well placed within that category.

The other group classified by the government as falling into the Annexure Two OBC category within the village is the Koeri caste, largely

consisting of agriculturalists specializing in vegetable cultivation. The
Koeri Tola was in the center of the village with compact houses and narrow lanes. The Dalit Tola, on the southern edge of the village, included a
mixture of different castes, largely Chamar, Paswan, and Dhobi, sharing
a history of oppression related to untouchability and consisting largely of
laborers and very small cultivators with a small number of families engaged in government service. The Musahar Tolas, one on the northern
edge of the village and the other located in a hamlet outside the village,
were without doubt the most economically depressed sections of the village. Musahar literally means "rat-eater," a title testifying to the malnutri-
tion and hunger that plagued these impoverished villagers. The continued
extreme poverty of the Musahar Tolas distinguished them from the other
Dalit communities. The Rajput Tola, the seat of the powerful *zamindars*
who controlled most of the village during the colonial period, was distinguished from the rest of the village by its large, well-built *pucka* (brick)
houses.

The caste names of these *tolas*, however, did not exhaust the caste composition of the village. There were twenty-four castes within the village,
and every *tola* that I have described had residents from different castes
even if they were all numerically dominated by the caste of its name.
In addition, there was a *tola* located in the center of the village—where
I lived with my Muslim host family—that was not named after a given
caste. This *tola* had a significant number of Muslim households as well as
service castes that were largely engaged in nonagricultural village occupa-
tions such as blacksmiths (*lohars*), shopkeepers (*bania* or *teli*), and gold-
smiths (*sonars*).

The castes that formed part of the names of most of the *tolas* reveal
the major forms of caste territoriality within the village. The smaller
castes that lacked their own named *tola* also lacked a strong independent political base within the village. This is true in every case except the
Musahar Tolas, where extreme poverty had prevented its sizable number of residents from wielding influence. With this most notable exception, the major political groupings within the village largely corresponded
to the caste *tolas* that I have described. When villagers discussed politics in
the village, I often heard the words "the Rajputs," "the Yadavs," "the Harijans," or "the Koeris" referred to as groups imagined to possess a degree
of cohesion and agency and local territorial control—somewhat similar
to the regional "caste belts" discussed in the previous chapter. These were
considered the politically important castes within the village, with the

many other smaller castes often relegated to unspecified "others," despite the fact that these other castes made up a significant portion of the village population. As we shall see, however, Yadav villagers had come to occupy a privileged place within village power relations.

The empowerment of backward-caste villagers in Rajnagar, and Yadav villagers in particular, effectively dislocated Rajput Tola from the center of Rajnagar's political, social, and ritual life. In the twenty-first-century Rajnagar that I encountered, no locality could be said to be the undisputed center of the village. Rather, there were multiple centers and meeting spots within the different *tolas*. These centers, located within a particular residential area (*tola*), were usually associated with a particular caste or section of a caste. Rajput *garh*, with its large pillared houses and the post office, is the center of Rajput Tola. Dalit Tola had the *panchayat* house (*bhawan*) and another community house, both built by a previous *mukhia*. The tea stall in the Koeri Tola was a popular meeting spot. Each of the three Yadav Tolas had their own meeting spots as well as the numerous Yadav owned tea stalls and shops that lined the main road in front of the village. Most of these sites were public or semipublic spaces: tea stalls, village shops, the veranda of a local politician's house, a temple, or the house of a particularly sociable villager. At these places men would gather and talk, often about politics.[6]

It is tempting to see the combination of all of these sites as the "public sphere" of the village, but none of these sites was socially or politically neutral. All of them were tied to specific forms of territoriality; sometimes as an extension of the surrounding residential space—spaces usually overlapping with caste divisions—sometimes related to the owner of the space and the owner's caste or political activities, sometimes as spaces of interactions that opened the village to wider influences. My "field site," in effect, was a constructed assemblage of these sites. I quickly became aware that there was no single "village" that could be studied as an organic whole. Rather, there were numerous micro-villages, sometimes competing, sometimes complementary, sometimes in open conflict.

So the role of Rajnagar in my analysis differs in important ways from the role of the village in most people's political understandings. Most people did not just view democracy through the prism of their village, but in relation to their specific social positioning within the village. This is not to say that I did not also have a distinctive social positioning that undoubtedly influenced my interactions (and, of course, my analysis), but it was somewhat ambiguous and fluid.[8]

This ambiguity allowed me at least partial access to the entire village, the ability to cross boundaries in ways that no one else did. The Rajnagar that I present, and that I experienced, therefore, is different from that of any resident of Rajnagar (each of whom could be said to have their own "Rajnagar," shaped by their specific social positioning). This wider perspective highlights both the actively constructed nature of my analysis— it's not a simple reflection of the way that other people see things—and, I would claim, its utility. By constructing an analytical vantage point that attempts to synthesize very different perspectives, I thereby map the ways in which the dynamics of larger-level party politics intersected with the social contradictions and struggles that were defining aspects of everyday village life.

The presence of such diversity makes almost any generalization about village life untenable. Moving between these micro-villages, I had to be careful to consider everyone's statements in proper context, since nobody could convincingly claim to speak for the village as a whole. My methodology, in attempting to understand the many political spaces found within the village, required me to constantly move across caste, faction, party, and territorial boundaries. I had to spend a lot of time roaming around the village, making friends and contacts in diverse residential areas and within many different caste groups. I was compelled constantly to leave the relaxed comfort of my host's veranda and actively engage with as many sites and as many interlocutors within the village as possible, collecting my "data," having ethnographic interactions within very diverse living spaces, and constantly physically moving among the various bases of social and political power within the village. This was not easy; everyone I interacted with knew that I also was interacting with his or her political rivals. Still, I eventually managed to gain contacts and a degree of confidence within all of the major party, caste, and factional bases within the village.

Village Rituals and Caste Divisions

Although the village must be critically examined as a natural category and site of analysis, I found that Rajnagar residents frequently referred to "the village" (*gaon*) in a variety of contexts. This is the case even though there was no clearly dominant caste in the village, and patron-client relations had largely disintegrated, the two factors that Dumont claimed underlie the village's apparent importance.[9] Especially in the early days of my work, villagers from all castes were very concerned that I produce a positive representation of Rajnagar. People frequently remarked how special and peaceful Rajnagar was, and initially, I found it very difficult to get people to discuss the social tensions that permeated the village. They seemed to fear that such discussions might negatively color my representation.

In addition, major festivals were usually conducted as village festivals, which served ritually to produce "the village" as a meaningful construct.[10] Even during the performance of these village festivals, however, the multiple centers of power that had emerged within Rajnagar were evident. At the time of my fieldwork, the management of major village festivals in Rajnagar was effectively divided among the different caste groups that had achieved a degree of territorial dominance. Villagers from Rajput Tola organized Durga Puja, the annual festival of the Goddess, villagers from the Yadav Tolas organized Govardhan Puja, the festival of the cow associated with the god Krishna, and villagers from Koeri Tola organized Chhath Puja, the festival of the Sun God that is specific to Bihar. There were other minor festivals managed by other groups as well. These festivals included construction of large clay idols that were later submerged in the river following riotous processions, along with evening drama and music performances. Collections were taken from households throughout the village, and even my Muslim host would contribute to these Hindu festivals as a sign of goodwill to the village.

Chhath Puja was the most dramatic of these festivals, with almost the entire village, including women who normally lived in relative seclusion from public life, walking a few kilometers down a festively lit path to the banks of the Sone River at sunset, and then the next sunrise, bathing and worshipping the sun with rituals and fireworks. My public presence at Chhath Puja, about a month after my arrival in the village, facilitated an ethnographic breakthrough after which I was treated less like an outsider. In the days after the festival, villagers commented again and again on my participation, especially the fact that I also bathed in the river. My contacts and access within the village multiplied because people regarded my participation in the festival as a sign of inclusion in village life.

Yet even an occasion as unifying as Chhath Puja could reveal significant tensions. In the midst of the festival, youths from near where I was living, organized a raffle and asked me to perform the ceremonial role of drawing the winning tickets. The proceedings began adjacent to the idol of the Goddess when Keori villagers angrily approached and small scuffles broke out. The Koeri villagers asserted that the management of the festival was under their control and the raffle was an infringement of their rights. After a day of tension and whispered threats, the raffle was eventually moved to a field on the other side of the village.

Shifts that had occurred in the relationships between caste and territoriality were even more clearly expressed during frequent *bhajans*— gatherings of village men engaged in often passionate devotional singing that not only served to mark the sacred geography of the village, but also reflected geographies of power by demonstrating territorial control over spaces within the village. On many nights the sound of devotional singing, loudly amplified and accompanied by vigorous drumming, clapping, and yelling, reverberated throughout Rajnagar. Unlike in the past, however, the Rajputs and Brahmans of the village no longer dominated this type of public worship. There could not be a more graphic representation of recent political change than when these *bhajans* occasionally took place at the small Devi Temple on Rajnagar *garh*, at the heart of Rajput Tola. I attended one such *bhajan* on a cold winter night in Raput Tola that lasted until early morning and included dozens of participants, as well as copious amounts of *ganja* and alcohol in blatant disregard for the "Sanskritic" norms that characterize Brahman-led *bhajans*. The attendance was usually almost entirely from the Yadav caste, including mainly small *kisans* (farmers) and laborers. It was truly an unruly scene—I myself was engaged in minor conflicts with drunken participants. Members of other castes, including the Rajput ex-*zamindars* whose houses surround the temple, were conspicuously absent, as most were inside their houses. These *bhajans* struck me as a vivid image of Yadav power—farmers, local politicians, laborers, drunks—roaming the village freely while most other people remained hidden away.

I do not view these *bhajans* as another example of Srinivas's "Sanskritization," the emulation of practices associated with upper-caste status by backward-caste groups attempting to raise their status, which ethnographers have widely observed. The overt, even aggressive performances were not as an attempt to emulate higher-caste practice or even an assertion of equal status, but rather a demonstration of a new dominance, a performance marking territorial control.[11] Although the Yadav *bhajans* were the most dramatic, *bhajans* were also held by other lower-caste groups, including many Dalits, in different areas of the village. These performances demonstrated the multiplication of centers of power within Rajnagar that served to profoundly transform perceptions of the village.

Democracy didn't just alter power relations within the village; it reconfig-
ured the ways in which the village was itself imagined.

This profoundly altered local perceptions of who controlled the village,
of everyday honor and respect. On one typical occasion, for instance, I observed a Dalit laborer leisurely sitting in the middle of a village path while
a Rajput landlord was forced to walk around him in the mud, a scene that
would have been unthinkable a few decades earlier (when the laborer
would have been expected to stand to the side and bow as the landlord
walked past). As a Dalit activist friend in the village put it, "They [Raj-
puts] used to beat us frequently. Now they are scared of us."

The village was clearly an important unit of identification with its own
territorial boundaries, but other forms of territoriality also crisscrossed
the village. The village was more than a container; it was a site of struggle
where particular territorial boundaries condition the political activities
that occurred within. It was the prize as well as the medium of grassroots
political activity. I turn now to party politics in the village. For most of the
electorate in Bihar, the political discourse and practical implications of
party politics were firmly grounded within the territorial spaces of the village, the place where politics derived much of its meaning, where the majority of the electorate lived, and where the most intense struggles were
waged.

The Political Village

With the rise of lower-caste politics in the 1990s, Rajnagar, like many villages in Bihar, was deeply divided politically. The *panchayat* (local government) in Rajnagar, which was elected in 2001 after a gap of twenty-three
years, more or less represented those groups willing to publicly support
the RJD (most of whom were Yadavs)—the Rajputs not only did not participate, but actually held their own parallel *panchayat* meetings. Under
these circumstances, *panchayat* resource allocation was largely driven by
political compulsions.[12] The institutional framework for inclusive *panchayat* governance is based on providing a central role in planning and
allocation decisions to the *gram sabha* (village assembly that is supposed
to be attended by every adult in the village). Given the divided social
landscape of Rajnagar, it is not surprising that *gram sabhas* occurred
mainly on paper, attended by a handful of village politicians close to the
mukhia. Female members had never participated, even though a third of

panchayat posts were reserved for women. The poor participation was not unique to Rajnagar; even reasonably well-attended *gram sabhas* remained extremely rare in Bihar's divided villages. In the absence of functional *gram sabhas*, the *panchayat* "ward" (more or less parallel to the village *tola*) was the most cohesive and inclusive level of the *panchayat* system, although elected ward members enjoyed very little formal power, acting mainly as local political leaders and middlemen.[13]

The political change resulting from lower-caste politics was perhaps most visible in the changing caste and class backgrounds of local political leaders (*netas*). In almost every section of the village, at least one or two local *netas* represented the interests of their caste and residential community, many of whom became ward members in 2001. When people in Rajnagar referred to "politics," either using the English word or the Hindi *raajniti*, they usually were referring to these local *netas*. Most local *netas* in Rajnagar were people with the ability to mobilize sections of their own castes and residential communities. Although they often had a very local field of operation, articulating the immediate interests of their surrounding section of the village, most *netas* were also part of Koilwar's political society examined in the last chapter, connected to Lal Bihari or Mohan Yadav, with a few connected to other parties such as the CPI(ML) and the JD(U). And through these very local leaders, the RJD's state-level and regional hegemony was articulated with the political dynamics of the village. Many people with whom I spoke commented on the multiplication of these local leaders. As one villager in Rajnagar put it, "There is only politics here. In this village even children are politicians (*bachche log bhi neta hai*). There is only politics here, nothing else." Another person, referring to the rise of backward-caste politicians, said, "Forward-caste people no longer like to wear *kurta pajamas* [the attire associated with politicians in India]; they consider politics dirty. Now mainly backward-caste people wear these clothes, especially Yadavs."

An example of this type of local leader was Ram Bachan, a ward member of the *panchayat* who represented the immediate interests of the twenty-five Yadav households of "East Yadav Tola." He was a part-time politician, spending the majority of his time farming. Partly due to the localized nature of their influence, leaders like Ram Bachan tended not to be strongly associated with any particular party or politician. Ram Bachan was always very ambiguous when I asked him about his political affiliations, and other people also were unsure of his political connections, which remained something of a mystery (although he did maintain a tenuous relationship with Mohan Yadav's Social Justice Pariwar). This political ambiguity was not accidental; much of the power of local leaders like Ram Bachan lay in their ability to negotiate with larger political agents, to shift their support at the last minute, if required.

From the perspective of these local leaders, politics appeared as instrumental and profit oriented. Much of the activity of local leaders and contractors involved negotiating exchanges of votes for development works. When I asked the elected ward member of Koeri Tola about his relationship with the *sarkaar* (the state), he boasted, "If I call, the local MLA will come at once." He claimed that this was why a new road was going to be built in this section of the village. It is important to note that these local leaders mediated most people's interactions with political parties, with larger-level politicians, and with state institutions.

The most important mediator between villagers and governmental institutions in Rajnagar was undoubtedly the *mukhia*. In addition to the *mukhia*, there were thirteen ward members of the *panchayat* (representing smaller sections of the village), although only five of these ward members were actively involved with the *mukhia* in *panchayat* business. The members of this inner circle were all RJD activists and, with one exception, were all Yadav villagers. Rajnagar *panchayat* also included a small village on the banks of the Sone River where sand mining was being performed illegally. Because trucks involved in the mining had to pass over *panchayat* land to reach the mining sites, this group of *panchayat* members imposed a "tax" of fifty rupees on every truck that passed over this land. In this way, the "*baloo* (sand) mafia" that was operating in Koilwar (Chapter 4) was replicated on a much smaller scale within the *panchayat*.

Another *thikadar* in the village, Sundar Rai, had no connection with the block administration or with the *panchayat*, but was connected with the local police station (*thana*) on the main road between Rajnagar and the next village. A retired police officer, Sundar worked with the police to extract what he termed an "agency" (English) tax of ten rupees from buses and passenger Jeeps that passed by the railway station situated on the main road on the southern edge of Rajnagar. Other villagers jokingly referred to this small operation as the "station mafia."[14] These local leaders connected diverse spheres—access to state institutions and higher-level politicians with village realities. In effect, they translated the RJD's state-level and regional hegemony (a hegemony that, as we have seen, was partial and at times internally conflicted) into territorial control over key spaces in the village.

I now turn to an examination of the ways in which party politics intersected with caste and territoriality to explore how lower-caste politics transformed Rajnagar.

Caste Divisions and Party Politics

In Rajnagar, previous supporters of the Congress before 1990 emphasized the broad base of their earlier support that cut across caste boundaries. As one Congress activist recounted, "The whole village was with us." Such statements seem impossible now within Rajnagar's fragmented political landscape. For most of the postindependence period, however, the Congress was the dominant political force in the village. All of the previous *mukhias* were said to be supporters of the Congress, as were village brokers, and most of the older villagers, from all castes that I spoke with, said that they were Congress supporters in the past.

Still, the village had a history of opposition to the Congress, an opposition strongly associated with the anti-Congress socialist tradition discussed in Chapter 1, and especially with Bihar's most important socialist leader, Jayaprakash Narayan. An alternate political center developed in one area of the village, largely due to the activities of Sanjay Sinha, a Kayasth (traditionally a caste of scribes and considered a forward caste in Bihar) villager who later became a highly successful industrialist, a member of parliament, and an important politician within the socialist movement. Sanjay's political career began as an activist with Jayaprakash Narayan's movement, at one point serving as JP's personal secretary. Sanjay met his wife, who was also an activist with JP, during this time. Their marriage was the first publicly acknowledged intercaste marriage in Rajnagar.[15] Although Sanjay left the village, his presence left its mark.[16] A beautiful old temple to the god Shiva marks the area of the village around Sanjay's old family house. A number of older residents in the area around the temple told me about their activities with Sanjay. At one time this area appeared to be an alternate center of politics in the village. All of the villagers I spoke with, who claimed association with Sanjay's politics, were older backward-caste villagers drawn from a number of different castes residing in this section of the village. Some of these villagers still spent considerable time sitting in front of Sanjay's empty house, although they were no longer an important force in village politics. This center of the village had faded, existing now as a residue of an earlier political era. The important point is that even opposition to the Congress crossed caste lines, and its geographical space in the village had more to do with Sanjay than with specific caste considerations.[17]

Another important politician from Rajnagar during this time was Ramji Singh, a Rajput villager who became the second *mukhia* of the village. Ramji was a Congress activist who went on to become the MLA for the local Barahara constituency.[18] I was surprised to hear older Yadav villagers speak highly of Ramji; people told me that Ramji had widespread support in the village that cut across caste lines. Considering the political fragmentation of the village while I lived there, such widespread support of a Rajput *mukhia* was hard to imagine. The first *mukhia* of Rajnagar, a Yadav villager from an educated, landholding family, was also a Congress activist with widespread support in the village. In fact, he was elected uncontested, a prospect even more difficult to conceive in the Rajnagar that I experienced nearly fifty years later.[19]

With the emergence of the backward-caste movement in the late 1960s, caste-based polarization began to emerge. But since Rajput dominance was still strong, they were able to maintain effective control. During the *panchayat* elections of 1977—held amid widespread tension generated by then–chief minister Karpoori Thakur's decision to implement the caste-based reservations recommended by the Mungeri Lal Commission—Rajputs prevented the emergence of a Yadav *mukhia* by supporting a Dalit candidate and Congress leader, Tapeshwar Ram. As a prominent Rajput patriarch explained, "We searched for a candidate who would do what we (Rajputs) wanted, that is why Tapeshwar Ram always gave Rajputs a great deal of attention" (*isiliye mukhia tapeshwar ram hamesha babu sahib logoko zyada mante the*). So while the caste of the *mukhia* changed, effective political control of village institutions did not. In fact, this alliance was a village-level reflection of the upper caste–Dalit alliance that was the core of the Congress party's hegemonic alliance (see Chapter 1).

With the lower-caste politics of the 1990s in the wake of Mandal, the village became clearly segmented in terms of party support, a segmentation that overlapped with caste-based residential divisions. Most villagers generally assumed that the "caste equations" operating in state-level politics also applied to the village. Yadavs and Muslims were expected to vote for the RJD; Koeris were supposed to vote for the JD(U); Rajputs and Brahmans were generally assumed to support the BJP; Paswans were expected to vote for LJP, and so on.

These generalizations, of course, did not always reflect the complexities of actual practice. In the last chapter, I examined the political base of Barahara's MLA, Lal Bihari (within whose constituency Rajnagar lies), as a compromise between Rajput regional territorial interests and the RJD's all-Bihar caste support by Yadavs, Muslims, and other backward-caste groups. I described the ways in which Lal Bihari combined his status as a Rajput caste leader with the sphere of party politics, serving as a minister in the RJD government. The activities of caste-leader politicians complicated and often disrupted the "caste equations" of state-level politics. This was as true in the village as within larger political spaces.

In the case of Rajnagar, however, very few of the Rajput villagers with whom I spoke expressed support for Lal Bihari or the RJD. In fact, I encountered only one case, and he was a *thikadar* who required a relationship with Lal Bihari to get contracts. Almost all of the Rajputs in the village expressed support for the BJP and said that they intended to vote for the joint JD(U)-BJP candidate in both assembly as well as parliamentary elections. The areas in Koilwar block where I observed significant Rajput support for Lal Bihari all appeared to be villages that had strong Rajput territorial dominance. Without territorial interests to defend and strengthen, a caste-leader politician like Lal Bihari would be of little use. In Rajnagar, as I have described above, Rajput territorial dominance was more or less a thing of the past. Rajnagar's Yadav villagers were the main rival group exercising territorial dominance, making the kind of compromise that Lal Bihari articulated unpalatable to either group. Most Rajput villagers in Rajnagar did not have a local territorial dominance to defend, and they had no reason to forge an electoral compromise with the very group that had effectively dislocated them from their previous position.

Rajput Tola was now largely devoid of farmers with the younger generation finding jobs outside the state. But three households were still cultivating fairly substantial plots. It was no coincidence that these cultivators differed to some extent from most other Rajput villagers who almost all claimed to support the BJP and tended to distance themselves from political activities. In addition to the *thikadar* mentioned above (who, not surprisingly was from one of these Rajput cultivator families), I became well acquainted with another politically active family. This household possessed around ten acres of land cultivated by two brothers with the assistance of their tractor (the only non-Yadav-owned tractor in the village) and seasonally hired laborers. Ramesh, the older of the two brothers, was the village postmaster. Their father had served in the state excise department, part of the expansion of Rajputs into government service since the late 1930s, service that buttressed their territorial interests and agricultural operations in the village. Kamlesh, the younger brother, was markedly more politically active than most other people living in Rajput Tola. I often saw him in the company of other local *netas* of the village, *netas* almost exclusively from lower castes.

One day, I met Kamlesh in Patna, and he asked me to accompany him to the home of a member of the legislative council (MLC). This MLC, whom I later got to know quite well, was elected on a special ticket from a constituency restricted to voters with a university degree. Kamlesh, although economically dependent on cultivation, had a degree from a college in Patna and had served as a local organizer for this MLC during his election. Kamlesh had made the trip to Patna to invite the MLC to his son's wedding. I later met the MLC again as the guest of honor at the wedding ritual (*tilak*) in Rajnagar, a visit serving as a public display of this family's political connections.[20]

As the 2004 parliamentary elections approached, Kamlesh joined Ram Vilas Paswan's recently created Lok Janshakti Party (LJP), a party associated with the empowerment of Dalits, whose supporters are thought to be largely drawn from the Paswan caste. Such a move made sense because there was little conflict between Dalit and Rajput villagers in Rajnagar, village dominance being increasingly in the hands of Yadav villagers. During the election there was an electoral alliance between the LJP and the RJD, an alliance pictorially represented by photos plastered on election posters everywhere of the towering leaders of each party, Lalu Yadav and Ram Vilas Paswan, warmly embracing. Because both of these leaders were widely perceived as caste leaders, these photos represented a political alliance between the Yadav and Paswan electorates. The LJP also attracted numerous leaders, Kamlesh being a good example, who wanted access to state power but who were unwilling to join the RJD. The LJP enabled Kamlesh to be active within Koilwar's political society without having to make a direct compromise with the RJD, a party dominated by Yadav villagers in Rajnagar. Kamlesh was one of three Rajputs who attended the RJD rally in the village with Kanti Singh (described in the last chapter), and he was the only non-Yadav from the village to give a speech. This speech, however, highlighted Kamlesh's precarious position. Beginning his speech with the customary naming of the notable political figures present, he conspicuously omitted mention of any of the Yadav *netas* present, except Kanti Singh, mentioning only Lal Bihari. Standing on the makeshift stage he said, "The president of India has stated that we should give our vote to the best candidate, and therefore, I support Kanti

Singh." Kamlesh was emphasizing that his support was not caste-based; his political position, in fact, was contrary to most other Rajput villagers in Rajnagar.

Having a sizable agricultural operation required access to the state, and therefore politicians, for credit and development resources. Most Rajputs had given up cultivation, and the younger generation sought job opportunities outside the state. They therefore had little interest in engaging in a political environment dominated by their households' previous clients. But the few families still cultivating had little choice. While Ramesh always voiced strong support for the BJP during our many discussions, he tolerated Kamlesh's political activities. The inability of the BJP to provide access to the state and to protect his interests was apparent. This, I think, explained his flirtation with the Ranvir Sena, a landholder private militia whose members were almost exclusively drawn from the Bhumihar caste. A *sena* activist in the run-up to the parliamentary elections told me of Ramesh's support of the *sena*. He was the only person in the village that I know of who had any association with the Ranvir Sena, although this association was probably confined to the election and was a subject that he was understandably reluctant to discuss. Whatever the case, any such association with a Bhumihar caste militia that had very little support in Koilwar block underscores the need for territorial protection that Kamlesh and Ramesh must have felt.

The important point, however, is that Kamlesh and his brother were exceptions within Rajput Tola, and their agricultural operations largely necessitated their political activity. Most other Rajput villagers relied on fixed land rent that was paid up front, remittances from family members working outside the village, and government pensions. They did not have strong economic interests within the village, and therefore, had little need for territorial protection. A cultivator like Kamlesh, however, needed to protect his crops, control labor, and have access to credit and agro-development resources provided by the state. These needs explained his political activities, activities that expressed the ambivalent position that he occupied within the village.

A Communist Pocket

Rajnagar and the southern areas of Bhojpur, where the Naxalite movement and counter landlord/caste militias had been strong, provide an interesting comparison. In these areas, agriculture tends to be large-scale commercialized production, and most of the laborers are Dalits. Although Naxalite territory is only a few kilometers from Rajnagar, I found no evidence of actual paramilitary activity in this area. A road separates Koilwar from Sandesh block, and villagers told me that on the Sandesh side of the road, the CPI(ML) levied *rangdari* "taxes," yet Koilwar block appeared to be completely free from these practices.

There was, however, quiet support for the CPI(ML), including a secret committee in the village.[21] This support had not become militarized, but it remained an ever-present potentiality, a threat hovering in the background of village political life. As a communist activist stated, "If someone here beat or oppressed (*dawa karte*) a Dalit, with a phone call I could have 200 activists in the village within an hour." One local leader of the CPI(ML) had led a village agitation in 1991. At the time, Chamars in the village refused to carry away cow and buffalo carcasses from village land, a polluting task that involved the skinning and tanning of hides. When I lived in Rajnagar, farmers were forced to bury their own cows and buffaloes or hire Chamars from outside the village at high prices.

Only a handful of villagers openly acknowledged membership in the CPI(ML). Most of these men were involved in a business transporting automobiles, often stored for a few weeks in Dalit Tola, to other states where the vehicles were sold. Although I was unsure where and how they acquired these cars (some questions are better left unasked), the important point is that their income, like most Rajput villagers, came from sources outside the village. One of these activists would say, "If they have the self-respect to vote for their own, every Dalit would vote for *male* (CPI-ML)." It was acknowledged, however, that many Dalits' votes went to other parties either for immediate gain (vote purchasing) or because the RJD government controlled access to much-needed development and welfare funds. Laborers told me that there had been substantial support for the CPI(ML) in Dalit Tola as well as in Koeri Tola five years before, but that in recent years many people had begun supporting the RJD. A labor organization (*mazdoor sammiti*) existed in the village, but to my surprise the chairman was the *mukhia*, who was far from being a laborer, and the vice chairman was his wife! Some villagers told me that this organization had been important in the past in pressing for higher wage rates, but by the time of my fieldwork, it was defunct, an outcome that demonstrated the increased influence of Yadav local leaders as well as the RJD.

Yadav Dominance and the RJD

Almost all Yadav villagers with whom I interacted, from all three *tolas*, said that they voted for the RJD, despite the fact the these Yadav Tolas were quite distinct and had a history of conflict. I deal with variations between Rajnagar's Yadav Tolas at some length in the next chapter, but I want to point out the importance of the RJD in politically uniting Rajnagar's Yadav villagers in order to exercise local hegemony. Although a small number of Yadav villagers sided with the Social Justice Pariwar's candidate during the 2000 assembly elections (see the last chapter), when it came to the parliamentary elections I did not encounter a single Yadav villager who did not claim to support the RJD candidate.

The most important politician from the village was Rameshwar Singh Yadav from West Tola. Rameshwar was a socialist activist during the JP movement and was a member of the legislative council (MLC) with the RJD. His family were the largest landowners in the village outside of Rajput Tola, acquiring much of their land in the period of *zamindari* reform. Rameshwar began his political career in Ara, the district headquarters where he had lived since his college days. The legislative assembly indirectly elects the members of the state legislative councils, requiring no grassroots political support. Unlike many other politicians, therefore, MLCs do not require a strong base of support from their village. Rameshwar was basically an urban politician: he was respected within political circles in Ara and Patna, and even Lalu Yadav held him in high esteem. Many villagers in Rajnagar, however, complained to me that Rameshwar did not make enough use of his political influence to benefit his village. He was accused of being an absentee villager, and during my stay, I only saw him in the village a few times. Although Rameshwar was an important link between the village—particularly West Yadav Tola—and the RJD government, he was not a major player within village politics. His influence was indirect even if substantial.

Other, more localized RJD activists in the village had a much more visible presence. These included the contractors (*thikadars*) described above who perform development works in the village through government contracts, politicians' development funds, or increasingly through the local *panchayat* bodies. The important point is that all of these people were associated with the RJD and most were Yadavs. These connections, both direct and indirect, served to reinforce both RJD dominance as well as the dominance of Yadavs within the village, and this differential access to state resources gave villagers who supported the RJD a distinct advantage over other party supporters.

Yadav dominance in Rajnagar was predicated on the political dominance of the RJD and vice versa. The RJD served to unite Rajnagar's Yadavs in a way that was previously inconceivable and provided access to state resources and relationships with regional politicians that reinforced this dominance. This mutually reinforcing relationship between the RJD and Yadav dominance in Rajnagar is what effectively dislodged the Rajput ex-*zamindars* from their previous position of influence.

I must emphasize, however, that this territorial dominance really only mattered for people with economic interests within the village or nearby. The cases that I have described of rival centers of party support—particularly Rajput Tola's strong support for the BJP and the small number of CPI(ML) supporters among Dalits—were largely composed of supporters whose prime source of income came from outside the village and region. These groups were not dominated in a physical sense; they had simply been dislocated from power (many having relocated their interests to urban areas outside Bihar) and politically weakened within the space of the village.

Party Politics and Village Realities

The hegemonic alliances reflected in the "caste equations" that operated in state-level party politics actively shaped social relations in the village and people's perceptions of one another. Although RJD support in Rajnagar was largely drawn from Yadav villagers, there were other supporters, most notably the Muslim support following the M-Y alliance that operated in state-level politics. This political relationship also extended into the social realm, and I often saw Muslim and Yadav villagers together. The RJD's emphasis on secularism supported this relationship, and in the village, the shop operated by the *mukhia*'s father combined Hindu, Christian, and Muslim images. In front of this shop, in fact, I first met my Muslim host, Jafar.

Jafar had a deep, long-standing association with the RJD. Jafar's activist involvment went well beyond relationships with village leaders, and he sometimes gave election speeches in nearby towns. On one occasion in the room in his house where I was staying, Jafar engaged in a heated debate with the previous RJD president of the village, Kedar Yadav. Kedar, along with a small section of Yadavs, had voted for the independent Yadav candidate fielded by Mohan Yadav's Social Justice Party in the previous assembly elections instead of the RJD candidate, Lal Bihari, who is Rajput (see the previous chapter). Jafar, visibly angry, said, "MLAs come and go. Your vote should be for the party, not for these leaders." People like Jafar were extremely useful to their party because they could be trusted and counted on in times of crisis. He was a party man, a reputation which itself carried its own sense of respect. Other *netas*, such as the *mukhia* (head of the elected *panchayat*), often would consult Jafar for advice on political matters, referring to him as an elder brother (*bhaiya*) or political guru (*guruji*). Jafar and a handful of other people were the organizers of the village unit of the RJD. Anyone involved in these activities, even if not Yadav, were seen as political players in the village; involvement with the RJD automatically generated a sense of importance because people saw association with the RJD as association with Koilwar's political society and with sources of governmental and informal power (such as the *baloo* mafia).

I was often surprised when political assumptions originating from state-level political practice influenced how people interpreted—and sometimes misinterpreted—the behavior of people living in close proximity. Sitting on a veranda with a group of Rajput villagers, for example, I was told that the *mukhia*'s father had been employed to tend the animals of a wealthy Kayasth villager. These Rajput villagers complained about how the *mukhia* of their village had come from an uneducated, poor background. I was struck by this story because, knowing the *mukhia*'s father quite well, I knew that it was completely fictitious. The *mukhia*'s father was a retired government employee in the Patna secretariat, and his father had also been a government servant. This story was more likely drawn from the life of Lalu Yadav than from village realities. The life story of the Yadav chief minister was imaginatively superimposed on the life of the village's own Yadav *mukhia*. The centrality of the figure of Lalu Yadav within village political conversation related to a widespread perception of the government in Bihar as "Yadav Raj," an image that also shaped the ways in which people perceived village realities.

Yadav Raj

As on many days, I was sitting at the fertilizer shop owned by the *mukhia*'s father, Bhagawan, participating in a conversation that included Bhagawan, myself, and two other Yadav men whom I did not know well, one from Rajnagar and the other, Sanjay, from a nearby village. They were discussing the corruption of various RJD politicians in the region and the immense amounts of money that they believed were being illegally appropriated. The conversation then shifted to a much-repeated joke about Lalu Yadav: "The prime minister of Japan came to Bihar and told Lalu, 'Give me four years and I will turn Bihar into Japan.' Lalu replied, 'You are so inefficient. Give me four weeks and I will turn Japan into Bihar!'"

After the joke I asked my three interlocutors, all supporters of the RJD, why they voted for people whom they believed to be corrupt. Sanjay, sounding surprised and perhaps irritated by the naivety of my question, replied self-evidently, "This is Yadav Raj." He went on to discuss how easy it would have been to loot booths in his *panchayat* during the previous election to the local bodies, in which he was a losing candidate. "They were completely unguarded. Next time . . ."

The "Yadav Raj" that Sanjay referred to was not local. Sanjay comes from Ranabhigha, a village that was the site of the largest Rajput estate in the region during the late colonial period. Members from this *zamindari* family continued to have a great deal of influence after independence.[22] Although the fortunes of this family were now in decline, nobody would refer to Ranabhigha as a Yadav-dominated village; there was no "Yadav Raj" in Ranabhigha. The "Yadav Raj" that Sanjay referred to was imagined to exist at a higher level, related to the RJD's state level and regional hegemony. People like Sanjay were engaged in a project to translate this larger-level hegemony into Yadav territorial control of the village (in this case, through controlling the voting booths).

Although these conceptions were diverse and people who seasonally migrated to cities for employment often had rather more complex perspectives, I found many of the poorer Yadav petty cultivators hardpressed to criticize the state government. The government was often referred to using kinship metaphors emphasizing "Yadav Raj." Lalu Yadav was often referred to as "Lalu *bhai*" (brother Lalu). For example, when I asked one petty cultivator why he voted for the RJD he pointed to his house and replied, "I vote for my own family. Why would someone from another house help me?"

Contrast this perspective with the frequent ethnographic accounts of poor people in India viewing the state as *maa-baap*, a maternal/paternal patron. For example, Gupta quotes a backward-caste villager as saying, "We consider the government which supports us small people as if it were our mother and father (*Usi ko ham maa-baap key samaan maantey hai*). If it weren't for the Congress, no one would pay any attention to the smaller castes (*chotee jaat*). Not even God looks after us, only the Congress" (1995, 390). Although this account also uses the kinship terms mother and father (*maa-baap*), these terms refer to a patronage relationship that connotes verticality. In this account, the government "looks after" its supporters and is, therefore, conceptualized as a separate entity. When Yadav cultivators in Rajnagar referred to Lalu *bhai* (brother), they were speaking of a horizontal relationship. Instead of supporting the government because it "looked out" for them, Yadavs in Rajnagar frequently commented to me that the current government was *their* government, and they would support it regardless of what it delivered. This perspective reflected a radical caste-based notion of popular sovereignty less concerned with what government does than with *who* does it—how the hegemonic alliance that the regime expressed shaped local power.

However, among educated, politically active Yadavs, a group that arguably benefited the most from the RJD government, I sometimes sensed a strange unease about the political situation. For example, one day when Bhagawan, the *mukhia*'s father, was speaking with me about corruption and the widely perceived breakdown of the state in Bihar, he said, "There is a difference between *raaj* and *saasan*. Politicians are now only concerned with *raaj*, they know nothing about *saasan*." While both words can refer to government and political power, Bhagawan used *raaj* here to refer to the outer, representational and symbolic aspects of power. *Saasan*, on the other hand, was used as "administration," as the tightness of bureaucratic control.

I heard a similar sentiment expressed by Anil Yadav, an advocate in the Patna High Court and the only person in Rajnagar who was actively involved with the Yadav Mahasabha, the national Yadav caste association. We were discussing politics on the veranda of his house in the village when he said, "Whatever awakening has occurred among Yadavs has only been external appearance. This is our *mukh mantri* (chief minister), our *raaj*, nothing else." I found these statements compelling. They both accept and support the political changes that have occurred, but at the same time critique the lack of an institutionalism that would provide legitimacy for these political changes. The specific social positioning of these conceptions needs to be stressed. Bhagawan is a retired clerk at the state secretariat, and Anil is a High Court advocate. They have both spent a good portion of their lives working within state institutions. It is possible to view their uneasiness as a conflict between their professional lives working within state institutions in Patna among mostly upper-caste bureaucrats and the village life to which they both were still very much connected. It may also reflect their awareness of the extent to which Lalu was unable to control the Bihar bureaucracy.

As we could expect, there were other criticisms of "Yadav Raj" as well. In Rajput Tola, as I sat with Kamlesh and Ramesh on their veranda, the conversation frequently turned to caste and politics. The brothers' frequent comment was: "Rajputs are *nyaya priye*, 'lovers of justice.' Yadavs are professional thieves," and Ramesh often asserted, "Even the British had written this." He also referred to a recent and much-discussed incident that occurred when a train carrying wheat had stopped at the edge of Rajnagar and was looted—the police believed this was done by one of the nearby Yadav households. As another example of Yadav thievery, Kamlesh frequently referred to the theft of his crops from the fields at night. He often juxtaposed these caste stereotypes at the local level with larger level political discourse, linking local Yadav theft with state-level political corruption. Ramesh continued, "Ragwendra Prathap Singh (the local MLA, who happens to be a Rajput) is just like a Yadav. There is no difference. . . . They are all thieves."

A handful of villagers, therefore, overtly criticized the entire system of democracy, sometimes cynically stating that "democracy is rule of the fools, by the fools, for the fools," in a critique of popular sovereignty that invoked the colonial-era ethic of rule by a "worthy" upper-caste minority. This discourse was marginal, however, because nearly all of those expressing such views were ex-*zamindars* who had been displaced from power and whose children had left the village. In fact, there were really no important "languages of power" (as West 2008, citing Mbembe [2001], describes in Mozambique) that were in opposition to democracy. Rather, anyone who sought power did so through the medium of democratic practice. Even Dalits, whom I knew sympathized with the Maoist movement—the leadership of which does, of course, oppose a democratic system in India—saw democracy as an important pathway to power and enthusiastically took part in elections, without perceiving any contradiction in their simultaneous participation in an armed insurgency and the democratic process.[23]

Electoral Practice and Village Power

I have described how the village, while maintaining its own form of territorial identification, is divided into distinct caste *tolas* with their own social
and political centers. These centers often entered into direct interaction
with larger-level politicians. In this sense, the village was fragmented, differentially traversed by larger political forces. Still, villages remained the
central territorial space for political practice in Bihar. Without a history
of Rajput domination within Rajnagar, for example, lower-caste politics
would have had no contextual basis.

In Rajnagar, the RJD helped to strengwthen the dominance of Yadav
villagers, and this Yadav dominance is precisely what reinforced RJD support in the village. This is how local power relations and electoral practice became intertwined in Bihar. To further highlight the relationship
between caste, territoriality, and party politics, let us return to the 2004
parliamentary election examined in the last chapter. I described how two
of the three polling booths in Rajnagar had been "peacefully captured"
and were being "managed" by supporters of the RJD. Almost all of these
"managers" were Yadavs, with one significant exception. The two most
prominent people were the *muhkia*'s brother Bipin, who was also a *thikadar*, and the brother of Ramji Singh, the previous Rajput *mukhia* of Rajnagar, introduced above, who went on to become a Congress MLA. Ramji
Singh's brother was a Congress leader involved with municipal politics in
Ara, the electoral alliance between the Congress and the RJD explaining
his presence. Both of these "managers" were, therefore, seen as associated
with the state government. When I asked some villagers who were wit-
nessing the bogus voting why the election officials were cowering in the
corner instead of stopping unfair practice, they responded that the officials were scared of these *netas*. One of these "managers" even asked me
to cast a vote. Thinking they were joking, I went along because I wanted
to see the inside of the booth. Once inside, I realized that a voter slip had
been given to the election official, and I was escorted to the voting machine. Suddenly, my hand was grabbed and propelled toward the RJD
button. I managed to wrestle free without being forced to cast a bogus
vote (although they cast it the moment I left), but I was able to experience
firsthand what it means to have your vote "managed." When I asked why
villagers from the adjacent Rajput Tola, who support the BJP, were not in-
tervening, they replied that Ramji Singh's brother made sure that Rajput

voters were all allowed to caste genuine votes in the morning without harassment.

After observing the "voting," I walked to Rajput Tola to attend a funeral feast. The Rajput villagers, clearly agitated about what was happening in the nearby voting booths, quietly complained. The feast was held on the roof of one of the large *zamindari*-era houses on the very top of Rajnagar *garh*, with panoramic views of the entire village. We could still see the "operation" winding down at the voting booths below us. The guests avoided political discussion, even as the election was still taking place before our eyes. I felt a silent despondency, sitting on top of a fortress that was no longer a seat of power. Except for impoverished Musahars, there were only a handful of the lower-caste villagers who, at one time, would have thronged to an event like this for a free feast. Yadav villagers were totally absent. They were reveling in their victory in the fields below.

CHAPTER SIX

A Multiple Caste

Intra-caste Divisions and the Contradictions
of Development

Rajnagar is not a remote village; it is located a mere two kilometers from the main Patna-Ara road, just inland from the banks of the Sone River, with a small railway station bordering its fields. According to villagers, the railway station was built soon after the enormous bridge (one of the largest railway bridges in Asia) that crosses the Sone River at Koilwar was built in 1875, and the road that connects Rajnagar to the main Patna-Ara road was built in 1956. Many villagers told me that Rajnagar was first electrified soon after independence, making it among the first electrified villages in India, much less Bihar. Those days of distinction are gone, and "electrified" now means an unpredictable hour or two of light current per day, if any at all. Toward the end of my stay, theft of wires resulted in a complete cut of electricity in the entire region for months. Similar to stories circulating in the media and all over Bihar, people in Rajnagar often complained about what they perceived to be the deteriorating condition of state services, including electricity, state-built irrigation pumps, fertilizer subsidies, availability of credit from cooperatives, agricultural procurement prices, and, above all, the deplorable condition of the main road connecting Rajnagar with the outside world. This deterioration was most often blamed on corrupt politicians, bureaucrats, and contractors.

I participated in hours of discussions with villagers involving lengthy speculation about how public money was being misappropriated. One such occasion took place in front of Bhagawan's (the *mukhia's* father) fertilizer and seed shop and included Bhagawan and my Muslim host, Jafar. Bhagawan's shop was a common site for heated discussions, and everyone present, including me, were frequent—even core—participant in these debates. Conversation turned to the deteriorating main road that stretched out in front of us, providing a visual backdrop for the exchange. Bhagawan discussed in detail the different ways that the money for the road, which everyone agreed had been spent on paper, had been "looted." He discussed the use of inferior materials, and speculated on the percentage of "commission" that the involved politicians, contractors, and government servants each received. Jafar disagreed with Bhagawan's assessment that most of the fraud came from the use of inferior materials. "The best method is to begin the work for one-and-a-half kilometers, finish just one kilometer, and then collect payment for the entire contact. Thirty-three percent profit!" The blame for these failures was most often directed toward politicians and the contractors—themselves often petty politicians—who were connected to these politicians. Frequently, Lalu Yadav was personally blamed. "Look at the condition of the road! This is Lalu's Bihar." Or, as people would sometimes remark, "Look at Lalu's road!"

This public discourse emphasizing a perceived deterioration of development works and state services was often extended to describe the social and economic condition of the village itself. Soon after I first arrived, a Yadav villager who was introduced to me as a "village intellectual" asked me what I had come to study. When I replied, "Politics," he cynically asked, "The politics of poverty?" Although people generally expressed pride for their village, many villagers asked me why I had chosen to come to such a bad part of India, where conditions had reached such a low point. A main complaint was endemic unemployment, and it was certainly true that among people not engaged in agriculture, a substantial number—many of them educated—were unemployed, spending their time loitering about the village, often drinking and playing cards. For every person earning, a common saying went, there are fifteen eating (*ek kamanewal aur pandrah kaanewale*).

With so much pessimism, I was surprised to see a great deal of unexpected dynamism and even excitement in certain key areas. Agriculture appeared to be far from stagnant; in fact a "silent revolution" in relations of production appeared to be taking place, with lower-caste, mostly Yadav, petty cultivators progressively taking over direct cultivation from larger, mostly Rajput, landholders. These expanding petty cultivators had a reputation for hard work in the village and expressed to me a strong desire to increase productivity and profit. I also observed dynamism in other domains in the village as well; in the myriads of new shops that were opening along the road and in almost every section of the village, in the increase of labor migration among many castes (to better jobs and wages than in the past), in the new sense of pride and improvement that I felt within the Dalit areas of the village, and above all, within the domain of politics.

The last chapter explored the ways in which the RJD's lower-caste politics influenced the context of a single village, resulting in the emergence of multiple centers of power. This chapter extends this analysis to explore the multiplicity within a singe caste, the Yadavs of Rajnagar. In doing so, I examine the class basis of lower-caste politics. I explore three Yadav caste *tolas* in Rajnagar, the caste that most people agreed had emerged as the most dominant caste in Rajnagar by the time of my fieldwork. As discussed in preceding chapters, the Yadav caste had also become the most important and powerful of the "backward castes" in Bihar's state-level politics. Examining the class heterogeneity among Yadavs in Rajnagar, I argue that a homogenizing caste identity—"Yadav"—conceals this internal heterogeneity, which, I suggest, demonstrates the political efficacy that results when increasingly heterogeneous class groups act as a politically united community.

Most academic as well as journalistic accounts analyze lower-caste politics primarily as "politics of identity" benefiting politicians in their pursuit of power. This type of analysis explicitly downplays any class basis of these new political formations. The frequent assertion is that if the poor among the lower castes have benefited at all from the emergence of parties claiming to represent "backward-caste" interests, the benefit is largely symbolic; the general consensus is that although the self-respect of lower-caste people may have increased, their economic conditions have not.[1]

Within contexts where state institutions are intertwined with territorial dominance in local contexts, issues such as honor and voice become central because of the prevalence of social exclusion, humiliation, and subjugation. We must recognize, however, that these are not merely "symbolic" issues in opposition to concrete material interests for economic growth and development-related public goods. Rather, issues such as "voice" represent very material interests for the poor: the interests of freedom from arbitrary physical assault, molestation, or rape, and economic freedoms to work where one decides (promoting labor mobility), to collectively bargain for wages (since minimum wages are very rarely enforced), to freely cultivate one's own land, and to receive a fair share of development-related resources (especially those targeted to below-poverty-line households). In one survey conducted in the mid-1990s in five villages in central Bihar that represented extreme but not uncommon cases, for example, the dominant castes in these villages collectively owned 96 percent of the land while making up less than 50 percent of the villages' households (Nedumpara 2004).[2] There were no less than twenty-six wage arrangements in these five villages, differing by caste, gender, and the presence or absence of attached labor, revealing the ways in which caste dominance can distort labor markets.

This is not to say that symbolic and psychological aspects are not involved, but that these aspects of subordination are inseparable from material impacts. An attached laborer who is compelled to perform unpaid work for his or her landlord (*begar*), and to sell milk at below-market rates, will certainly experience humiliation, but will also suffer economic losses (equal to the difference between the market rate and "subsidized" rate for the milk). In fact, the perpetuation of caste as a central identity in Indian public life stems precisely from the ways in which caste inequalities weave social, political, and economic inequalities together. "Untouchability," for instance, has been an intensely demeaning form of humiliation, but also has perpetuated a class of bonded or semi-bonded laborers who, because of extreme social and political marginalization, have generally possessed very limited economic bargaining power.

The account that I offer here involves a rather different argument. Although there is not always a direct connection between caste as political identification and organized class interests, when viewed from the local level, a complex assemblage of class interests emerges. I am not arguing that the economic changes that I have examined benefited all, or even most, of the poor among the lower castes; however, I am arguing that certain sections of poorer lower-caste agriculturalists, such as Yadav petty cultivators in Rajnagar, did benefit, and this must be taken into account if we are to understand the implications of lower-caste politics. In the next section I briefly sketch the history of agrarian change in Rajnagar.

Agrarian Change in Rajnagar

As discussed in the last chapter, during the colonial period Rajnagar was dominated by Rajput *zamindars* who had the right to collect revenue on all cultivated land within their *zamindari*, which included most land in Rajnagar as well as a substantial amount of land from nearby villages. This land was divided into a portion that was cultivated by laborers directly supervised by the *zamindars* (land known as *zirat*) and other land that was cultivated by tenants (*raiyat*), with the *zamindars* extracting rental income or taking a portion of the product.[3] I was told by older former Rajput *zamindars* in the village that as early as the 1920s, the biggest *zamindar* of the village had begun to extend the portion of land that was cultivated by supervised labor, beginning an expansion of commercial cultivation using labor-intensive traditional irrigation techniques requiring laborers to be brought to, and settled in, the village. Consequently, he earned the reputation as being the "father of agriculture" for the region. Commercialization of agriculture occurred even earlier in many parts of what is now Bhojpur district through the colonial administration's creation of the Sone Canal system of irrigation in the late nineteenth century, partly in response to agrarian unrest and a large-scale revolt of 1857 led by Kunwar Singh, the *zamindar* of Jagdishpur (about thirty kilometers from Rajnagar).[4] Although only two kilometers from the Sone River, Rajnagar and surrounding villages have never had access to canal irrigation, and this early expansion of commercial cultivation was, therefore, a limited one.

In the 1930s, the Kisan Sabha, under the leadership of Swami Sahajanand Saraswati, pressed for *zamindari* abolition and land reform.[5] The Kisan Sabha was active in Bhojpur (then part of Shahabad district), and Swami Sahajanand's headquarters was located just over twenty kilometers from Rajnagar. I found no evidence, however, of a Kisan Sabha organization in the village from this time, probably because of the influence of the Rajput *zamindars*. Partly because of the activities of the Kisan Sabha, in 1950, Bihar became one of the first states in India to pass *zamindari* abolition legislation, although this was not implemented for another decade. Land ceiling laws have continued to be disregarded in many parts of Bihar, although not in Rajnagar.[6] After independence and *zamindari* abolition, *kisan* politics declined in Bihar and has not had the same force as in other parts of north India, especially Harayana, western Uttar Pradesh, and Punjab (although I emphasize the importance of a *kisan* identity to many Yadav villagers below).

In the years after *zamindari* abolition, the *zamindars* of Rajnagar were forced to sell their lands in other villages; a portion of their land in Rajnagar went to previous tenants as well as to some Rajput families that migrated to Rajnagar at this time. This loss of land and rental income was compensated, however, by the increased profitability of agriculture in the 1970s after the introduction of high-yielding seeds (first introduced in Rajnagar in 1970), tractors (the first one bought in 1971), and tube-well irrigation (from 1966), as well as government subsidies associated with the "green revolution" that Indira Gandhi initiated in the late 1960s.[7] After the green revolution, Bhojpur district had some of the most profitable agriculture in Bihar and experienced some of the highest growth rates in agricultural productivity in India (Brass 1990, 327).

In many areas of Bhojpur, particularly in canal-irrigated areas, growth in agriculture led to agrarian tension as landlords attempted to oppress laborers to decrease labor costs and thereby expand areas of supervised cultivation. The Naxalite movement, however, had begun before this in 1967 in Ekwari, situated in the south of Bhojpur about one hundred kilometers from Rajnagar (Das 1983, Louis 2002). Tensions and agrarian violence increased in the 1970s and 1980s although Rajnagar, lacking canal irrigation, had a limited presence of both Naxalite groups as well as landlord caste *senas*, as discussed in the last chapter.

By the time that I arrived in Rajnagar in late 2002, only three Rajput households were still cultivating their own land. These families constantly complained to me of the high cost of labor, the breakdown of three of the four government-built irrigation pumps (the only one operating was in North Yadav Tola), the increasing cost of inputs (especially chemical fertilizer), and the lack of price controls and government subsidies. The lack of reliable electricity, which everyone stated had been much more reliable in previous years, meant that tube-well irrigation required diesel, an additional and increasingly costly input. As one farmer complained, "We have to depend on the market and the brokers of the market. Agriculture has become unprofitable." The two main crops in Rajnagar are wheat and potatoes and, especially for the latter, which was considered a "cash crop," profit completely depends on market fluctuations. Despite this increased risk, Rajput farmers complained to me that credit from the cooperative banks (see Chapter 3) had become much harder to obtain.

Remarkably, around ten years previously almost all of the large landowners of the village gave up direct agricultural cultivation through the supervision of labor. The previous Muslim landowners sold all of their land, and all but two families permanently moved to urban areas. The previous Rajput *zamindars* have not sold much land in recent years, but nearly all of this land was now being either leased to tenants, mostly from the Yadav caste, for cash rents, or it is sharecropped (*batai*), dividing both input costs, excluding labor, and profits fifty-fifty. The significant increase in cash rents, paid up front, is particularly revealing. While the potential profits of sharecroppoing were far greater (since rents were relatively low), this required the ability of the landlord to protect their interests vis-à-vis tenants. Many Rajput households had given up even this level of engagement with agriculture, relying on fixed rents. Villagers told me that in the early 1990s, there was an agitation for minimum wages—the labor wage in Rajnagar was a relatively good fifty to sixty rupees per day for male laborers at the time of my fieldwork—and that most male laborers refused to work for less.[8] As related in the last chapter, landholders in Rajnagar repeatedly told me of crop theft, of the inability to effectively enforce shareholding arrangements with Yadav tenants, and other challenges to landlord authority. Although these forms of resistance were certainly not new, the landowners' accounts indicated that by the early 1990s these "weapons of the weak" (Scott 1985) had escalated into a profound challenge of the social and economic order in the village.

In the political climate of the 1990s, the landowners did not have access to the local police and administration and no longer had the ability to subdue these agitations by force. The types of control over labor described above had ceased and most lower-caste people credited Lalu Yadav's coming to power as the catalyst.[9] The dramatic transformation of political representation, and the weakening of state institutions controlled by upper castes, did succeed in at least partially displacing upper-caste dominance. Under RJD rule, upper-caste landed elites found themselves without access to subsidized credit from cooperative banks (most of which became effectively insolvent), cut off from sources of patronage and "commissions" that they had long enjoyed through the control of development funds and, above all, deprived of the connections with politicians and the police (the later seriously weakened) that had enabled them to effectively control labor, protect standing crops from theft, and enforce exploitative sharecropping arrangements. The result was a "democratization of agriculture" as lower castes progressively took over most cultivation. In addition, many lower-caste villagers now had their own connections to a new class of lower-caste politicians within Koilwar's political society, as well as to the criminal networks with which these politicians were affiliated. Not only did upper-caste landlords lose many of their sources of influence outside the village, but also lower castes gained their own, and this opened up economic opportunities. In the following sections, I examine the Yadavs of Rajnagar to investigate the micro-dynamics of this process of democratically facilitated economic change.

Yadavs in Rajnagar: Multiplicity within a Single Caste

Three residential areas of Rajnagar are generally referred to as Yadav Tolas: East Tola, South Tola, and West Tola. All of them have seen a great deal of economic dynamism in recent years, demonstrated by the dramatic spatial expansion of these settlements, an expansion particular to the Yadav settlements in Rajnagar. While East Tola was completely relocated from the center of the village to a series of large cluster settlements in the nearby fields, South Tola shot a straight line of expansion from its previous location contiguous with Dalit Tola, deep into the fields. West Tola, in turn, had colonized the entire stretch of semipaved road running along the village, resulting in both Road Tola, a new residential settlement, as well as a long stretch of Yadav-owned shops and tea stalls. Although many Rajput villagers were leaving the village altogether and other caste settlements appeared to be retaining spatial continuity, Yadav settlements had been expanding in all directions.

As we shall see, there are substantial differences between these *tolas* in class terms as well as political, ritual, and social practices. Even with such differences, however, I was struck by how people often spoke of Yadavs within Rajnagar as a single, homogenous identity. Despite sharing a common caste name—"Yadav"—as well as a commonly acknowledged support for the RJD government, each of these *tolas* had its own distinct modes of economic organization, social practices, and political engagement.

East Tola

Many of the Yadav settlements of Rajnagar, located on the periphery of the village coextensive with the fields, had begun to acquire new political, ritual, and social importance. These settlements consisted of small clusters of large houses that were usually one story, of simple brick and concrete construction, with a large enclosed space and many rooms—some for living and some for crop storage—that branched off from a central open courtyard. In front of the houses were sheds for buffaloes, the number ranging from one or two to as many as fifteen for a single household. These were mostly joint households with multiple brothers, their wives, children, and elderly parents, often as many as forty people, all living in the same house.

Seven of these large settlements, collectively referred to as "East Tola," were the product of Yadav families migrating from overcrowded residential areas in the center of the village during the 1970s. These multiple separate settlements just to the east of the village were in the midst of the agricultural fields and were populated by people engaged in intensive family-based cultivation, mainly on rented land, as well as dairy production—the traditional occupation of the Yadav caste being cattle, and especially buffalo, herding. Although still relatively poor, these settlements held a real sense of economic dynamism, and many people expressed pride that their family had largely given up working as wage laborers and had become small cultivators.

In East Tola, there was an important social distinction between the new Yadav *kisan* (farmer) as opposed to the *mazdoor* (laborer) within these settlements. I was often introduced to people with the remark, "He is a Yadav, a *kisan*," but I was never introduced to someone who was explicitly referred to as a Yadav *mazdoor*. People here used the word *kisan* constantly to refer to themselves and to praise the success of others. It was easy for me to spot these *kisans* in the fields, holding the *laathi* (staff) with a distinct sense of pride. In practice, however, the distinction between *kisan* and *mazdoor* can be quite blurred. Yadav households in East Tola are large and tend to rely on diverse income sources, including petty cultivation, migratory employment that is often seasonal, dairy production, and short-term agricultural labor, although the latter is minimized within East Tola and publicly discouraged. This diversification of income sources seemed to be central to the economic movement and expansion of these settlements.

In the past, Rajput *zamindars* were generally prohibited from touching the plow.[10] I often found Yadav *kisans*, in contrast, to be proud of their direct contribution to production. At a *gram sabha* meeting (open to all villagers in the *panchayat*), for example, Ram Bachan, a Yadav *panchayat* ward member from East Tola, told me with pride how, unlike the other "lazy" ward members, he had plowed his fields himself before engaging in political activities for the day. I discovered that almost none of these households in East Tola had luxury items like televisions, even when their income was relatively high (little also seemed to be spent on education). As Ram Bachan put it, "What do I need a television for? Those things make you lazy and corrupt the minds of the children. I would rather have a cow.... We [Yadavs] have become so strong because we drink so much milk. Not that watered down junk sold in the market, the pure stuff, *ekdum garam* [totally warm, straight from the cow/buffalo]" After purchasing a buffalo, he said he would use any extra money to rent more land for cultivation or even buy a small amount if possible.

I heard Rajputs in the village often remark with disdain and apparent incomprehension that the new Yadav *kisans* had "not improved their standard of living," even after acquiring increased incomes. These Yadav cultivators, however, seemed much more interested in directly reinvesting their capital in agriculture and dairy production. There seemed to be an emergent Yadav-*kisan* work ethic, a kind of "Weberian spirit" built on cow veneration and muscular manliness. It is interesting, in this context, to recall the ways in which the late colonial caste movements claiming *kshatriya* status had sought to provide a positive status to the labor of direct cultivation (see Chapter 1).

Little agricultural profits seemed to be invested in urban pursuits, unlike in other areas of commercial agricultural production in Bihar where upper-caste cultivators enjoyed greater dominance. Expansion within the agrarian economy was the main priority within these Yadav settlements, and it was common for capital accumulated from activities outside the village—such as remittances from family members working in factories in other states—to be reinvested in agriculture.

South Tola

A similar situation existed in South Tola where Yadav petty cultivators and dairy producers had steadily expanded their settlement in more or less a straight line into the agricultural fields. Along with East Tola, these settlements were slowly but surely buying up a significant amount of village agricultural land (this was also taking place to some extent in Road Tola). Still, there were significant differences between South Tola and East Tola. Although East Tola's expansion dates to the early 1970s, South Tola's is much more recent, mostly taking place since the 1990s. Also, the economic and spatial expansion of South Tola was occurring without the introduction of many of the practices aiming to translate economic gains into higher status that I observed in East Tola. For example, the distinction that I noticed between *kisan* and *mazdoor* in East Tola appeared much less marked in South Tola. Many petty cultivators engaged in wage labor during gaps in the agricultural cycle, especially in labor-intensive but relatively highly paid work in sand mining on the banks of the nearby

Sone River. Rather than expressing a sense of shame in these activities, people often noted the resulting increase in household incomes, an increase that could be reinvested in agriculture.

Another striking social difference between the Yadav *kisans* of East Tola and of South Tola relates to gender practices and how economic activities were influencing these relations. In East Tola, I observed the seclusion of women within the household in a manner somewhat similar to upper-caste and Muslim homes—veiling (*parda*) was still very much practiced in Bhojpur—even if this seclusion was not nearly as strict as in the upper-caste/Muslim households.[11] In South Tola, however, this seclusion was absent, and women were easily approachable and spoke with me as openly as men. In contrast, I never once spoke to a woman in East Tola, even after months of almost daily visits. In South Tola, women also more easily engage in wage labor to supplement household income. More importantly, these fewer restrictions allow women to sell milk while the men are in the fields or working in the sand mines. Consequently, South Tola was largely the main location in the village where people without their own livestock would purchase milk, and in the morning and evenings many people from other areas of the village would gather, waiting for milk. One household would even deliver milk daily all the way to Patna. I also frequently observed a much more open consumption of alcohol and *ganja* in South Tola than in East Tola, where such practices were more actively concealed.

Another striking difference between East and South Tola related to the annual Govardhan Puja, the day for the worship of the cow that has become increasingly associated with the Yadav caste and the god Krishna. Lucia Michelutti (2008) describes the importance of the replacement of local caste deities with the cult of Krishna in the forging of a unified Yadav identity and the importance of Krishna as a common ancestor. In recent years Govardhan Puja has acquired an explicitly political significance, with Yadavs from different villages competing with each other, trying to secure the presence of powerful Yadav politicians. In East Tola this *puja* has become a large and extravagant affair. It is practiced at a *govardhan pahar*, built for the purpose, a concrete seven-layered pyramid connected with Krishna mythology. These *govardhan pahars*, most built recently, can be seen all over rural Bihar. After the ritual, performed by a Brahman priest assisted by the organizers, festivities included a large vegetarian feast, wrestling, and speeches by attending politicians, including the *mukhia* as well as Nagendra Rai, the member of the legislative council whose family lives in West Tola.[12]

In South Tola, Govardhan Puja was practiced in a strikingly different way. The *govardhan pahar* was constructed using mud, and the climax of the ritual involved the sacrifice of a pig, speared with the horn of a cow—a long and somewhat dangerous process that took place in an open field as a boisterous crowd of villagers looked on. The pig was then cooked and eaten at a feast, a practice that Yadavs from the other *tolas* in the village would consider polluting. When, after observing this ritual, I asked Bhagawan about it, the *mukhia*'s father (from West Tola) narrated an interesting story about the colonial origin of the pig sacrifice. According to the story, Yadavs, engaged in active resistance to colonial power, fled to the jungle where they were forced to eat pork to survive. The story lends the practice, remembered in this ritual context, a nationalistic justification. Perhaps even more interesting, I never heard any such story from the Yadavs living in South Tola who practiced this ritual and described it without shame or justification. Such a mythic justification allows the diverse and even contradictory ritual practices of the different Yadav Tolas to be diminished in favor of a larger, homogenous Yadav identification, a point to which I shall return.[13] Remarkably, these stark differences exist in the practice of a ritual that itself is a symbol of Yadav unity.

Comparing East Tola with South Tola reveals a difference between processes of expansion beginning in the 1970s and those beginning in the early 1990s. Interestingly, the more recent expansion lacked what could be called "Sanskritizing" practices—practices that were meant to reinforce claims of *kshatriya* status (see Chapter 1). This is indicative of widespread changes occurring in Bihar, changes in the entire modality of mobilization. The system of reference for caste mobility had been largely overturned; the aim was no longer to attain equality of status with upper castes by emulating upper-caste systems of morality and social practice. It is also important to note the economic effectiveness of these new modes of practice; although South Tola was very poor in the not-so-distant past, many people conceded that it had become perhaps the most economically dynamic area of the village.

Agriculture and the Weakening of State Institutions

Most of the large landowners in Rajnagar, almost all of them Rajput villagers, often complained to me that agriculture had become unprofitable for them. The main reasons they cited were usually the high cost of labor, the high cost of basic inputs such as gasoline for generators to operate the irrigation pumps and fertilizer, and the unpredictability of the market. The specific modes of economic practice that I encountered in East and South Tola seemed able to reduce many of these disadvantages through the use of household labor as well as community labor exchanges, and the diversification of income sources providing some insulation from the uncertainties of the market. Some of these diversified income sources are complementary, particularly dairy and petty agricultural production. In contrast to the previous *zamindari* and Brahman households (with one recent exception), which claimed to prohibit the selling of milk, most of the milk produced by Yadav households was sold, providing a valuable supplement to farming. Not only did agricultural fields yield fodder for buffaloes, but shortages of chemical fertilizer could be supplemented with organic manure. In addition, milk production provided a daily, relatively stable source of household sustenance that, if not directly consumed, could easily be sold, along with the sale of dung cakes used for fuel, complementing the uncertainty and periodicity of agricultural production. In general, Yadav cultivators enjoyed slightly higher yields than their upper-caste counterparts (see Table 4), despite much less capital to invest. This was complemented by the recent entry of many small cultivators who owned or rented tiny plots to supplement other economic activities. This "democratization" of cultivation not only positively impacted income distribution, but also may have contributed to agricultural growth because smaller operational landholdings enjoyed significantly higher yields in the village (see Table 5).[14]

In addition, because most households in these *tolas* were moving—economically as well as physically—from a relatively poor economic past

TABLE 4. **Rajput versus Yadav Wheat Cultivation**

Caste Group	Yield (kg per acre)
Rajput	311.9
Yadav	326.8

TABLE 5. **Wheat Yield by Operational Landholding Size**

Landholding Size (acre)	Yield (kg per acre)
Less than 0.5	352.3
0.5 to 1.0	319.2
More than 1.0	310.7

that relied heavily on the sale of labor, they were able to function, and even thrive, on profit margins that would be unacceptable to the economic ventures and standard of living of Rajput villagers. The presence of diversified income sources meant that these Yadav households could profit from the increasing rate of wage labor, while still engaging in small-scale cultivation relying on household and community labor exchanges. As a result, these households were less vulnerable to the effects of the breakdown of state subsidy programs such as the cooperative societies (chapter 3), many of which were controlled by upper-caste middlemen who pocketed a large portion of these resources and favored Rajputs. So not only were Yadav farmers able to prosper despite the weakening of state institutions, but the exit of Rajputs from the village economy provided space for their economic expansion.

West Tola

The shift of power in Rajnagar in recent years has not been accomplished by Yadav cultivators alone. A handful of Yadav households, mostly located in West Tola, have owned land for some time, mostly acquired in the immediate period after *zamindari* abolition. A significant number of households in West Tola received their main incomes from government jobs, which dates back to the 1940s, when West Tola established links with service in the railways, at the lowest level of recruitment (class 4).[15] While this is the same period that Rajput villagers began securing higher-paying and more influential government jobs, particularly with the police, over time these low-level government jobs transformed this section of the village. Almost every house in West Tola contained at least one government servant, especially in the lower levels of the railways, but now also the police, military, and various posts at the Bihar secretariat. A significant amount of this employment dates from the late 1970s (coinciding with the implementation of the Mungeri Lal Commission discussed in Chapter 2), and many people in this area were now pensioners. Many of these retired Yadav villagers spent considerable time at a local tea stall that I jokingly referred to as the "Rajnagar Yadav Pensioners Club." Yet, access to government jobs within South Yadav Tola seemed to be more or less a thing of the past. Although almost every month during my stay there was a party for someone retiring from government service in West Tola, I could not find anyone who had been recruited into government employment during the previous decade. A great deal of the income that sustained

West Tola was coming from government pensions, an income source destined to end with the death of the retired workers.

West Tola, which has existed as a Yadav residential area for some time, was recently extended to form Road Tola. New houses were built along the road as railway workers retired and relocated, investing their savings in the surrounding land and engaging in petty agriculture and dairy production. Of the twenty-five or so households in Road Tola, all of them had at least one member drawing a salary or, more frequently, pension from the railway department. Many of these people were employed in lower-scale positions (class 4), and it was amazing to see the impact of even lower-level government service when refracted back into the village economy. People with jobs with the potential for extra-legal payments (jobs said to "have scope"), such as a ticket collector, often owned a large house and substantial land by retirement.

Many of the households in West Tola, therefore, had relatively stable incomes along with a growing number of educated and unemployed youth. These conditions partly explain the emergence within the last decade of myriads of village shops and tea stalls owned by families from West Tola: pensions were invested in pursuits that could be managed and eventually taken over by these youths. The presence of large numbers of educated, unemployed young people also explains the relatively high number of contractors and small politicians that I encountered in West Tola. The *mukhia*, for example, came from an educated household at the inner edge of West Tola. In stark contrast with his father, who often distanced himself from village affairs and constantly reminded me of his past employment in Patna, the *mukhia* was very much at home within the village context. This *tola* was also home to the family of Nagendra Rai, a family with one of the largest landholdings in the village. West Tola, with its longer history of land ownership, relatively high degree of education, and long association with government service, was obviously very different from both East and South Tola. Still, it was considered very much a "Yadav" Tola and it generated a great deal of Yadav leadership and larger-level connections.

Caste as Assemblage

The diversity of economic conditions, educational levels, and lifestyles of people living in these three Yadav Tolas was striking. If they did not all claim to be Yadavs, it would be difficult to imagine what link could possibly exist between such diverse groups. I found many Yadavs, however, reluctant to acknowledge their internal diversity. When I asked one Yadav, for example, about the diversity that I was observing, he replied, "We are all brothers; there is no difference between us." All Yadavs in the village claimed to be, and were widely acknowledged to be, *krishnavansh* Yadavs, claiming descent from the common ancestor Lord Krishna, although some suggested that numerous outsiders had been allowed to merge freely into this status. As one Yadav villager put it, "All Yadavs came here from Mathura [the mythological birthplace of Krishna in Uttar Pradesh]."

One should not overemphasize this feeling of Yadav unity, however. Rather it should be viewed as an essentially political identity—the result of a hegemonic project—coexisting with distinct internal divisions. In fact, East and West Tola have an interesting history of factional conflict, which apparently culminated in the late 1980s in a huge confrontation between members of the two camps, armed with *laathis* and spears. In the ensuing melee, the declared leader of East Tola, Danpath Palwan, an almost legendary wrestler (people told me stories of him lifting a car), was speared to death. A prolonged legal battle followed, advancing to the High Court before finally being thrown out. Although conflicts had settled, I still noted subtle tensions between the two groups, and very rarely did people from these different *tolas* attend each other's weddings.[16]

Despite such intense and public rivalry in the not-so-distant past, it took me a remarkably long time to find out about the conflict. It was not for months after my arrival, following the Govardhan Puja ritual, that I heard the first indications of this conflict. The *mukhia*, although from West Tola, had attended the large function at East Tola. He had been very excited about presiding at the ritual, saying, "This is the first time a Yadav *mukhia* will be inaugurating Govardhan Puja in Rajnagar." Afterward, while relaxing in my room, I asked about the symbolism of the ritual and the relation of the *govardhan pahar* with Krishna. The *mukhia*, a bit drunk, replied angrily, "It is not Krishna, it is only Danpath Palwan!" Only then, armed with the name Danpath Palwan, was I able to inquire and discover that the *govardhan pahar* in East Tola had been built as a type of memorial after Palwan's violent death. It is significant that both the *mukhia* (as well as the MLC) from West Tola attended the festivities, suppressing his anger in favor of political expediency and a larger Yadav unity. It is hard to imagine this happening if Govardhan Puja had not acquired a political significance. This example highlights how internal diversity and conflict was publically concealed by a homogenizing political identity.

In Chapter 1, I described the emergence of a homogenous Yadav identity in the late colonial period through caste associational activity. A handful of older villagers from North Tola told me that their parents, all of whom had been lawyers or government servants, had been active in Yadav caste *sabhas* and the Triveni Sangh in nearby Ara town in the 1930s and 1940s. They said that it was from this time that many Yadavs in Rajnagar started wearing the sacred thread worn by "twice-born" castes.[17] Only one person in the village, however, was actively involved in a Yadav caste association at the time of my research, and as an advocate in the High Court, he normally resided in Patna. A politically unified Yadav identity had become salient in Rajnagar, not through caste associational activities, but through electoral politics. It is easy to see the political potency of such an internally diversified, yet politically homogenized caste; there were abundant leaders, with connections to state resources and important politicians, organically connected to the most dynamic agricultural cultivators in the village, as well as a mass of laborers. This internal class differentiation within Yadavs in Rajnagar is precisely what enabled Yadav dominance to emerge.

It does not seem possible to analyze the changes of power relations that have occurred in Rajnagar as either the simple empowerment of homogenous caste communities, or as the product of new class forces. Rather, there was a complex configuration of multiple, often contradictory, class components, "overcoded" by a homogenous Yadav identity that effectively masked this internal heterogeneity. Local politicians and contractors, such as the *mukhia*, came from more educated Yadav households with histories of government service, and this new generation of local politicians and contractors received a very large percentage of the benefits of having connections with state power, such as contracts and the ability to distribute development patronage. These benefits served somewhat to offset the losses that this class of Yadav villagers suffered because of the contraction of job opportunities in the public sector. I have also demonstrated, however, that poorer Yadav villagers were also economically benefiting, although not through state intervention. In fact, it is precisely the weakening of the institutions of planned development that enabled an economic expansion of Yadav petty cultivators in Rajnagar. As I discussed above, this was linked to aspects of economic organization that I observed in East and South Tola, such as the diversification of income sources, the ability to survive on smaller profit margins, and the advantages of small-scale family-based cultivation. Yadav *kisans* found a space to maneuver as the older Rajput dominance was weakened.

But, at the same time, one should not overemphasize the changes that occurred in agrarian relations. Active cultivation was taken over by lower castes, especially Yadav farmers, as was the ownership of tractors and agri-

TABLE 6. **Caste and Landholding in Rajnagar**[18]

Caste Category	Caste Name	Population (Households)	Average Landholding (acres)	Total Landholding (acres)[19]
Upper Castes	Brahman	40 (3%)	1.33	53.1 (6.1%)
	Rajput	60 (4.5%)	3.20	192.2 (22%)
OBC (Annexure 2)	Yadav	510 (38.3%)	0.92	464.8 (53.1%)
	Koeri	185 (14%)	0.53	84.1 (9.6%)
	Other Annexure 2	135 (10.2%)	0.13	17.3 (2%)
Annexure 1[20]	Muslim (OBC)	75 (5.6%)	0.12	4.7 (0.5%)
	Hindu Annexure 1	60 (4.5%)	0.17	12.7 (1.5%)
Scheduled Castes	Pasi	65 (4.9%)	0	0 (0.0%)
	Paswan	55 (4.1%)	0.63	34.5 (4%)
	Chamar	35 (2.6%)	0	0 (0.0%)
	Musahar	90 (6.8)	0	0 (0.0%)
Total		1,330 (100%)	0.67	875.2 (100%)

cultural supply shops. But, although a significant transfer of landowner-ship had occurred (Table 6), this had reached its limit. In fact, an informal boycott of selling land was observed by Rajput landlords, and a significant amount of land was also owned by a politically connected Yadav family that lived in Ara and also did not cultivate. And the RJD government was unable to alter this scenario since the implementation of land reforms proved to be politically impossible precisely because of the class hetero-geneity of the RJD's lower-caste base that included substantial landown-ers (see Chapter 2). Many farmers found this situation deeply frustrating. For instance, Ram Bachan, the consumption-eschewing Yadav farmer in-troduced in the previous chapter, wanted nothing more than to buy land, and he had the financial means to do so. But over the decade that I have known him, he has been unable to find sellers in the village. The result was that many households that actually cultivated did not own much land, and many of those that owned land did not cultivate, inhibiting crucial invest-ment in irrigation and land improvement necessary for sustained agricul-tural growth.

The inability of the RJD to alter the agrarian structure through policy explains why primacy was given to caste-based democratization while state-directed development, including agricultural development, was mar-ginalized. But this did facilitate an OBC takeover of cultivation and of the village economy. When viewed from the perspective of the heterogeneous class groups that supported the RJD, it becomes clear that, despite limita-tions, many people actually benefited from the breakdown of state institu-tions and the marginalization of development in Bihar.

CHAPTER SEVEN

The Fall of Lalu Yadav and the Meaning of Lower-Caste Politics

This book has sought to demonstrate that the logic and impact of lower-caste politics can only be appreciated when analyzed according to the specificities of India's postcolonial democracy. Long processes of state formation shaped identities, local power, state institutions, and the relationships among them. Lalu Yadav's populist politics responded to this context: since caste identities had served to perpetuate established power, "backward-caste" political solidarity would shatter it; since state institutions had long reinforced this dominance, they were systematically weakened; since "development" had legitimized this social order, it was displaced by a discourse of popular sovereignty predicated on the rule of the lower-caste majority. I have sought to demonstrate the hybrid character of postcolonial democracy—wherein the sphere of institutional politics is intertwined with relations of dominance and subordination—by examining the ways in which larger-level politics is "plugged into" struggles over local power and local frameworks of interpretation. Viewed "from above," the politics of caste empowerment weakened and destabilized state institutions, resulting in sharply decreased public expenditures, increased corruption, and a widespread deterioration of public services such as health and education. But when viewed from below, this destabilization facilitated profound transfers of power in many local sites, such as Rajnagar, including a shift within the agrarian economy.

Lower-caste politics cannot be reduced, therefore, to a "politics of identity," divorced from material interests and broader structures of power. Much popular and academic treatment of lower-caste politics has analyzed it as an opportunistic patronage politics. And while this politics did involve "looting the state," as so many commentators and analysts have emphasized, I also argue that this is only part of the story. In Rajnagar, as we have seen, the specificities of local power relations conditioned how party politics played out within the village. While people did vote strategically, voting was conditioned by the specific power relations present within local sites and connected to long histories of dominance and struggle. And in myriads of contexts, long histories of upper-caste dominance were undone.

But even if the politics of patronage does not provide a satisfactory explanation for the RJD's electoral success, it is useful for understanding the context within which the politics of caste empowerment emerged. Lalu's populism articulated popular opposition to the discretionary use of state resources and state power to sustain the dominance of mostly upper-caste, landed groups within local contexts. India's "patronage democracy" (Chandra 2004) is the context within which the backward-caste movement emerged and explains why backward-caste leaders primarily focused on gaining control of the state through electoral politics. If the discretionary use of state resources by upper-caste actors is what enabled the continuance of upper-caste hegemony, the coming to power of lower-caste politicians undermined this hegemony. The RJD government did not attempt to transform the system of "patronage politics"; on the contrary, RJD leaders often were explicit about their patronage transactions. Backward-caste leaders highlighted the ways in which the discretionary allocation of state resources had reinforced upper-caste hegemony, and they sought to use patronage politics to benefit their own constituencies. The result was the widespread perception of politics as a "naked dance" (*nanga naach*), as the open practice of forms of corruption with a long history, but which had previously remained implicit, masked with the rhetoric of development. Within this context, many people supported politicians not only despite perceptions that they were corrupt, but precisely because they were perceived as corrupt, and therefore capable of using their positions to benefit their supporters.

And many people did benefit. Remarkably, the poverty rate fell significantly during the Lalu period in Bihar, more than in most other states. In fact, during this period Bihar shed its long-standing distinction of having the highest poverty rate of any state in India (Orissa briefly gained that distinction).[1] This decline in poverty occurred despite very low rates of economic growth, a flight of capital, the departure of much of the educated population, almost no new corporate investment (in a period defined by competition for investment among states), the general collapse of state-directed development, and a surge of criminality. The only way to explain this outcome is to take seriously the impact of democratization as an agent of change. The expansion of Yadav cultivators in Rajnagar, for instance, many of whom had been impoverished laborers in the recent past, was clearly part of a widespread process wherein the displacement of upper-caste landlords opened opportunities for many among the lower-caste poor.

The idea that democratization can have economic impacts independent of policy interventions, I think, would have been easier to digest for earlier generations of scholars—a reflection of how technocratic thinking about democracy and development has become in the neoliberal era. The theorization that Bihar's economy was crippled by a "semifeudal" (Chattopadhyay 1972, Prasad 1973) or a "postcolonial" (Alavi 1975, 1981, Banaji 1972) mode of production, for instance, explicitly argued that political change from below was the only effective path to development (see Chapter 1). While most advocates of this school of thought privileged land reforms, the "institutional reform" that the socialist left within the Congress (including Nehru) advocated in the early years after independence also included democratization within the Congress Party's organizational structure and within cooperative societies, although these never materialized (Frankel 1978, see also the case study of cooperative societies in Chapter 3). And Prasad (1980), writing in the immediate aftermath of the backward-caste movement's upsurge in the 1970s, predicted that the semifeudal mode of production was being undone by the democratic rise of the OBCs. While in retrospect this prediction was a decade early, such a process did unfold during the 1990s. But the transformational potential of lower-caste politics had serious limitations, as the next section examines.

Limitations of Caste-Based Democratization

If, as I have argued, the efficacy of Lalu Yadav's caste-based populism can only be understood within the context of India's postcolonial democracy, its limitations were equally shaped by this context. These limitations relate to several factors: Bihar's position within a large federal polity wherein caste-based struggles play out almost exclusively at the state level and yet many powerful institutions are national; the essentially oppositional logic of a populism predicated on a broadly construed "backward-caste" base of support that, faced with an uncooperative bureaucracy, prevented an institutionalization of the political change that occurred (in contrast to neighboring West Bengal under the cadre-based Communist Party of India [Marxist]); and the inherent limitations of caste identities that were constructed in the late colonial period as a means to achieve social justice. Since the first two factors were examined in depth in Chapter 2, I turn to the third factor.

I have examined the ways in which RJD rule profoundly altered local power relations, instilling a sense of participation and empowerment among many lower-caste people. In many ways, this represented a meaningful deepening of democratic participation. This democratic empowerment was dependent, however, on leaders whose functioning was markedly undemocratic. It created a new class of politicians and *thikadars* who came from different caste backgrounds than their predecessors, but who continued to effectively mediate ordinary people's access to government. As was examined in the previous chapter, the homogenous political identity "Yadav" in Rajnagar concealed a great deal of internal diversity, class heterogeneity, and a history of violent conflict. Such an imagined collectivity could function politically only when represented by politicians; caste, as political identity, was only effective when mediated by self-styled caste leaders. This is a continuation of the colonial "sociology of rule" through "representative men" identified by Cohn (1983, see Chapter 1)—it's just that the relative positioning of the "communities" involved has changed. The empowerment of lower castes in Bihar, following a postcolonial logic, was a "mediated empowerment," an empowerment dependent on the authority of this new class of politicians.

The destabilization of state institutions, therefore, while facilitating a broad transfer of power, did not result in a true democratization of power. Or, rather, it could be said that a "democratization" of power did not result in an equal empowerment for all, or even most, subaltern groups. With public institutions destabilized, and power transferred from the bureaucracy to democratic networks, the larger, more populous and better organized among the lower castes inevitably gained the most. Yadavs, and other populous castes with access to leadership and resources, enjoyed a disproportionate dominance, often at the expense of weaker castes. This is precisely what Ram Manohar Lohia, the ideologue of the backward-caste movement, had warned against; that instead of lower-caste politics eliminating caste oppression, some castes would taste empowerment but oppression would continue.

These limitations can be easily seen in the case of Rajnagar. The Musahar Tolas, one on the northern edge of the village and the other located in a hamlet outside the village, were undoubtedly the most economically depressed sections of Rajnagar, and the only lower-caste areas that did not see their position improve significantly during the Lalu period. Most of these families did have simple brick homes built during the early Lalu years through the Indira Awaas Yojana development scheme. Since these *tolas* were visible from the main road, officials probably felt compelled to provide them since Lalu would have traveled on this road, and he had given orders that all Musahars should receive Indira Awaas houses. But by the time of the 2005 elections, Musahars often complained to me that Yadavs had become worse oppressors than Rajput landlords, and they voted against Lalu's RJD for the first time.

In Rajanar, the lower-caste empowerment that resulted from RJD rule translated largely into Yadav empowerment, alienating other lower-caste groups who, freed from the coercive influence of the Rajput ex-*zamindar*s, often found themselves on the receiving end of a new Yadav dominance. This disadvantage was especially true for the many small castes whose limited numbers denied them political clout (although collectively they made up more than a third of the village). Many people from these groups generally supported the displacement of upper castes in the village and believed that meaningful change had occurred, but most also had become quite antagonistic to the newly dominant Yadavs and to the general breakdown of state institutions. A defunct public irrigation pump just outside Rajnagar, for instance, was the site of numerous robberies during this period, reflecting both the increase in criminality and the decline of state-directed development (in addition to the dilapidated main road described in Chapter 5). But instead of desiring a return to the old order—the politics of caste empowerment had become too entrenched for that ever to be an imaginable option—most non-Yadav lower-caste people with whom I spoke expressed a desire for a broader-based democratic empowerment from which they might also materially benefit.[2]

Equally important to the insight that a destabilization of the institutions of state-directed development resulted in some positive outcomes, then, is a realization of the limitations of such a project. The RJD's fall can be seen as a symptom of the relative success of many of its core political aims—displacement of upper castes and the defeat of Hindu nationalism—which, being purely oppositional in nature, could not be institutionalized. For example, while Yadav family farms in Rajnagar ex-

perienced a remarkable expansion during the Lalu era, once this transfer had occurred it is hard to see how such an expansion could continue
without supportive policies, especially land reform. And as we have seen,
it was precisely the class heterogeneity within the RJD's backward-caste
support that made such reform politically impossible.

And the upwardly mobile among the lower castes became increasingly
aware of the limitations of a mode of governance that weakened state institutions. Bihar has the highest rate of outmigration of any Indian state,
with migrants increasingly heading to informal manufacturing centers in
states that benefited the most from the post-liberalization economy, especially Gujarat (Gujarat, followed by Delhi, were the main destinations
for migrants from Rajnagar). During the Lalu period, the image of Bihar
outside the state had become so maligned that to call someone a Bihari
became a generalized insult (Bihari laborers whom I met in places like
Dehli routinely lied about where they were from until I revealed my fond-
ness for the state). The contrasts and discrimination that migrants experienced in other states must have also played a role in changing perceptions, increasing demands for education, health, and infrastructure.

Increasing popular resentment toward the RJD government was accompanied by the political mobilization of marginalized groups. During
the first of two state assembly elections held in 2005, for example, Ram
Vilas Paswan's Lok Janshakti Party attempted to forge a third front with
a "Dalit-Muslim" alliance. The electoral success of this party resulted in a
hung parliament, and the imposition of President's Rule. Furthermore, the
emergence of a third front led by a Dalit leader weakened the "backward-
caste versus forward-caste" dichotomy that had underpinned Lalu Yadav's political support and also reflected the emergence of a caste divide
among Muslims (most Muslims in Bihar are lower-caste) that threatened
to split the core of the RJD's "M-Y" alliance.

During the second assembly elections, held just eight months later,
"Extremely Backward Castes" (EBCs, Annexure One castes within Bihar's unique system of reservations) emerged as a decisive political force
for the first time. As pointed out in Chapter 2, although these castes represent an estimated 32 percent of the population in Bihar, there were only
11 MLAs from these castes at the time of my fieldwork (out of a total of
243). The weak political position of these castes contradicted the RJD's
claim to have empowered the "backward castes" as a whole. Many politicians from the opposition saw this contradiction as an opportunity, as
they believed that new social forces would eventually emerge to destabi-

lize RJD rule. In previous elections, Extremely Backward Caste votes had been crucial, but they were split among different parties, with the RJD receiving a significant percentage. Lalu Yadav's personal support from these castes during the early years of his tenure as chief minister helped him outmaneuver other Janata party leaders and gain control of the party. By 2005, this was no longer the case. As Nitish Kumar clearly saw:

> There is no question of a hung assembly this time. This way or that way, it will be a clear verdict. If the EBCs [extremely backward castes] have voted for us, then we will form the government; if they voted for RJD, Lalu will. . . . The EBCs were divided even last time—in places where they were directly against Yadavs, they came to us. And where the forwards were their main exploiters, they went to RJD. But this time, they have decisively voted for change.[3]

Jagannath Mishra, the chief minister preceding Lalu Yadav, complained to me during an interview at his house in 2003 that in Bihar "development is delinked from the electorate." He blamed the political salience of caste and especially the empowerment of the Yadav caste, stating "everything is being captured by them [Yadavs], by the *laathi*, where might is right." He continued, "For a long time the forward castes have ruled. Now has come the time of the backwards, this time the intermediate backwards. The intermediate will be replaced by the more depressed backwards. This is how the social forces are operating." In many ways Jagannath Mishra, a Brahman Congress leader who was first installed as chief minister during the Emergency and whose brother, L. N. Mishra, was Indira Gandhi's closest adviser in Bihar, represents everything that the socialist and backward-caste movements had fought against, making this concession all the more profound.

His prediction proved accurate. In the 2005 state assembly election, these discontented groups in Rajnagar, like in villages across Bihar, collectively mobilized for the first time in alliance with the Rajputs and voted for Nitish Kumar's NDA coalition. As Table 7 below demonstrates, a profound shift of voters occurred from the RJD to the NDA between the 2004 parliamentary and the 2005 assembly elections, mirroring the shift that occurred across Bihar.[4] As part of this wave, Lal Bihari lost his long-held seat to the JD(U) candidate for the Barahara constituency within which Rajnagar is located. Reflecting this larger trend, the RJD candidate also received fewer votes in Rajnagar and surrounding villages than the JD(U) candidate (see Table 7, and local RJD politicians told me that

TABLE 7. **Election Results for the 2004 and 2005 Elections in Rajnagar and Surrounding Villages**[6]

Election	JD(U)	RJD	LJP	CPI(ML)	Other	Decline to State	Don't Remember	Total
2004 Parliamentary Elections	393	722	15	20	2	28	26	1206
2005 Assembly Elections	669	482	4	17	10	22	9	1213

they had "lost" Rajnagar, a remarkable result considering that Rajnagar had long been considered an RJD stronghold.[5] Lalu Yadav's long rule had ended.

Nitish Kumar and the Discourse of Development

Nitish Kumar came to power, following a decade of spearheading the opposition in the state after he broke with Lalu Yadav in 1994 (see Chapter 2). In many ways, the Nitish government appeared to be the polar opposite of Lalu's, highlighting the opposition between the caste-based democratization that this book has focused on and top-down development. Following Chatterjee's terminology (2004), this was a dramatic shift from a mode of governance that privileged "political society" to governance according to technocratic models drawn from an elite "civil society" and implemented by bureaucrats. I briefly sketch the main features of the Nitish period—a new discourse of development, the "resurrection" of state institutions (and corresponding weakening of political society), and the use of new categories in an attempt to empower the marginalized among the lower castes—in order to reveal insights about Bihar's longer democratic trajectory.

The Nitish government's ambitious development agenda benefited from India's high rates of economic growth from 2005, resulting in the Bihar government's budget more than doubling over five years and its budget for "plan expenditure" (funds used for productive investments) more than quadrupling. The bulk of this windfall was from nondiscretionary devolution of the central tax pool (through the Finance Commission) that had expanded along with India's high growth rates (and some success with tax reform by the central government).[7] Of course, a state government has to be able to spend effectively, but having access to such increased funds is what has enabled Nitish Kumar's aggressive development agenda even to be an option. This is in stark contrast to the fiscal crisis that followed structural adjustment soon after Lalu Yadav took office in the early 1990s. In addition, multilateral institutions such as the World Bank and Asian Development Bank, which had avoided the state during the Lalu period, came to consider Bihar under Nitish Kumar to be one of the most important laboratories for development interventions in South Asia, extending billions of dollars in development loans.

Bihar went from one of India's slowest-growing states to trailing only Gujarat as the fastest-growing state. The government was especially successful with an aggressive road-building scheme (the main road that borders Rajnagar was rebuilt from its long state of horrible disrepair).[8] In fact, a significant portion of Bihar's economic growth from 2005 to 2011 was in road construction and other infrastructure: Bihar's construction sector more than quadrupled over five years and demand for cement grew faster than that of any other state (and the "sand mafia" examined in Chapter 4 flourished). This extra cash also provided a ready source of alternative sources of "revenue" for entrepreneurial politicians and the compulsions of campaign finance, some of which had previously been generated by the kidnapping-for-ransom industry, the arms trade, drugs trade, and other criminal activities, with some of Bihar's infamous mafia politicians becoming contractors (a process that helped reduce criminality).

Nitish also embarked on an aggressive law-and-order campaign relying on fast-track courts and a strengthened police force, resulting in a reported 52,343 criminal convictions between 2005 and 2010—many times that of any comparable earlier period.[9] As a very senior police officer explained to me, "For the first time the Bihar government took the role of prosecutor seriously."[10] The public display of guns, which had earlier been something I had seen nearly every day, almost completely disappeared.

With the return of the discourse of development and "good governance" (*sushasan*), Bihar's image outside the state improved. In complete contrast to the media's disdain for Lalu, Nitish was showered with awards, especially by the English-language media.[11] In fact, while Lalu constantly complained about the bias of an "upper-caste media," the coverage of the Nitish government was so positive that the Press Trust of India launched a formal investigation to ascertain whether press freedom was being curtailed by the state government's "media management."[12]

A new political logic undergirded the return of development. The effort of the socialist/backward-caste movement to build a united backward-

caste front that was central to Lalu's discourse of lower-caste empowerment was abandoned in favor of focusing on new categories of beneficiaries. This fragmentation of backward-caste unity was inevitable once
upper castes had been partially displaced, and certain groups benefited
more than others (paralleling the Bahujan Samaj Party's seemingly contradictory Dalit-Brahman alliance in Uttar Pradesh in 2007). As Ram
Vilas Paswan explained to me, "Reservations were not for employment.
They were for empowerment. How could we gain empowerment? Scheduled Castes cannot do it [alone]. Therefore there was the Dalti-Backward-
Minorities alliance.... Unlike Nitish, Lalu in the past was the true leader
of the Dalits-Backwards-Minorities [united front]. Because of Mandal
they all united. But once Mandal was implemented, they were divided....
They started looking towards their own interests [individual castes]—'how
much is my share?'"[13]

There was a shift from what Laclau (2005) termed the "logic of equivalence" underlying populism to the "logic of difference" underlying bureaucratic modes of governance. The Nitish government introduced 20
percent reservations for the "Extremely Backward Castes" (EBCs) that
were crucial to his party's election victory, and an unprecedented 50 percent reservations for women in local *panchayats*. The NDA combined the
BJP's upper-caste supporters—who after spending such a long time in
political wilderness were willing to rally behind a lower-caste chief minister—with Nitish's EBC supporters, together with his own Kurmi caste
and a new constituency of lower-caste Muslims who felt that they had
benefited little during the Lalu period. This was the first time that either
EBCs or lower-caste Muslims emerged as consolidated political forces,
reflecting the rise of nondominant castes. Although Kurmis are arguably
the most socioeconomically well positioned among the OBCs, the Kurmi
caste is not populous enough and is too regionally concentrated to exercise a statewide dominance, in contrast to Yadavs during RJD rule. If the
M-Y alliance provided Lalu's core base of support for fifteen years, EBC
castes formed the core of Nitish's support. Nitish broadened this already
formidable base to include a category that he termed "Maha Dalits,"
Scheduled Castes excluding the populous Paswan caste, which was already aligned with the opposition Lok Janshakti Party headed by Ram
Vilas Paswan. A Maha Dalit Commission was formed, and Nitish stated
to me during an interview at his official residence in 2007 that he intended
to "saturate them [Maha Dalits] with development funds."

But, since political society had been weakened, EBCs, Backward Muslims, and Maha Dalits did not emerge as active political formations. While a handful of leaders did gain some prominence, nothing like the politicization of OBCs in the wake of Mandal occurred. In fact, given the new electoral indispensability of these groups, it was striking how little popular mobilization ensued—the transformation in political representation that occurred in the 1990s was not replicated and these groups remained grossly underrepresented in the state assembly. In fact, the main shifts in political representation from Lalu Yadav's peak in1995 to Nitish Kumar's overwhelming victory in 2010 was a precipitous decrease in Yadav representation (from 27 percent of legislators to 16 percent), an increase of representation by Nitish's Kurmi caste (from 4 percent to 7.4 percent) and a rebound of upper-caste representation (from 18 percent to 32.3 percent), although still considerably less than during the Congress period (Chaudhary 2011, 163).

A prominent Yadav JD(U) leader offered this remarkably clear explanation of the logic underlying the NDA's alliance: "We had the masses with us but I am not sure that we would have won such a landslide [in 2005] without the BJP. Although some JD(U) members kept wanting to break from the BJP, we realized that it is the BJP which has the support of the system, the upper-caste press, bureaucracy and judiciary. Though Nitish led from the front, the BJP played its part in this win."[14] This emphasis on the support of an upper-caste "system" points to the continued influence of upper-caste actors, even after fifteen years of rule by a self-declared "backward-caste" state government. This and the presence of the Hindu nationalist BJP in the ruling coalition could be taken as regressive developments, an undoing of Lalu Yadav's political project. Both the new chief minister and the deputy chief minister, however, were from lower-caste backgrounds, and if upper-caste leaders increased their political position, this was only possible by aligning with more powerful lower-caste leaders. And neither upper castes nor Hindu nationalists managed to increase their influence in the state as much as they had hoped (to their frustration).[15] In order to maintain the support of lower-caste Muslims, the JD(U)'s alliance partner—the Hindu nationalist BJP—had to be kept as weak as possible in the state.[16] In fact, a member of Nitish's inner circle told me that the alliance with upper castes was a "crutch" that Nitish had to rely on to come to power and to jump-start long-defunct state institutions, a crutch that he was in the process of "systematically abandoning" (although, at the time of writing, the outcome of this process is uncertain).

Faced with corrupt and even criminal legislators in his alliance and own party, Nitish Kumar responded by shifting power from elected politicians to recruited officials.[17] As during the Lalu period, power was centralized in the post of chief minister. In stark contrast to Lalu, however, who weakened the bureaucracy and ruled through informal political networks, Nitish sought to revive the bureaucracy by operating through a "core team" of senior IAS officers and by forcibly weakening the political class. In key departments, while Nitish distributed ministerial posts out of political compulsion, corrupt ministers were teamed with secretaries with honest reputations, constraining the influence of the former. Circulars instructed officials at all levels, including police *thanas* and block offices, to resist interference from politicians, including those from the ruling party. The government threatened to arrest politicians, including those from the ruling party, who were caught unduly influencing administration. As we would expect, a broad governing alliance enjoying both upper-caste as well as lower-caste support resulted in greater cooperation and cohesion between different state institutions, in contrast to the endemic intrastate conflict during the RJD period. But this shift from the political class to the bureaucracy also entailed distinct disadvantages—bureaucrats, unfettered from political pressure, often became more corrupt. And the dynamic political society that this book examined in places like Koilwar, and even in Rajnagar, more or less disappeared since the links between state institutions and party politics (including the ruling party) were largely severed.

Nitish's discourse of development was centered on a single leader promising to implement change "from above" despite the widely recognized corruption of his own party and the state bureaucracy. Nitish was popularly described as a *vikash purush*, a "man of development," widely perceived to be above, and struggling against, the corruption of his own government. As a result, the return of development to the center of political discourse in Bihar did not involve public debate on development "issues" or the proper allocation of public resources; people voted exclusively for a man, not a set of policies. Nitish's reputation as a *vikash purush*, as well as consolidation of the social/caste factors examined above, led to an even larger victory in the state assembly elections in 2010. Further consolidation of "Extremely Backward Castes" behind him (providing around half of the NDA's votes), combined with upper-caste support and, once again, a split of the Muslim vote along caste lines, enabled the NDA to capture two-thirds of the seats in the Bihar assembly. The once unassailable RJD was reduced to near irrelevance, winning less that 10 percent of the assembly seats.

But, even if Nitish Kumar's development agenda was successful in bringing some of the fruits of India's post-liberalization economy to Bihar, this project was bound to face severe constraints, as we would expect given the reliance on state institutions that had long served elite interests. As during the Lalu period, the most important policy intervention—land reform—proved to be politically impossible. Despite a high-profile commission that recommended reforms, an intense political backlash prior to the 2010 elections spearheaded by upper castes (and, in a deviously opportunistic move, fanned by Lalu Yadav) ensured that any efforts at serious reforms were abandoned.[18]

But the most startling outcome, especially considering that more than half of Bihar's population falls under India's very austere poverty line (around $.40 per day at the time of writing), was that during the period of Nitish Kumar's first term the poverty rate barely moved, and poverty in absolute terms actually increased. Bihar reclaimed its position as India's poorest major state.[19] This is despite having high rates of economic growth, a massive increase in public spending, the initiation of the largest national antipoverty scheme in India's history (the National Employment Guarantee Scheme), and a chief minister widely considered to be among the most competent and development-oriented in India (so much so that people spoke of the "Bihar model of development"). Especially when considering that poverty decreased during the Lalu period, many people would find such an outcome inexplicable.

While a thorough examination of the reasons for the lack of poverty reduction during the Nitish period is beyond the scope of this book, the analysis developed here suggests that it likely had something to do with the weakening of "political society" in a context in which state institutions remained ineffective. If, as I have argued, caste-based democratization, despite its limitations, did have transformative impacts that facilitated lower-caste economic expansion, the weakening of this process and a shift to "development" through state institutions had unintended consequences. This is despite attempts to facilitate lower-caste empowerment through policy. For instance, enacting reservations in *panchayats* for Extremely Backward Castes and women was a potentially transformative policy intervention. But in practice, in most of the *panchayats* that I am familiar with, these reserved positions were effectively controlled by someone else. In the case of elected women, their husbands usurped their official power to such an extent that the term *mukhia-pati* (husband of the *mukhia*) was routinely used in administrative contexts, while in villages such as Rajnagar the unelected husband was simply referred to as *mukhia.* (While the former *mukhia*'s wife was officially *mukhia* from 2006 to 2011, he remained the functional *mukhia*, and I never even met the actually elected mukhia.) In a neighboring *panchayat,* the new EBC *mukhia* was little more than an employee of the previous Rajput *mukhia* who supported his election and who maintained effective control over the *panchayat.* While these policies may prove to have longer-term impacts (with women, for instance, slowly increasing engagement in public affairs), the immediate effects were limited, while the weakening of regional political society closed opportunities for bottom-up political mobility.

Even if the modes of governance of the Lalu and Nitish regimes could not have been more different, much of what Nitish put in place was only possible because of the transformations of the Lalu period. It is no accident that Lalu and Nitish began their political careers together during the JP movement and that Nitish was Lalu's right-hand man during the early years of his rule. As one senior JD(U) leader put it,"They were educated in the same school."[20] It was only fifteen years of rule by a militantly lower-caste leader that made rallying behind an alternative OBC leader palatable for upper castes, even as the government's policies targeted EBCs, Maha Dalits, and Backward Muslims. And it was only the weakening of upper-caste dominance during the Lalu period that made relying on upper-caste bureaucrats palatable for lower-caste leaders (many of whom were now more concerned about Yadav dominance). But even if there are underlying continuities and even the same ultimate goal of lower-caste empowerment, the means utilized by the two governments to achieve their ends could not have been more different. This reveals a longer process of politically driven state formation involving an alternation of disrupting caste-based democratization and attempts to implement state-directed development, a movement between the relative hegemony of "political society" and "civil society" (Chatterjee 2004), of a populist logic of equivalence and the differential logic of governmentality (Laclau 2005).

Understanding Postcolonial Democracy

What does the case of Bihar teach us about democracy in the postcolonial world? I have argued that in order to understand the impact of democratic practice in postcolonial contexts, analysis of democracy must be separated from normative evaluations based on liberal values, which would invariably reduce Bihar to the status of a "failed democracy."

Liberal frameworks cannot empirically capture the complex dynamics of electoral practice and the widespread presence of relations of dominance and subordination that have been shaped by long processes of state formation. And if inapplicable models of democracy prevent an understanding of the dynamics of postcolonial democracy, the very real transformations resulting from processes of democratization are likely to be overlooked. For instance, as examined above, most analysts would have great difficulty explaining why poverty rates decreased more under Lalu Yadav's "antidevelopment" government than under Nitish Kumar's "prodevelopment" government unless democratization is recognized to be an agent of change independent of the functioning of state institutions (which collapsed during the former government and were strengthened during the latter).

Once we take into account the central importance of caste—not just as identity but also as caste networks and caste-based territorial dominance—a longer history of democratically driven state formation emerges as political change altered the relationships between caste, state institutions, and local power. During the Congress period, landed upper castes were central to the political process in Bihar, resulting in a "passive-revolution" development regime controlled by dominant groups who enjoyed a discretionary allocation of public resources. But the stability of the first state governments after independence was followed by instability during the late 1960s (interrupted by the Emergency) as lower-caste politics and the issue of caste-based reservations first emerged with force (see Chapter 1). While a decade of Congress rule in the 1980s was based again on the promise of state-directed development and an expansion of welfare schemes, starting in the 1990s, the upsurge of post-Mandal OBC politics dismantled this system. Yadavs and other politically organized, populous lower castes actually benefited from the breakdown of state-directed development because this weakened upper-caste control over state institutions and facilitated transfers of power. But, as was noted above, many lower castes were left behind. In contrast, the small, geographically dispersed lower castes that make up the core support base of the Nitish Kumar government demanded "law and order," a more impartial administration, and the provision of education, health, and infrastructure because these castes are unable to become dominant actors within local sites (as Yadavs did in the 1990s), or gain discretionary control over development resources (as upper castes did for decades). Democratization in Bihar resulted in progressively changing relationships among state institutions, electoral politics, and caste dominance, with state institutions ebbing between periods of relative weakness and strength that have produced cumulative social change, albeit slow, uneven, and still partial, and yet nonetheless substantial.

The specificities of this process make comparison difficult, even across Indian states. Take, for instance, the most obvious comparison—Uttar Pradesh (UP). India's most populous state (with a staggering two hundred million people) was the other great laboratory for the backward-caste movement, from Lohia to the post-Mandal period when Mulayam Singh Yadav created his own Muslim-Yadav alliance (Hasan 1998). But there are also fundamental differences. While eastern UP was under the *zamindari* system during the colonial period, and therefore has an agrarian structure similar to much of Bihar, western UP was not and has very different class and caste formations (Lerche 1998). Partly because of this division, Mulayam Singh Yadav never had the broad populist appeal of Lalu Yadav among the lower-caste poor, and a separate Dalit politics spearheaded by the Bahujan Samaj Party (BSP) emerged in the east. Such a Dalit politics has never emerged with force in Bihar (despite Ram Vilas Paswan's attempts), and the BSP has made almost no inroads. The relatively larger numbers of upper castes in UP also provided the base for the rise of Hindu nationalism, focused on the Babri Masjid dispute (located in Ayodhya in UP, see Chapter 2), a political force that has also remained weak in Bihar. So while there is obviously a common national and global context that shapes political developments across states, regional variations can be acute as exemplified by the Lalu period in Bihar (Corbridge 2011).

And since national politics is ultimately shaped by what happens in the states—with Uttar Pradesh and Bihar being historically two of the most influential—there is no substitute for ethnographically informed analysis of trajectories of politically driven state formation for an understanding of India's democracy. Although one has to be careful in making generalizations about India, much less other postcolonial contexts, I conclude by suggesting that the case of lower-caste politics in Bihar reveals three dynamics that may be useful for understanding postcolonial democracy in other places.

First, as a result of the processes of state formation examined in Chapter 1, a state autonomous from local power, as assumed within liberal theory, has always been more idea than reality (Abrams 1988). And while the intersections between state institutions and local power vary greatly in form and degree, such intersections exist in most postcolonial contexts. The intertwining of state institutions and local power has important implications for understanding postcolonial democracy. Policy debates and rational dialogue are meaningful only to the extent that state institutions have the capacity to implement policy, which is determined by a complex political economy. Within Bihar's postcolonial democracy, the lack of anything resembling a Habermasian "public sphere," as well as a dearth of policy-oriented debate among a nonetheless politicized populace, makes models of "deliberative" (Bassette 1994, Habermas 1996) or "dialogic" (Giddens 1994) democracy inappropriate to apply. Instead of democracy providing a forum for rational debate among citizens, the politics of caste was unashamedly focused on capturing power and challenging upper-caste dominance. And even if the means employed may at times appear remarkably "undemocratic" from a liberal framework, these practices were perfectly "rational" from the perspective of India's postcolonial democracy.

Secondly, I have sought to show the ways in which lower-caste politics cannot be reduced to a politics of identity, and I suspect the same is true of other colonially constructed identities. Colonial and postcolonial modes of governance shaped democracy both through governmental strategies that favored group identities over individual citizenship, but also through an interweaving of caste networks, state institutions, and caste-based territorialities backed by routine violence within local contexts. But this does not mean that India's democracy is overdetermined by the colonial legacy. The case of Bihar demonstrates that, precisely because of the relationships between caste identities, state institutions, and local dominance, democratization based on caste did partially transform structures of power shaped by the colonial legacy.

Lastly, the case of Bihar cautions that we should not assume the hegemony of dominant discourses, explaining why the liberalism of "liberal democracy," even if endowed with global normative force (Paley 2008) that is embraced by India's middle class, does not enjoy a central role within Indian political life. The ways in which colonial processes of state formation set the stage for distinct processes of democratization, as we have seen, often play out in quite unexpected ways, reflecting the inherent indeterminacy of democracy (Lefort 1988) and of hegemonic practice (Laclau and Mouffe 1985). Part of this distinctiveness is reflected in the fact that hegemonic practice is grounded in struggles over local dominance that operate according to their own logic. The discourse of development (Escobar 1995, Ferguson 1990), as we examined, was effortlessly marginalized when lower-caste leaders perceived it as impeding lower-caste empowerment, precisely because of the ways in which state-directed development reinforced upper-caste territorial dominance. While this dramatic displacement of development discourse did not occur to the same extent in other states, the fragility of hegemonic discourses that intersect with local power configurations and the tension between democratization and state-directed development exist to varying degrees across India. And the discourse of lower-caste empowerment that attained hegemony during the long reign of Lalu Yadav was displaced just as quickly by a new discourse of development centered on Nitish Kumar. While this new discourse was shaped by India's post-liberalization economy, it was undergirded by new political alignments at the local level and included categories—"Extremely Backward Castes," "Maha Dalits," and "Backward Muslims"—that reflected the emergence of new political forces.

Instead of a democracy conjoined with (and constrained by) liberalism, then, I suggest that democratization in India, especially since the 1990s, privileged a discourse of popular sovereignty construed as rule of the lower-caste majority. India's "alternate" political modernity (Nugent 2008), therefore, does not just represent an adaptation of a universal democracy or its culturally contextualized deployment, but rather a divergent articulation with concepts such as "popular sovereignty" and a caste-based notion of "social justice" taking prominence at the expense of concepts such as "individual liberty." And since there was little pretense of a state autonomous from local power, elected representatives did not "represent" their supporters through policy, nor were they popularly perceived (or even asked) to do so. Rather, they combined influence over state institutions with informal sources of power in order to directly intervene in struggles within local sites. Elections, therefore, were not so much about choosing political "representatives" as about determining the very contours of power.

If one response to the realities of postcolonial democracy was to attempt centralized, top-down development, the other was a disruptive attempt to use the force of sheer numbers to undermine elite dominance through the electoral process. And while these two political projects appear contradictory—just as Lalu Yadav and Nitish Kumar would seem to represent opposite political projects—over the *longue durée* they unfolded as alternating phases of a single process. Democratization in Bihar may have played out according to dynamics that liberal democratic theorists would find difficult to explain in positive terms, but it produced meaningful change nonetheless, revealing the need for new frameworks for understanding the realities of democratization in the postcolonial world. This also suggests that, despite all of the very visible shortcomings of India's democracy that are nowhere more visible than in Bihar, this may all be part of a distinctly postcolonial but very real trajectory of democratization that continues to unfold in unexpected directions.

Notes

Introduction

1. Massive congregations of people, assembling for often disruptive political activities, have a long history in India, going back to Gandhian civil disobedience of the independence movement. In Bihar, huge rallies took place during Jayaprakash Narayan's movement against Indira Gandhi in the mid-1970s, which spread from Bihar and culminated in the imposition of emergency rule in India in 1975. In fact, Jayaprakash Narayan spoke to enormous crowds of protesters at the same Gandhi Maidan, and Lalu Yadav, then the Patna University student union president, was also present. But whereas Jayaprakash had been agitating against the Congress governments in Bihar and Delhi, the ruling party in the state was itself the organizer of the *laathi* rally.

2. The subtheme was "Bush *bhagao dhuniya bachao*" (get rid of Bush and save the world), capitalizing on widespread popular opposition to the American invasion of Iraq.

3. In the past, Lalu has been spelled in English as "Laloo." In 2004, Lalu claimed that his opponents were responsible for promoting this misspelling. ("Laloo" could be mistaken for the Hindi word *lalloo*, meaning "fool"). The national media now routinely spells his name as "Lalu," a practice I also follow.

4. Despite the chaos, there were remarkably few reports of violence. I was easily able to roam unarmed amidst the *laathi*-wielding crowds on motorcycle and on foot.

5. George K. Varghese, "'Like Gandhi Chased the British Away with His Laathi, Lalu Will Chase the BJP Out,' Said a Man on the Mike." *Indian Express*, April 30, 2003.

6. Quoted in ibid.

7. Lalu Yadav termed the event the "*laathi railla*," *railla* replacing the English "rally" because the "y" ending in Hindi is feminine, while "a" is masculine—here meant to denote muscular strength.

8. I heard many people in attendance comment on the difference between this rally and the even more massive *garib* (poor) rally held by the RJD in 1997, remarking that the composition of this crowd was visibly different. The rural poor were largely absent and many supporters arrived on new motorcycles. I ran into dozens of regional and village-level politicians, contractors, and newly elected members of village-level (*panchayat*) bodies, many of whom I knew from my fieldwork in Bhojpur district. Rather than representing a call for empowerment, the rally's composition reflected the newly empowered, a new class of local leaders that had emerged during the previous thirteen years of RJD governance.

9. While much of this criticism was urban in origin, I heard many villagers' criticism of the amount of oil used to lubricate the *laathis* when many poor families cannot afford enough oil with which to cook.

10. Amranath Tiwari, "Federal Rule Improves Bihar Life," Patna: *BBC News*, April 23, 2005. A common local joke that I heard many times referred to kidnapping as the most profitable industry in Bihar, having "low capital investment with high returns."

11. Anthropologists Bailey (1957, 1960, 1963), Srinivas (1962), Mayer (1960), and Carter (1974) tried to understand the changes that electoral democracy were effecting in local experiences of caste. See also Cohn (1987b). Yalman's inherently political conception of caste allowed him to write somewhat prophetically, "It does not seem to me likely, then, that there will be any early abandonment of caste principles, even under conditions of improved physical mobility and urbanization" (1960, 111). For compilations relating to caste published in recent years see Fuller (1996), D. Gupta (2000), Searle-Chatterjee and Sharma (1994). See Michelutti (2008) for an excellent recent study of the ways in which democracy has shaped modern Yadav identity.

12. The only lapse was a twenty-one-month period during 1975–77 when Indira Gandhi imposed emergency rule.

13. For a similar point, see also Wood (1995, 227–237).

14. See Bate (2009), Coles (2007), Goankar (2007), Michelutti (2008), Paley (2002, 2008), Spencer (2007).

15. Khilnani (1997, 58–60) similarly emphasizes the instrumentalism of a caste politics seeking to capture the state, arguing that "the meaning of democracy has been menacingly narrowed to signify only elections. . . . The conflicts [of caste and community] in India today are the conflicts of modern politics; they concern the state, access to it, and to whom it ultimately belongs."

16. Electoral incentives do help to explain patterns of Hindu-Muslim violence. Wilkinson's (2004) excellent analysis of this demonstrates, however, that a Hindu-Muslim divide is usually promoted as a "wedge issue" by politicians representing the minority interests of upper-caste elites. This is why Corbridge and Harriss (2000) refer to the rise of Hindu nationalism as an "elite revolt."

17. The first "democratic upsurge" began in the mid-1960s with the growing strength of opposition parties.

18. See Dirks (2001, 275–276) for a graphic account of these protests. The decision was stayed by the Supreme Court but eventually implemented in 1992.

19. See Corbridge and Harriss (2000).

20. As Hasan (2000, 26) puts it, " The unmistakable aftermath of Congress decline has been the displacement of upper castes from positions of power and the rise to power of backward and lower castes. This is nothing short of a quiet social revolution."

21. Jaffrelot (2003) focuses on documenting the changes that occurred within the caste backgrounds of members of state assemblies and government ministries. Hansen (1999) invokes the radical transformations of recent democratic experience in order to situate his analysis of a reactionary Hindu nationalism.

22. Partha Chatterjee's (2004) analysis of the "politics of the governed" is a rare attempt to theorize the colonial influence described above on contemporary political practice in India. See Mbembe (2001) and Mamdani (1996) for reflections on the ways in which the colonial legacy impacts contemporary African politics.

23. See Rao's (2009) excellent account of the ways in which Dalit "caste radicalism" shaped colonial liberalism through collective action aimed at creating a political consciousness of group rights, such as Ambedkar's movements for temple entry and, later, religious conversion.

24. This also applies to urban contexts in India where modes of governance are not necessarily organized around caste networks. For example, Hansen (2001) describes the ways in which the Shiv Sena maintains control over much of Mumbai not only through public spectacles of violence, but also through informal political networks that penetrate state institutions.

25. In fact, the apparent autonomy of the institutional political sphere only exists, as it were, from the outside looking in; a fiction created not only by political theories modeled on Western-style liberal democracy that posit a separate "political sphere" and autonomous state, but also by an overwhelmingly upper-caste Indian media catering to a still small but expanding urban middle class. The origin of this fiction can be traced to the colonial "civilizing" project and the creation of a narrow "civil society" in the shadow of the Raj that was contrasted with the alleged "incivility" of "native politics" (Chatterjee 2004).

26. As Mamdani (1996, 18) observes in relation to a similar division in Africa between an urban-based "civil society" and strategies of indirect rule in the countryside, "We need to consider them separately while keeping in mind that each signified one face of the same bifurcated state."

27. For example, see the volumes edited by Das and Poole (2004), and Benei (2001), Hansen and Stepputat (2001).

28. See also Hansen's (2001) account of the central importance of spectacle and public performance in Mumbai politics.

29. See Laclau and Mouffe (1985, Chapter 1) for a detailed discussion of the concept of hegemony.

30. Corbridge and Harriss write of an encounter with Lalu Yadav, "Mr. Yadav

told one of us in an interview in December 1999, that he was not interested in providing development for the poor in Bihar. Development, he said, was a 'foreign and polluting' ideology; what people needed was the respect and 'honor' that was due 'to all human beings'" (2000, 269, fn 22).

31. See Edelman (1999) for a similar point drawn from social movements in Costa Rica.

32. Chatterjee (2011, 144) recognizes this, stating that "within the strategic field of the politics of governmentality, there is always a tussle between the differential [politics of the governed] and equaivilential modes [populist democracy]," although this conception remains undeveloped.

33. For instance, areas under the landlord-based *zamindari* system of land tenure differ from those that were under the peasant-based *raiyatwari* system. Regions that had been part of the Mughal Empire obviously had different precolonial governmental structures than the princely states. The caste composition of south India, where Brahmans were less populous, owned relatively little land, and were much easier to displace, differs from north India where upper castes were landed, more populous, and have enjoyed a more entrenched dominance (see Jaffrelot 2003). This list could easily be multiplied.

Chapter One

1. The eighteenth-century historian Sayyid Ghulam Hussain Khan Tabatabai chronicled the increasing power of *zamindars* in his "View of Modern Times." See Yang (1998, 66–69). As Prakash (1990) points out, "The term zamindar emerged in the fourteenth century to characterize the group of ruling magnates at the local level absorbed into the ruling class under the Turkish Sultans. But this group was really subordinate to the imperial ruling class" (85).

2. See Yang (1989, 161) and Hill (1997, 89–93). In many cases *patwaris* and *chaukidars* actually had to pay *zamindars* for their positions (Hill 1997, 90).

3. Interview with Darampal Singh in Rajnagar, November 13, 2012.

4. Citing an 1872 study, Yang (1989) notes that "a differential rent system existed that demanded less from higher castes—Brahman, Rajput and Bhumihar raiyats—even though they occupied the best lands" (50).

5. See Hill (1997) for an interesting account of how the presence of unsettled forests made administrative control over Purnea district nearly impossible, with the district collector having very little actual influence in much of the district (51–84).

6. "Because its local connections were landed magnates with their own networks of power and control, it was in the state's best interests to see that the power of its allies remained localized within the framework of the Raj and that their impositions on rural society were restricted so as not to cause any major peasant

outbreaks.... Not until the advent of the nationalist movement in the twentieth century was there any real danger at the suprolocal level" (Yang 1989, 95).

7. Quoted in A. Das (1997, 62). See also Appadurai (1996) and Dirks (2001) for treatments of the colonial census and the enumeration of caste in colonial India.

8. See Dirks (1987, 309–384).

9. See Appadurai (1996), Dirks (2001, 212–224). See Rudolph and Rudolph (1967) for a classic analysis of the politics of caste associations as instruments for democratic participation.

10. The colonial census used the scriptural representation of caste derived from the fourfold *varna* system of *brahmans* (priests), *kshatriyas* (warriors/rulers), *vaishnas* (merchants/farmers), and *shudras* (servants) found in the Vedas, the "Laws of Manu" and other texts. This overarching fourfold schema is quite different from actual social life, however, with dozens of distinct castes (*jati*) residing within most villages.

11. See Walter Hauser, *Peasant Organisation in India: A Case Study of the Bihar Kisan Sabha, 1929–1942* (unpublished doctoral dissertation, University of Chicago, 1961).

12. See Pinch (1996, 135–136). Swami Sahajanand's birthday is still commemorated in Bihar by the Bhumihar Brahman Sabha.

13. While "upper-caste" associations' support for colonial rule resulted from the influence of *zamindars* within the organizations, lower-caste associations relied on the colonial state to further their ambitions. Pinch even suggests that there was a "subtle alliance being forged between the new *kshatriya* peasants on the one hand, and local and regional administrators" (ibid., 128).

14. James Kerr, a colonial administrator wrote, "It may be doubted if caste is on the whole unfavorable to our rule. It may even be considered favorable to it, provided we act with prudence and forbearance. Its spirit is opposed to national union" (quoted in A. Das 1997, 61). See also Bayly (1999, 234–239).

15. Frankel (1989). A. Das writes, "The Awadhiya Kurmis or Koeris of Patna, the Dhanuks of north Bihar, and the Mahatos of Chhotanagpur were till then discrete groups in social terms with inter-dining and inter-marriage between them being prohibited. However, with the politicisation process [of caste associations], all of them started to refer to themselves as Kurmis" (1997, 61).

16. Michelutti (2008) has described how in addition to changing kinship practices, including arranging marriages across linguistic regions, the Yadav caste movement has been accompanied by a conversion of local caste shrines to the Krishna cult, who is an important symbol of Yadav power. The All India Yadav Mahasabha is today the largest caste association in India.

17. I discuss the effects of this history of Yadav caste *sabhas* within Rajnagar village in Chapter 6.

18. Chattopadhyay (1972), Prasad (1973); for an overview of the debate see Thorner (1982).

19. See Frankel (1989), Mishra and Pandey (1996).

20. On a similar hegemony based on caste networks in rural Uttar Pradesh, Jeffrey (2002, 38–39) writes, "Farmers' efforts to co-opt local marketing institutions are comparable with their successful attempts to colonize or influence local panchayats, the local police force, and the judiciary."

21. See Bhatia (2005), A. Das (1983), Louis (2002).

22. See also Jaffrelot (2003, 260–265), Mishra and Pandey (1996).

23. See Michelutti (2008) for examples of the ways in which claims for Kshatriya and backward-caste status are reconciled by Yadavs in Mathura.

24. Quoted in Frankel (1989, 84).

25. See Chandapuri (2003).

26. "Bihar has been the cradle and birthplace of socialism in India since the foundation of the CSP [Congress Socialist Party] in Patna" (Jaffrelot 2003, 265).

27. In 1974, JP told a group of opposition leaders, "The struggle in Bihar is not just a flash in the pan of history but a continuing process of revolutionary struggle. That is why I have called it a struggle for total revolution" (quoted in Chandra 2003, 43).

28. See Chandra (2003). See also Khilnani (1997, 188) for a brief comment to this effect.

29. Jaffrelot (2003), for example, does not even mention the JP movement in his detailed account of the "rise of low castes in north Indian politics."

30. Chakravarti (2001) provides a very detailed examination of how commercialization of agriculture in a village in Purnea district in Bihar coincided with increased social control over laborers, a distinct process of capitalist penetration that increasingly relied on un-free labor.

31. Lenin (1977, 377) termed landlord-driven-based agrarian capitalism "semi-feudal capitalism," since feudal privilege was retained, and a more desirable and transformative peasant-based alternative "democratic capitalism." And, in fact, democratization made the later path the only viable one.

Chapter Two

1. My aim here is not to take part in wider debates about what constitutes "populism." For instance, some definitions of populism have emphasized an opposition to representative politics that clearly does not apply at all to the case of lower-caste politics (although it does apply to the JP movement, where most lower-caste leaders began their careers). Rather, I draw here from Laclau's particular theorization, which I argue is useful for analysis of certain key aspects of lower-caste politics. As noted below, the populism associated with lower-caste politics exhibits the particularities of postcolonial democracy.

2. See Shah (2008) for a critique of Chatterjee's theorization of India's political

economy as elite-driven, downplaying the central role of popular struggles, especially those related to lower-caste politics, as well as the unpredictability of an electoral process that "contains within it the seeds of totally unexpected outcomes" (81).

3. Chatterjee (2011, 140–144), reflecting on Laclau, recognizes the ways in which populism operates according to a different logic than a politics of the governed. Furthermore, he also recognizes that populism "*is* the *effective* form of democratic politics in the contemporary world" (140, italics original), but this effective form of democracy remains marginal within his analysis.

4. When I spent a few days in Phulwaria during the *panchayat* elections in 2001, the village had obviously benefited from its famous son, with a new health clinic and good village roads. But Brahman landlords still maintained dominance, even if less overtly than in the past. And Lalu's relative was defeated in the elections by a Brahman opponent, reflecting the incompleteness of political change during this period, a theme that I will return to.

5. Quoted in Thakur (2000, 96–97).

6. Interview with Yadunand Rai, 1/2012.

7. While there are many biographies of Lalu Yadav, none of the ones that I am aware of are written from anything approaching an impartial perspective. This is an indication of how controversial Lalu Yadav's career has been. Titles range from *Lalu Yadav, Prophet of Social Justice* to *The Making of Lalu Yadav and the Unmaking of Bihar*. I have drawn from the latter because it is the best researched, written by a well-known journalist. It does, however, need to be situated within the partisan perspective that the book's title explicitly indicates.

8. He later, however, made himself very much at home in the chief minister's residence, complete with custom-built deluxe stables for his reported two hundred cows and buffaloes.

9. Interview with Dr. Razi Ahmad, Patna, 1/2012. Translation mine.

10. V. P. Singh, "Power and Equality—Changing Grammar of Indian Politics," quoted in Jaffrelot (2003, 350).

11. Raj Kamal Jha and Farzand Ahmed, "Laloo's Magic," *India Today*, April 30, 1995, 54.

12. Taken from Chaudhary (2001, 316).

13. Jha and Ahmed, "Lalu's Magic," 52.

14. Yadavs, as traditional dairy producers, are thought to have a special role as "protectors of the cow." Thus many of the earlier communal riots that were related to cow protection movements were documented as occurring largely between *ahir* (Yadav) activists and Muslims. See Pandey (1990) and Pinch (1996, 118–121).

15. The National Elections Studies and Bihar Assembly Election Studies conducted by the Center for the Study of Developing Societies show that during the period of Lalu's rule, a full 80 percent of Yadav voters consistently voted for the RJD, while around 60 percent of Muslim voters did so, providing strong evidence for the validity of the so-called M-Y (Muslim-Yadav) equation (Kumar 2004).

16. Interview with Ramanand Yadav, Patna, 1/2012.

17. "If Laloo Goes, Naxals Will Surround the Cities," *Outlook*, March 22, 1999.

18. See also Jaffrelot (2003, 377–384).

19. Raj Kamal Jha and Farzand Ahmed, "Laloo's Magic," *India Today*, April 30, 1995, 54.

20. I once observed Lalu refuse to drink bottled water that an attendant handed him because it was what he termed "multinational" water, which he saw as fit only for washing his hands.

21. A widely circulated joke was that instead of "information technology," Lalu mistook IT to stand for "income tax," a reference to the corruption allegations that would explode in later years.

22. Jaffrelot (2003, 235), quoted from Rao (1978, 156) and Rao, "Political Elite and Caste Association," *EPW* (1968): 779–782.

23. A Yadav caste publication states, "Lord Krishna gave them three principles: democracy, social justice and commitment to equality. These are the bases of our future. He was a democratic leader. He used to respect the views of his citizens. He used to believe that the person who is elected by the citizens has the right to rule. He was the first person to begin a 'democratic way of governance': but others say that France gave birth to democracy" (Michelutti 2008, 253).

24. Quoted in Michelutti (2008, 118).

25. "Love Him or Hate Him, You Can't Ignore Lalu in Bihar," *Indian Express*, April 4, 2005.

26. See Jaffrelot (2003, 357) and Chaudhary (2001, 325), for a caste breakdown of the Bihar assembly in 1995 (although the two accounts differ to some extent).

27. "No Longer Backstage," *Indian Express*, November 30, 2005.

28. Interview with Ramanand Yadav, Patna, 1/2012.

29. Farzand Ahmed, "Crippled By Confrontation," *India Today*, April 15, 1995, 64–65.

30. Ibid., 64.

31. Ranjit Bhushan, "Curious Paranoia," *Outlook*, March 27, 1996.

32. Anonymous source, January 29, 2006.

33. "I'll Fight It Out in the Court and the Streets," *Outlook*, July 2, 1997.

34. These two Yadav leaders engaged in a drawn-out electoral battle for the Madhepura Lok Sabha seat in Bihar. Lalu beat Sharad in 1998, only to lose in 1999, and then reclaim the seat in 2004.

35. "The Charges Are Political," *Outlook*, November 20, 1996, italics added.

36. "I Won't Allow CBI to Plot My Removal," *Outlook*, May 14, 1997.

37. George Fernandes was defense minister; Yashwant Sinha was finance and then foreign minister; Nitish Kumar was railway minister; Ram Vilas Paswan was communications and then coal minister; Sharad Yadav was civil aviation and then labor minister; and C. P. Thakur was health minister.

38. Interviewed by Francine Frankel, quoted in Witsoe (2006).

39. Poornima Joshi, "Fatal Gaffe Arms Lalu in EC War," *Telegraph*, October 27, 2005.

40. Extremely Backward Castes refers to castes officially classified as "Annexure One" within Bihar's unique system of reservations implemented by Karpoori Thakur, which divides the OBC category into two annexes with the aim of providing the most benefits to the most marginalized OBC groups.

41. Sanjay Kumar, "The Return of the RJD," *Frontline*, vol. 17, issue 6, March 18–31, 2000.

42. Sanjay Kumar and Muneshwar Yadav, "It Was Laloo's Charisma That Tilted the Scales in Bihar," *The Hindu*, May 20, 2004.

Chapter Three

1. The DM is formally under the supervision of the divisional commissioner but the fact that the latter has the responsibility for ten districts and only is present in a particular district for periodic inspections means that the DM has more or less a free hand in day-to-day administration. Divisional commissioners have been criticized as "kings whose subjects are unaware of their existence" (Maheshwari 2005, 565).

2. The DM is responsible for the maintenance of law and order (as district magistrate), the collection of district tax revenue (as district collector), development works in the district (although there is also a district development commissioner), and postings in the district administration (as district officer). The DM also serves as the returning officer overseeing the conduct of parliamentary and state assembly elections in the district and as the district census officer in performing the decentennial census (see Maheshwari 2005, 579–584).

3. On one occasion, for example, I ran into Rai while meeting with the chief minister at his residence in Patna.

4. According to the Bihar Panchayat Raj Act, the *zilla parishad* should be responsible for most development works done in the district, including roads (other than national or state highways), agriculture, education, and health facilities. The act also, however, gives the state government discretion in providing funding (Bihar Panchayat Raj Act, 1993, Act No. 19, sections 67, 71, and 71). The result has been that the *zilla parishad* has received almost no funding and the district magistrate has retained control over district-level administration and development funds.

5. The DM and leadership of the CPI(Marxist-Leninist) were in frequent contact. I was once with the DM when he received a call from the district leader of the CPI(ML) and I was with this CPI(ML) leader when he received a call from the DM.

6. A survey of Bihar cadre IAS officers in 1992, for example, found that 80 percent were from urban backgrounds. See Singh (1997).

7. While there have been studies that have documented the caste background of the IAS, I am aware of no studies that highlight the divergence in the caste backgrounds of members of different state institutions. See Frankel and Rao (1989), Appendix 1, for a study of the caste backgrounds of members of the IAS.

8. During interviews with IAS officers, I went through the IAS personnel list, asking my informants to identify individual officers' caste backgrounds. Such a method can be criticized for "enumerating" caste, but I found it necessary to document divergences in the social and caste backgrounds of members of different state institutions. Although such enumeration has political implications (and could even be considered a political act), ignoring the caste backgrounds of actors within state institutions and the ways in which these actors participate in power configurations that extend beyond institutional boundaries also has political implications. It should also be noted that the caste backgrounds of bureaucrats had become a topic of intense popular interest and awareness, especially in the wake of the politics of caste empowerment. I used the caste categories that my informants referenced.

9. The relative "backwardness" of Bania castes in Bihar reflects the weakness of indigenous capital and the dominance of merchants from outside the state, especially Bengalis and Marwaris.

10. Kanshi Ram, "*Bahujan Samaj ke lye, asha ki kiran*," cited in Jaffrelot (2003, 398).

11. A scandal erupted in 2010 when a similar caste-based list of the Congress Party state committee was leaked and published by the press. Regional parties such as the RJD and JD(U) know this information so well that explicit lists are unnecessary.

12. I obtained these numbers by going through the IAS personnel list and asking senior IAS officers to identify individual officers' caste backgrounds. Much of the data is drawn from a single officer and it was not always possible to verify his account. In addition to its incompleteness then, I cannot guarantee that the numbers are completely accurate. The chart serves the more general purpose of indicating the basic social composition of the IAS in Bihar. I used the caste categories that my informants referenced.

13. See Jaffrelot (2003, 357) and Chaudhary (2001, 325) for a caste breakdown of the Bihar Assembly in 1995 (although the two accounts differ to some extent).

14. The most extreme example of this occurred during Mayawati's Bahujan Samaj Party–led government in Uttar Pradesh, a party claiming to represent the backward-caste *bahujan* (majority) and especially the Scheduled Castes. Within the first 136 days of her government, there were more than 1,500 transfers (Jaffrelot 2003, 416). Such occurrences highlight a high level of intrastate conflict. See "Bureaucracy Bashing," *The Times of India*, May 14, 1997, and "Depoliticize India's Steel Frame," *Hindustan Times*, July 25, 2004.

15. "Going with the Wind," *India Today*, February 28, 1995, 100.

16. N. C. Saxena, *Implementation of Poverty Alleviation and Food-Based Schemes in Bihar,* Supreme Court Commission on Food Security, 2003, 19.

17. Saxena (2003) referred to this fear as "fear paralysis."

18. See Mathew and Moore (2011, 9–14) for a detailed analysis of underspending by the Lalu government. They demonstrate that the full extent of underspending cannot be explained by fiscal crisis, center-state relations, or lack of basic state capacity (although these were all important factors), but points towards a strategy of what they term "state incapacity by design."

19. Saxena (2003, 17).

20. Saxena (2003, 27, 30).

21. The Bihar State Cooperative Bank is the apex institution connected to twenty-four district-level Central Cooperative Banks (CC Banks) and a multitude of village-level Primary Agricultural Credit Societies (PACS). This is considered the most important and powerful of the cooperative institutions; it is where the money is. The election was won by Satyendra Narain Singh. S. N. Singh was the Ara Cooperative Bank chairman and the nephew of the late Tapeshwar Singh, who was a major player in the cooperative movement as well as the Congress Party, both at the state and the national level. S. N. Singh, like most cooperative leaders, is connected to the Congress. He was the Bhojpur district Congress president.

22. The Housing Federation is also a three-tiered institution involved with extending credit for the construction of personal houses as well as to construction companies. This was the only society where open elections actually took place, perhaps because of the association of the strongest candidate with the BJP; in other cases the RJD-Congress alliance within the state government must have made compromise easier. The election was won by V. K. Mishra, a former Congress MP who is currently a BJP MLA, and the son of the late Lalit Narayan Mishra, the powerful Congress leader who was brother of former Bihar chief minister Jagannath Mishra. The overwhelming presence of L. N. Mishra's legacy in the Housing Federation, which was started late in 1969, is demonstrated by the federation's building being named "Lalit Bhavan." V. K. Mishra was the previous chairman of the Housing Federation. Ram Babu Singh (Rajput), connected to RJD, would receive only 15 votes compared with V. K. Mishra's 166. The Mishra family's previous dominance was easily maintained.

23. Of these, seven were general seats; two were reserved for women, and one each reserved for Scheduled Caste, Scheduled Tribe, Annexure One, and Annexure Two categories.

24. A sad postscript for this story is that Ajit Singh, who became a member of parliament in 2005, was killed when hit by a bus in 2007. Although no clear evidence emerged, there were many accusations (including by the then-chief minister Nitish Kumar) that hostile elements within the "cooperative mafia" had assassinated Ajit. His widow, Meena Singh, succeeded him as member of parliament, winning by a large margin.

25. The chairman election of the Bihar State Marketing Association is an exception, but only because S. K. Singh was able to establish a connection between the previously dominant Rajput network and the RJD. Sunil is from Chapra, and Lalu Yadav has a personal electoral interest in Chapra, from where he was elected MP in 2004. On one occasion a few weeks before the 2004 parliamentary elections, I visited Sunil in his office suite at the top of the Bihar State Marketing Association tower (BISCUMAUN). The office lobby was filled with Rajput villagers from Chapra whom Sunil was taking to meet Lalu. I asked Sunil what it was about Lalu that he liked and he unabashedly stated, "I like him because he is so powerful." Subhash Yadav, the chief minister's brother, was reportedly present at the time of Sunil's nomination with substantial muscle power. This combination of command over Tapeshwar Singh's Rajput network, as well as support from the RJD, created a very powerful position. Sunil Singh won uncontested. Even in this case, however, the RJD was forced to extend its support to a forward-caste candidate; backward-caste candidates were absent during all of the elections.

26. Sawshilya writes, "Bureaucrats can defeat politicians by obfuscation, delay, and by the use of rules, regulations, and procedures" (2000, 149).

27. My research assistant, Akhilesh Kumar, conducted twenty-five detailed interviews of corporation councilors. I then met with some of the key figures.

28. At the home of the mayor's brother and political ally, a failed project to redirect the course of the Ganges closer to Patna had cut a huge trench straight through his brick kilns, approaching his house. The logical course of the trench appeared to have been altered to cut into this land. Local residents claimed that this was an intentional act of the government and of Lalu Yadav in particular. I heard stories that the trench was stopped short of the house only by building a makeshift temple that the workers refused to destroy. Whether true or not, this left the impression that to go against Lalu Yadav could result in the earth literally swallowing one's house and livelihood.

29. Bihar Mayor Council v. the Union of India and others, C.W.J.C. No. 1019 of 2003.

30. World Bank (2005, 58).

31. Even the World Bank, an organization not known for political analysis, observes in a report: "About 80 percent of the judiciary belongs to the forward castes although they represent about 18 percent of the total population. It is reported that interests represented by the forward castes are reflected in judicial pronouncements, undermining the implementation of much socioeconomic legislation." World Bank (2005, 59).

32. Former parliament speaker Purno Sangma stated, "The judiciary was exhibiting a dangerous tendency to encroach on legislative and administrative foundations beyond its ambit [and] ... the judges were populists playing to the gallery in the recent spate of widely-publicized corruption trials." Quoted in Rudolph and Rudolph (2001, 136).

33. "By the mid-1990s, as the chorus of those malaffected by judicial decision-making grew louder, the judges defended their intervention as a temporary antidote to the collapse of institutions of governance and a weakening of the rule of law" (Dhavan 2000, 315).

34. This is a common perception among top-level bureaucrats. Sawshilya, for example, quotes a Bihar bureaucrat as saying, "Success is to make the system work. Individuals may come and go; the system will always be there" (2000, 147).

35. Vishwas was previously a university vice chancellor with continued publications even after his appointment to the IAS. See, for example, Vishwas (1998).

Chapter Four

1. Territoriality can overlap with ownership but it certainly is not identical. For example, it is possible for a family to legally own land (holding a formal title) but be unable to cultivate it because of the inability to protect standing crops and irrigation resources from theft. Likewise, it may be possible for land to be seized and cultivated without the possession of a legally defined ownership.

2. This relationship between caste and territoriality, of course, has been recognized before. Dirks (1987), in his ethnohistorical analysis of caste, asserts, "Territory is not restricted in its influence to the macro historical level, but intervenes at every level of social organization" (259). Even Dumont (1966), whose model of caste obliterated the role of territory, remarked that "we have been obliged to refer to the fact that actual caste systems, in contrast to the theoretical model, were organized within a fixed territorial area, were so to speak contained within a spatial framework" (152).

3. Srinivas's (1962) influential concept of the "dominant caste" asserted that "a caste may be said to be 'dominant' when it preponderates numerically over the other castes, and when it also wields preponderant economic and political power" (1962, 300). While Srinivas's concept of the dominant caste has been criticized (Dube 1968 and Oommen 1970 are early criticisms), I believe that the concept is still relevant, not least because the English term "dominance" is popularly used to refer to the strength of groups designated in caste terms within various contexts. See also Raheja (1988) and Quigley (1993), where caste practice is asserted to revolve around the "centrality" of the dominant caste. See Karanth (1996) for a more recent account of the dominant caste concept.

4. What Anna Tsing observes in Indonesia equally applies to what I observed in Bihar: "These are the men I call leaders because they are ambitious enough to tell the government that they represent the community and their neighbors that they represent the state" (1993, 72).

5. Chakravarti, in an analysis of material from a village in north Bihar in which he did fieldwork from 1978 to 1980, writes that it "seems plausible to argue that

local or village-based agrarian power structures are, at least in Bihar, interwoven with the power of the state. The vital agent in this relationship is the dominant caste" (2001, 292).

6. See Stuart Corbridge, Glyn Williams, Manoj Srivastava, and René Véron, *Seeing the State: Governance and Governmentality in India* (Cambridge: Cambridge University Press, 2005), 192–206.

7. See Louis (2002).

8. I was told that generally the MLA took a 10 to 15 percent "commission"; the BDO took 5 percent; the *panchayat sevak* (village-level official) took 5 percent; and the *thikadar* took 10 to 15 percent. I was also told that the local MLA, Lal Bihari (introduced in Chapter 4), did not take this "commission," relying solely on revenue from sand mining, which enhanced his public image.

9. In addition, most brick kilns in central Bihar are operated with laborers brought from tribal areas, working under very harsh conditions.

10. The Kulharia estate was purchased in the late nineteenth century and was the largest estate in the region in the late colonial period. After independence the importance of this family continued. They founded one of the most important colleges in Patna and a family member served as a High Court judge. There were other important families in the region, as well such as the previous Rajput *zamindars* of Rajnagar that we will meet in the next chapter. One can imagine regional political life in Koilwar in the colonial as well as in the early period after independence as completely dominated by these *zamindari* families.

11. The *panchayat* committee is the block level of the *panchayat* system with members elected from each *panchayat*.

12. The media establishment and almost every major political analyst appeared certain that an NDA victory was more or less a foregone conclusion. This was confirmed by preelection opinion polls, and even post-poll voter surveys indicated an NDA victory, although the margin narrowed as the five phases of voting progressed. The reasons for such confidence were many. The Indian economy was growing at an unprecedented rate; Prime Minister Atal Bihari Vajpayee was seen as the most popular leader in the country; the NDA had recently swept state assembly elections in Madhya Pradesh and Rajastan; and efforts to ease tensions with Pakistan appeared to be succeeding complete with a long-awaited India-Pakistan cricket tournament that India won just a few days before voting began.

13. Lalita Srinivasan, "Ad Firms See Big Bucks as Cong, NDA Plan Media Blitz," *Financial Express*, February 16, 2004. Adding to the NDA's confidence was the opposition's apparent disorganization, having no common policy platform worked out and not even a commitment of who would become prime minister if the alliance won. Sonia Gandhi, the party president of the Congress, the largest party in the alliance, was inexperienced and her Italian origin was an easy political target for ruthless NDA criticism.

14. In the intense introspection and analysis that inevitably followed such an

unexpected electoral debacle, a number of theories emerged. The BJP seemed to have lost touch with rural India, and everyone agreed, including the top BJP leadership, that the "India Shining" strategy had been a complete failure. For some within the BJP leadership, the loss was blamed on a neglect of the BJP's Hindu base; this interpretation implied the need to return to a more hard-line *hindutva* (Hindu nationalist) agenda. Others interpreted the loss as a popular rejection of the economic reforms that had been pursued since 1991. India was shining for the rising middle classes in major urban centers, and the Indian IT sector was surely shining, but for most rural Indians the "feel-good factor" did not seem to apply. As a taxi driver in Delhi was quoted as saying, "The BJP lost because it was not able to deliver goods to a poor man. How can one 'feel good' when the government decides to make cell phones cheaper and petrol dearer?" ("In Quotes—India's Election Results," *BBC News*, UK edition, May 13, 2004).

15. "Common Man Lalu to Take Shine Off BJP Campaign," *Indo-Asian News Service*, Patna, March 12, 2004.

16. Mark Tully, "Forget Charisma, Forget Hype," *BBC News*, World Edition, May 14, 2004.

17. J. P. Yadav, *D.H. News Service*, Patna, April 3, 2004.

18. "Heads She Wins, Tails She Wins," *Times of India*, Patna, April 13, 2004.

19. This is the problem with Chandra's (2004) notion of "ethnic head counting" as a rational calculation intended to maximize individual voters' access to development patronage. The crucial role of territorial dominance is absent.

20. See Witsoe (2011) for an example of violent booth looting.

Chapter Five

1. See for example, Chakravarti (2001), A. Gupta (1998), Jeffrey and Lerche (2001), Robinson (1988), Wadley (1994).

2. This is similar to the transformations in village power relations that occurred much earlier in many areas of south India. Andre Béteille's (1971) classic account, for example, describes a similar emergence of multiple centers of power, what he terms "power blocks" and the importance of party networks. The contrast between Béteille's village and the situation in Rajnagar is the history of *zamindari* land settlement (as I describe below) and the fact that Rajput ex-*zamindars* in Rajnagar still own a considerable amount of land as is the case in many, if not most, villages in Bihar.

3. The early work of Bernard Cohn (1987b) and, much later, of Akhil Gupta (1998) both represent attempts to deal with the multiplicity of the Indian village. Cohn, in an early article, wrote of "the pasts of an Indian village," demonstrating the fragmented and multiple nature of village historical consciousness. Gupta's account is interesting because it utilizes multiple and conflicting local historical

narratives as a means to analyze the articulation of development discourse, under-stood at national and global scales, within local-level political maneuvering and class differentiation. In effect, Gupta is able to juxtapose conflicting local historical accounts with a larger-level "conventional" historical narrative in order to demon-strate the ways in which larger historical trajectories play out locally within con-texts marked by differential power relations.

4. Harijan, literally God's people, was a title given by Gandhi. This term is now seen by many people as condescending and has been replaced by the more po-litically potent term Dalit, "the oppressed," as the "politically correct" term. The state's category is Scheduled Castes (SCs). Most people in Rajnagar used the term Harijan and occasionally the term Scheduled Castes. I heard the term Dalit used only in political contexts, emphasizing the mobilization and empowerment of the groups designated.

5. According to the 1991 census, out of the population of 5,086 in Rajnagar, 3,156 villages are classified as belonging to "Other Backward Classes"; 681 vil-lagers are classified as belonging to "Scheduled Castes"; and the remaining 1,248 belong to either "Forward Castes" or a handful of Muslim households (one domestic servant is classified as a Scheduled Tribe). The census figures combine the "Other Backward Classes" and "Scheduled Caste" categories in a "Backward Classes" category that numbers 3,838.

6. I never encountered women within these spaces in the village.

7. See Gupta (1995) for a discussion of how social positioning impacts peoples' perceptions of "the state."

8. When I first arrived in the village, people would constantly ask me about my caste. When I tried to explain that there is nothing exactly analogous to caste in the United States, many people (especially upper-caste people) disagreed: "You just call it something else" (an argument that does have some merits). Some people concluded that since I am American, I must be a "global Bhumihar" (the biggest landlord caste). But since I spent so much time with Yadavs and RJD politicians in the course of my research, other people gave me a Yadav nickname, Jeffrey Gope (using an older caste title that is now derogatory, or can also refer to a criminal status).

9. Dumont (1966), in an influential article, critiqued the entire concept of "the village community" and the theoretical reification of the village as a natural unit of analysis. This in effect was an attack on the entire tradition of village studies and opened the space for his structural methodology to gain dominance in South Asian anthropology. Dumont argued that the village had been given far too much sociological importance. The village, he claimed, only has meaning because of the "dominant caste" and when people refer to "my village," they are in fact actu-ally referring to either their caste or to their patron's caste. In writing this critique Dumont had, in fact, touched upon the multiplicity of the Indian village that we have been discussing. Still, he was wrong to believe that "the village" is unimport-ant or that we should focus exclusively on caste.

10. See Fuller (1992) for an overview of village rituals in India. He writes, "Village rituals are one manifestation of the social significance of the local community, and in much of India the unity and solidarity of the community is most strikingly expressed in the celebration of village festivals" (272).

11. For an interesting comparison, see Hansen's (2001, 106–108) account of the Shiv Sena's use of religious performances in the construction of a militant Hindu-Marathi identity.

12. There is substantial evidence that *panchayat* public resource allocation is influenced by political factors. See, for example, Besley, Pande, and Rao (2007). For a theoretical perspective on this, see Bardhan and Mookherjee (1998).

13. The post of *mukhia* enjoys a unique position of influence when compared to any other elected executives in India. While the *panchayat sammiti* and *zilla parishad* chairmen are elected indirectly by *sammiti* or *parishad* members, and can be removed through a vote of no confidence, the *mukhia* is directly elected with limited means for redress or removal.

14. Sundar had been a rival candidate for the post of *mukhia* but had lost by over six hundred votes. On one occasion in the village I was approached by a very drunk man known as Manager Yadav who claimed to be a *chela* (disciple) of Sundar. He insisted that I write down that he was opposed to the *mukhia* and that in the next election he would fight against the *mukhia* and perhaps beat or kill him. He worked himself into a drunken frenzy and eventually Yadav villagers living in the area had to restrain him for my safety. This was one of the few times that I witnessed public conflict between Yadav factions in Rajnagar.

15. Some informants claimed that there were other intercaste marriages but that the caste difference was concealed, the bride fictitiously assuming the caste of her husband. These stories were the stuff of village gossip and it was impossible to verify them.

16. Villagers told me that Sanjay used money given by the government after his marriage—the Indian government still gives money to promote intercaste marriages—to start business pursuits. Using his political connections to get contracts and inventing new materials used for laying railway tracks, Sanjay become one of the largest industrialists and one of the wealthiest men in the entire region. He also continued in politics, becoming the member of parliament for the neighboring Gaya district, where his factory and house were located. Sanjay died in a car crash the year before I arrived in the village, and all of his family members have left the village.

17. It should be noted, however, that both Sanjay and Jayaprakash were Kayasth by caste. I am not saying that caste did not play a role; only that caste was not the explicit organizing force of party affiliation in the village.

18. Ramji Singh was the MLA of Barahara until Lal Bihari's father defeated him in 1978.

19. I found many *panchayats* that in the past, in one case as late as 1978, elected their *mukhia* uncontested. In contrast, I do not know of a single case of an uncon-

tested *mukhia* election in the 2001 elections. This underscores the degree of electoral rivalry that has entered village contexts, a rivalry tied to caste-based territorial struggle.

20. This MLC happens to be the son of Tapeshwar Singh, the cooperative leader that I discussed in Chapter 3. This relationship reflected the long-standing links between Rajputs and key public institutions in Rajnagar.

21. This party is known as the CPI(ML) "Liberation" to differentiate it from splinter groups, most notably the CPI(ML) "Peoples' War." CPI(ML) "Liberation" is also known as *malay* and its political wing is called the Indian Peoples Front (IPF).

22. This family founded an important college in Patna, and a relative was a previous High Court judge.

23. When I accompanied the RJD-district president to a rally in Bhojpur in 2004, I was quite surprised when two Maoist area commanders (in what was then the "Peoples' War" faction) joined us for the trip, visibly excited to see Lalu Yadav speak.

Chapter Six

1. See Hasan (1998), Jaffrelot (2003).

2. In one village Rajputs owned 96.6 percent of the land with 58.8 percent of households; in another, Bhumihars owned 89.7 percent with 46 percent of households; Brahmans owned 68.2 percent with 34.2 percent of households; Kurmis owned 87 percent with 27.7 percent of households; and Yadavs owned 83.5 percent with 51 percent of households.

3. See Mitra (1985), Yang (1989).

4. An older Rajput ex-*zamindar* in Rajnagar told me that the Rajnagar *zamindars* had been opposed to Kunwar Singh, whom he accused of forcibly taking some of their *zamindari* lands in other villages.

5. On the Kisan Sabha see Walter Houser, *The Bihar Provincial* Kisan Sabha, *1929–1942: A Study of an Indian Peasant Movement* (unpublished doctoral dissertation, University of Chicago, 1961). See also A. Das (1983) and Kumar (2001).

6. According to informants, the largest two landowners in Rajnagar at the time of my fieldwork, both Rajput ex-*zamindars*, held fifty-five and fifty *bighas* (88 and 80 acres) respectively, well under the land ceiling of one hundred *bighas*. This is in contrast to nearby villages where big landlords legally held land at the one-hundred *bigha* limit and effectively controlled additional land (land registered in other peoples' names). Informants estimated Rajnagar's entire land to be around one thousand *bighas*.

7. See Gupta (1998) and Frankel (1978) for detailed accounts of the impact of the "green revolution" in India.

8. The rate of female labor, however, was half of this rate at twenty-five rupees per day. In addition, during labor-intensive periods such as harvesting of the potato crop, female and child laborers were brought in from other villages, as far as a hundred kilometers away. The rate given during the potato harvest in 2003 was five kilos of potatoes per day, which were selling in the village at that time for three rupees a kilo (2.5 rupees wholesale) providing a very low wage. This extreme gender bias in wage rate, the use of child labor, and the importation of outside labor allowed a partial circumvention of the relatively high adult-male wage rates.

9. This was the main reason given by respondents to a survey of one hundred households that I conducted in Rajnagar in 2010.

10. Most previous *zamindari* families still claim to maintain this prohibition, although the handful of Rajput households actively engaged in agriculture do not. One Rajput farmer stated this justification: "If I don't know the practicalities of agriculture firsthand, the laborers will cheat me." See also Gupta (1998) and Wadley (1994).

11. In fact, *kisan* women spend much of their time tending to the cows and buffaloes that serve as a significant source of income, not only from milk, but also from the sale of dung-cake fuel for cooking. See Wadley (1994, 52–55).

12. See Lucia Michelutti (2008) for the importance of wrestling within Yadav culture.

13. West Tola also has its own Govardhan Puja which was even more "sanskritized" than in East Tola. The ritual took place at the idol of Krishna that has been installed in the Durga temple next to the *tola*. It was, however, a markedly smaller-scale affair than in East Tola.

14. Biswanger, Deininger, and Feder (1993) persuasively argue that, given a minimum operation landholding, peasant family farms are more efficient than landlord farms, even when considering economies of scale.

15. Some villagers told me that there was a specific individual from West Tola who entered the railway service and then helped his neighbors join.

16. As noted in the previous chapter, a similar history of factionalism existed within the once dominant Rajputs, and this history was also downplayed in order to maintain political unity.

17. While one Yadav man claimed that all Yadavs in Rajnagar wear the sacred thread, most Yadav villagers whom I had seen wearing the thread were from West Tola, Road Tola, and to a lesser extent East Tola, with very few from South Tola. It was not a universal practice by any means, which fits with the diversity that I have been exploring in this chapter.

18. The data in Tables 4 through 7 is from a survey of four hundred randomly sampled households that I conducted in 2007.

19. Estimated from a sample of 20 percent of households.

20. Within Bihar's unique system of reservations, the Other Backward Classes category is divided into two annexes, with Annexure Two containing castes con-

sidered to be better positioned and Annexure One, popularly referred to as Extremely Backward Castes, containing the castes thought to be disadvantaged compared to Annexure Two castes.

Chapter Seven

1. From 1993–94 to 2004–5 the poverty ratio declined 14 percent (from 57.24 percent to 43.06 percent), compared to an 8 percent decline in India as a whole and a less than 2.5 percent decline in Orissa (which had now surpassed Bihar as the state with the highest head-count ratio of 47.76 percent). Even more surprising, the head-count ratio of the very poor halved in Bihar from 28.29 percent to 14.65 percent compared to a 5.74 percent decrease in India and an actual increase in Orissa (Mahendra and Ravi 2007, using data from the sixty-first round of the National Sample Survey for a reconstructed united Bihar).

2. This contrasts with Scott's (1985) research village in Malaysia, where the poor wanted a return to the "moral economy" of patronage obligations.

3. Manini Chatterjee, "Extreme Backward to Take Me Forward," *Indian Express*, November 19, 2005.

4. It should be noted, however, that people do have an incentive to over report or falsely report voting for the winning candidates, who were from the RJD in 2004 and the NDA in 2005, so the extent of this shift may be somewhat exaggerated in these figures.

5. These politicians said they had been passed this information indirectly from the booth-specific results observed during the vote computation in Patna (where party observers are allowed), although this obviously cannot be confirmed.

6. Data from a survey of four hundred randomly sampled households that I conducted in 2007.

7. In fact, one can make a strong case that Bihar is still discriminated against by the central government.While Bihar received more than 11 percent of devolved central taxes over the last five years (because this is done according to a fixed formula), it received only 3.87 percent of central investments. But since three-fourths of the Bihar government's revenue comes from central transfers, increasing central tax revenues is the most important source of Bihar's recent growth.

8. "13,000-Crore Plan for Bihar," *Hindu*, February 1, 2008.

9. The regional criminals who had been prominent and ever-present figures in Bhojpur's political life were nowhere to be seen when I returned in 2007, and villagers frequently recounted how once-feared "mafia dons" had been imprisoned.

10. Interview with Abhyanand, Patna, 6/2010. At the time of writing, he is director general of police for Bihar.

11. These include "Indian of the Year–Politics," 2008, 2010 (CNN-IBN), "Indian of the Year–Politics," 2009 (NDTV), "Economic Times Business Reformer of the Year, 2009," "Person of the Year–India," 2010 (*Forbes*).

12. A change in the structure of newspapers' revenue generation was a key factor in this shift. While during the Lalu period most revenue was generated from circulation (to a largely upper-caste readership), by the Nitish period the majority of revenue came from advertising, the bulk of which came from the state government itself (interview with anonymous newspaper managing director, Patna, 8/2011).

13. Interview with Ram Vilas Paswan, Patna, 1/2012.

14. Sabu Naqvi Bhaumik, "Easier Said," *Outlook*, December 5, 2005.

15. Several upper-caste landlords from different parts of Bihar with whom I spoke told me that their position vis-à-vis laborers had actually weakened under Nitish.

16. Anwar Ali, a prominent lower-caste Muslim leader in Bihar who became a member of parliament (Rajya Sabha) after Nitish came to power, told me during an interview in Patna in 2007 that he frequently asked Nitish to part ways with the BJP and assumed that he would do so at the earliest opportunity.

17. For the first time, the BJP topped the list of major parties fielding candidates with criminal backgrounds (nearly 50 percent). The BJP was followed by the RJD and then the JD(U). See "Criminals as Leaders—Yet Again?" *India Together*, November 19, 2005, http://www.indiatogether.org/2005/nov/gov-biharpoll.htm.

18. Based on interviews in 2010 and 2011 with anonymous sources.

19. The poverty rate declined from 54.4 percent to 53.5 percent from 2004–5 to 2009–10, but poverty increased in absolute numbers, with five million additional people falling under the poverty line (Planning Commission 2012). It should be noted that these numbers are based on the new Tendulkar methodology that attempts to take account of spending on education, health care, clothes, and food instead of just caloric intake. As we would expect given the collapse of public education and health care provision during the Lalu years, when this period (measured from 1993–94 to 2004–5) is reestimated using the new methodology, the reduction in poverty is far less dramatic—from 60.5 percent to 54.4 percent versus an 8 percent drop for India as a whole (Planning Commission 2009). But it was still considerably better than the subsequent five years.

20. Interview with anonymous JD(U) leader, Patna, 1/2012.

Reference List

Abrams, Philip. 1988. "Notes on the Difficulty of Studying the State." *Journal of Historical Sociology* 1(1): 58–69.

Alavi, Hamza. 1975. "India and the Colonial Mode of Production." In Miliband and Saville (eds.), *Socialist Register*, 160–197. London: Merlin.

———. 1981. "Structure of Colonial Formations." *Economic and Political Weekly* 16(10): 475–486.

Appadurai, Arjun. 1996. *Modernity at Large: Cultural Dimensions of Globalization*. London: University of Minnesota Press.

Bailey, F. G. 1957. *Caste and the Economic Frontier: A Village in Highland Orissa*. Manchester: Manchester University Press.

———. 1960. *Tribe, Caste and Nation: A Study of Political Activity and Political Change in Highland Orissa*. Manchester: Manchester University Press.

———. 1963. *Politics and Social Change*. Berkeley: California University Press.

———. 1969. *Stratagems and Spoils: A Social Anthropology of Politics*. Oxford: Basil Blackwell.

———. 1998. *The Need For Enemies: A Bestiary Of Political Forms*. London: Cornell University Press.

Banaji, Jairus. 1972. "For a Theory of Colonial Modes of Production." *Economic and Political Weekly* 7: 52.

Banerjee, Mukulika. 2008. "Democracy, Sacred and Everyday: An Ethnographic Case from India." In Paley (ed.)., *Democracy: Anthropological Approaches*. Santa Fe, NM: School for Advanced Research Press.

Bardhan, Pranab. 1984. *The Political Economy of Development in India*. Oxford: Oxford University Press.

———. 2001. "Sharing the Spoils: Group Equity, Development, and Democracy." In Kohli (ed.), *The Success of India's Democracy*. Cambridge:: Cambridge University Press.

Bardhan, Pranab, and Mookherjee Dilip. 1998. "Expenditure Decentralization and the Delivery of Public Services in Developing Countries." No. 90. Boston University, Institute for Economic Development.

Bassette, Joseph. 1994. *The Mild Voice of Reason: Deliberative Democracy and American National Government*. Chicago: University of Chicago Press.

Bate, Bernard. 2009. *Tamil Oratory and the Dravidian Aesthetic: Democratic Practice in South India*. New York: Columbia University Press.

Bayly, Susan. 1999. *Caste, Society and Politics in India from the Eighteenth Century to the Modern Age*. Cambridge: Cambridge University Press.

Benjamin, Walter. 1973. "Critique of Violence." In *Illuminations*. London: Fontana.

Besley, Timothy, Pande, Rohini, and Rao, Vijayendra. 2007. "Just Rewards? Local Politics and Public Resource Allocation in South India." Development Economics Discussion Paper Series, The Suntory Centre. London: London School of Economics and Political Science.

Béteille, Andre. 1971. *Caste, Class, and Power: Changing Patterns of Stratification in a Tanjore Village*. New Delhi: Oxford University Press.

Bhatia, Bela. 2005. "The Naxalite Movement in Central Bihar." *Economic and Political Weekly* 40(15): 1536–1549.

Biswanger, Hans, Deininger, Klaus, and Feder, Gershon. 1993. "Power, Distortions, Revolt, and Reform in Agricultural Land Relations." Washington, DC: The World Bank.

Brass, Paul. 1984. "National Power and Local Politics in India: A Twenty-Year Perspective." *Modern Asian Studies* 18(1): 89–118.

———. 1990. *The Politics of India since Independence*. Cambridge: Cambridge University Press.

Carter, Anthony. 1974. *Elite Politics in Rural India: Political Stratification and Political Alliances in Western Maharashtra*. London: Cambridge University Press.

Chakrabarty, Dipesh. 1999. *Provincializing Europe: Postcolonial Thought and Historical Difference*. Princeton, NJ: Princeton University Press

———. 2002. *Habitations of Modernity: Essays in the Wake of Subaltern Studies*. Chicago: University of Chicago Press.

———. 2007. "'In the Name of Politics': Democracy and the Power of the Multitude in India." *Public Culture* 19(1): 35–57.

Chakravarti, Anand. 2001. *Social Power and Everyday Class Relations: Agrarian Transformation in North Bihar*. London: Sage Publications.

Chandapuri, R. L. 2003. *The Second Freedom Struggle*. Patna: Mission Prakashan.

Chandra, Bipan. 2003. *In the Name of Democracy: JP Movement and the Emergency*. New Delhi: Penguin Books.

Chandra, Kanchan. 2004. *Why Ethnic Parties Succeed: Patronage and Ethnic Headcounts in India*. Cambridge: Cambridge University Press.

Chatterjee, Partha. 1986. *Nationalist Thought and the Colonial World: A Derivative Discourse*. Minneapolis: University of Minnesota Press.

———. 1993. *The Nation and Its Fragments: Colonial and Postcolonial Histories*. Princeton, NJ: Princeton University Press.

———. 1994. "Development Planning and the India State." In Byres (ed.), *State and Development Planning in India*. New Delhi: Oxford University Press.

———. 2004. *The Politics of the Governed: Reflections on Popular Politics in Most of the World*. New York: Columbia University Press.

———. 2008. "Democracy and Economic Transformation in India." *Economic and Political Weekly* 43 (16): 53–62.

———. 2011. *Lineages of the Political: Studies in Postcolonial Democracy*. New York: Columbia University Press.

Chattopadhyay, Paresh. 1972. "On the Question of the Mode of Production in Indian Agriculture: A Preliminary Note." *Economic and Political Weekly* 7: 13.

Chaudhary, Prasant Kumar "Shrikant." 2001. *Bihar mein samajik parivartan ke kuchh aayam (1912–1990)*. New Delhi: Vani Prakashan.

———. 2011. *Bihar: Raaj aur samaaj*. New Delhi: Vani Prakashan.

Chaudhary, S. N. 1999. *Power Dependence Relations: Struggle for Hegemony in Rural Bihar*. New Delhi: Har-Anand Publications.

Chhibber, Pradeep K. 1999. *Democracy without Associations: Transformation of the Party System and Social Cleavages in India*. Ann Arbor: University of Michigan Press.

Cohn, Bernard. 1983. "Representing Authority in Victorian India." In Hobsbawm and Ranger (eds.), *The Invention of Tradition*. Cambridge: Cambridge University Press.

———. 1987a. "The Census, Social Structure and Change in South Asia." In Cohn (ed.), *An Anthropologist among the Historians*. New Delhi: Oxford University Press.

———. 1987b. "The Pasts of an Indian Village." In *An Anthropologist among the Historians and Other Essays*. New Delhi: Oxford University Press.

Coles, Kimberly. 2007. *Democratic Designs: International Intervention and Electoral Practices in Post-War Bosnia-Herzegovina*. Ann Arbor: University of Michigan Press.

Comaroff, Jean, and Comaroff, John. 1991. *Of Revelation and Revolution*. Chicago: University of Chicago Press.

Corbridge, Stuart. 2011. "The Contested Geographies of Federalism in Post-Reform India." In Ruparelia, Reddy, Harriss, and Corbridge (eds.), *Understanding India's New Political Economy: A Great Transformation?* New York: Routledge.

Corbridge, Stuart, and Harriss, John. 2000. *Reinventing India*. Cambridge: Polity.

Corbridge, Stuart, Williams, Glyn, Srivastava, Manoj, and Véron, René. 2005. *Seeing the State: Governance and Governmentality in India*. Cambridge: Cambridge University Press.

Corrigan, Philip, and Sayer, Derek. 1985. *The Great Arch: English State Formation as Cultural Revolution*. New York: Blackwell.

Das, Arvind N. 1983. *Agrarian Unrest and Socio-Economic Change in Bihar, 1900–1980*. New Delhi: Manohar.

———. 1997. "Class Formation: Process and Product." In Verma and Lal (eds.), *Social Realities in Bihar*. Patna: Novelty.

Das, Veena, and Poole, Deborah. 2004. *Anthropology in the Margins of the State.* Santa Fe, NM: School of American Research Press.

Dhavan, Rajeev. 2000. "Judges and Indian Democracy: The Lesser Evil?" In Frankel, Hasan, Bhargava, and Arora (eds.), *Transforming India Social and Political Dynamics Of Democracy.* New York: Oxford University Press.

Dirks, Nicholas. 1987. *The Hollow Crown.* Cambridge: Cambridge University Press.

———. 2001. *Castes of Mind: Colonialism and the Making of Modern India.* Princeton, NJ: Princeton University Press.

Dube, S. C. 1968. "Caste Dominance and Factionalism." *Contributions to Indian Sociology* 2: 58–81.

Dumont, Louis. 1966. "The 'Village Community' from Monro to Maine." *Contributions to Indian Sociology* 9 (December): 67–89.

———. 1980. *Homo Hierarchicus: The Caste System and Its Implications.* Chicago: University of Chicago Press.

Dutt, R. C. 1981. *Socialism of Jawaharlal Nehru.* New Delhi: Frontis.

Edelman, Marc. 1999. *Peasants against Globalization: Rural Social Movements in Costa Rica.* Stanford, CA: Stanford University Press.

Escobar, Arthuro. 1992. "Imagining a Postdevelopment Era? Critical Thought, Development and Social Movements." *Social Text* 31/32: 20–56.

———.1995. *Encountering Development: The Making and Unmaking of the Third World.* Princeton, NJ: Princeton University Press.

Ferguson, James. 1990. *The Anti-Politics Machine: "Development," Depoliticization, and Bureaucratic Power in Lesotho.* New York: Cambridge University Press.

Ferguson, James, and Gupta, Akhil (eds.). 1997. *Anthropological Locations: Boundaries and Grounds of a Field Science.* Berkeley: University of California Press.

Foucault, Michel. 1977. *Discipline & Punish: The Birth of the Prison.* New York: Vintage Books.

Frankel, Francine. 1971. *India's Green Revolution, Economic Gains and Political Costs.* Princeton, NJ: Princeton University Press.

———. 1978. *India's Political Economy, 1947–1977: The Gradual Revolution.* Princeton, NJ: Princeton University Press.

———. 1989. "Decline of a Social Order." In Frankel and Rao (eds.), *Dominance and State Power in India,* Vol. 2. New Delhi: Oxford University Press.

———. 2005. *India's Political Economy 1947–2004: The Gradual Revolution.* New York: Oxford University Press.

Frankel, Francine, and Rao, M. S. A. (eds.). 1989. *Dominance and State Power in Modern India,* Vol. 1. New Delhi: Oxford University Press.

Fuller, Christopher. 1992. *The Camphor Flame: Popular Hinduism and Society in India.* Princeton, NJ: Princeton University Press.

———. 1996 (ed.). *Caste Today.* New York: Oxford University Press.

Fuller, Christopher, and Benei, Veronique. 2001. *The Everyday State and Society in Modern India*. London: Hurst.

Giddens, Anthony. 1994. *Beyond Left and Right: The Future of Radical Politics*. Stanford, CA: Stanford University Press.

Goankar, Ranajit. 2007. "On Cultures of Democracy." *Public Culture* 19(1): 1–22.

Goyal, Santosh. 1989. "Social Background of Officers in the Indian Administrative Service." In Frankel and Rao, *Dominance and State Power in Modern India*, Vol. 1. Oxford: Oxford University Press.

Gramsci, Antonio. 1971. *Selections from the Prison Notebooks*. New York: International Publishers.

Guha, Ranajit. 1996. *A Rule of Property for Bengal: An Essay on the Idea of Permanent Settlement*. Durham, NC: Duke University Press.

Gupta, Akhil. 1995. "Blurred Boundaries: The Discourse of Corruption, the Culture of Politics and the Imagined State." *American Ethnologist* 22: 375–402.

———. 1998. *Postcolonial Developments: Agriculture in the Making of Modern India*. London: Duke University Press.

Gupta, Dipankar. 2000. *Interrogating Caste: Understanding Hierarchy & Difference in Indian Society*. New York: Penguin Books.

Gupta, Shaibal. 1999. "A Messiah for Bihar?" *Seminar* 480 (August): 36–41.

Gupta, Tilak D. 1992. "Yadav Ascendancy in Bihar Politics." *Economic and Political Weekly* (June 27): 1304.

Guruswamy, Mohan, and Kaul, Abhishek. 2003. "Economic Strangulation of Bihar," research report, New Delhi: Center for Policy Alternatives.

Habermas, Jürgen. 1996. *Between Facts and Norms: Contributions to a Discourse Theory of Law and Democracy*. Cambridge, MA: MIT Press.

Hall, Stuart. 1986. "The Problem of Ideology—Marxism without Guarantees." *Journal of Communication Inquiry* 10(2): 28–44.

Hansen, Thomas Blom. 1999. *The Saffron Wave: Democracy and Hindu Nationalism in Modern India*. Princeton, NJ: Princeton University Press.

———. 2001. *Wages of Violence: Naming and Identity in Postcolonial Bombay*. Princeton, NJ: Princeton University Press.

Hansen, Thomas Blom, and Stepputat, Finn (eds.). 2001. *States of Imagination: Ethnographic Explorations of the Postcolonial State*. London: Duke University Press.

Harriss, John. 2011. "How Far Have India's Economic Reforms Been 'Guided by Compassion and Justice'? Social Policy in the Neoliberal Era." In Ruparelia, Reddy, Harriss, and Corbridge (eds.), *Understanding India's New Political Economy: A Great Transformation?* New York: Routledge.

Hasan, Zoya. 1998. *Quest for Power: Oppositional Movements and Post-Congress Politics in Uttar Pradesh*. New York: Oxford University Press.

———. 2000. "Representation and Redistribution: The New Lower Caste Politics of North India." In Frankel, Hasan, Bhargava, and Arora (eds.), *Transforming*

India: Social and Political Dynamics of Democracy. New Delhi: Oxford University Press.

Hill, V. Christopher. 1997. *River of Sorrow: Environment and Social Control in Riparian North India, 1770–1994.* (Monograph and Occasional Paper Series, number 55.) Ann Arbor, MI: Association for Asian Studies.

Jaffrelot, Christophe. 2003. *India's Silent Revolution: The Rise of the Low Castes in North Indian Politics.* New York : Columbia University Press.

Jameson, Fredric. 2002. *A Singular Modernity: Essays on the Ontology of the Present.* New York: Verso.

Jeffrey, Craig. 2002. "Caste, Class and Clientelism: A Political Economy of Everyday Corruption in Rural North India." *Economic Geography* 78(1): 21–41.

Jeffrey, Craig, and Lerche, Jens. 2001. "Dimensions of Dominance: Class and State in Uttar Pradesh." In Fuller and Benei (eds.), *The Everyday State and Society in Modern India.* London: Hurst.

Joseph, G. M., and Nugent, Daniel. 1994. *Everyday Forms of State Formation: Revolution and the Negotiation of Rule in Modern Mexico.* London: Duke University Press.

Karanth, G. K. 1996. "Caste in Contemporary Rural India." In Srinivas (ed.), *Caste: Its Twentieth Century Avatar.* New Delhi: Penguin Books.

Kaviraj, Sudipta. 1988. "A Critique of the Passive Revolution." *Economic and Political Weekly* 23(45/47): 2429–2444.

———. 1997. "The Modern State in India." In Doornbos and Kaviraj (eds.), *Dynamics of State Formation: India and Europe Compared.* New Delhi: Sage Publications.

Khilnani, Sunil. 1997. *The Idea of India.* London: Hamish Hamilton.

Knauft, M. Bruce. 2007. "Provincializing America: Imperialism, Capitalism, and Counterhegemony in the Twenty-First Century." *Current Anthropology* 48(6): 781–805.

Kohli, Atul. 1990. *Democracy and Discontent.* Cambridge: Cambridge University Press.

———. 1994. "Centralization and Powerlessness: India's Democracy in a Comparative Perspective." In Migdal, Kohli, and Shue (eds.), *State Power and Social Forces.* Cambridge: Cambridge University Press.

———. 2001. *The Success of India's Democracy.* Cambridge: Cambridge University Press.

Kothari, Rajni (ed.). 1970. *Caste in Indian Politics.* New Delhi: Orient Longman.

Kumar, Arun. 2001. *Rewriting the Language of Politics: Kisans in Colonial Bihar.* New Delhi: Manohar.

Laclau, Ernesto. 2005. *On Populist Reason.* New York: Verso.

Laclau, Ernesto, and Mouffe, Chantal. 1985. *Hegemony and Socialist Strategy: Towards a Radical Democratic Politics.* London: Verso.

Lerche, Jens. 1998. "Agricultural Labourers, the State and Agrarian Transition in Uttar Pradesh." *Economic and Political Weekly* 33(13): A29–A35.

Lefort, Claude. 1988. *Democracy and Political Theory*. Cambridge: Polity.

Lenin, V. I. 1977. "The Agrarian Question and the Present Situation in Russia." Lenin Collected Works, Vol. 19. Moscow: Progress Publishers.

Lohia, Ram Manohar. 1964. *The Caste System*. Hyderabad: Lohia Samta Vidyalaya Nyas.

Louis, Prakash. 2002. *People Power: The Naxalite Movement in Central Bihar*. New Delhi: Wordsmiths.

Mahendra, Dev S., and C. Ravi. 2007. "Poverty and Inequality: All India and States, 1983–2005," *Economic and Political Weekly* 42(6): 509–21.

Maheshwari, S. R. 2005. *Indian Administration*. New Delhi: Orient Longman.

Mamdani, Mahmood. 1996. *Citizen and Subject: Contemporary Africa and the Legacy of Late Colonialism*. Princeton, NJ: Princeton University Press.

Marcus, George. 1998. *Ethnography through Thick and Thin*. Princeton, NJ: Princeton University Press.

Mathew, Santhosh, and Moore, Mick. 2011. "State Incapacity by Design: Understanding the Bihar Story," Working Paper No. 366. Sussex: Institute of Development Studies.

Mayer, Adrian. 1960. *Caste and Kinship in Central India*. London: Routledge and Kegan Paul.

Mbembe, Achille. 2001. On the Postcolony. Berkeley: University of California Press.

Michelutti, Lucia. 2008. *The Vernacularisation of Democracy: Politics, Caste and Religion in India*. New Delhi: Routledge.

Mishra, G., and Pandey, B. K. 1996. *Sociology and Economics of Casteism in India*. New Delhi: Pragati Publications.

Mitra, Monoshi. 1985. *Agrarian Social Structure: Continuity and Change in Bihar 1786–1820*. New Delhi: Manohar.

Mouffe, Chantal. 1993. *The Return of the Political*. London: Verso.

Nedumpara, Jose. 2004. *Political Economy and Class Contradictions: A Study*. New Delhi: Anmol Publications.

———. 2008. "Democracy Otherwise: Struggles over Popular Rule in the Northern Peruvian Andeas." In Paley (ed.), *Democracy: Anthropological Approaches*. Santa Fe, NM: School for Advanced Research Press.

O'Hanlon, Rosalind. 1988. "Recovering the Subject Subaltern Studies and Histories of Resistance in Colonial South Asia Subaltern Studies." Modern Asian Studies 22(1):189–224.

Oommen, T. K. 1970. "The Concept of Dominant Caste: Some Queries." *Contribution to Indian Sociology* 4 (December): 73–83.

Paley, Julia. 2002. "Toward an Anthropology of Democracy." *Annual Review of Anthropology* 31: 469–496.

————. 2008. "Introduction." In Paley (ed.). *Democracy: Anthropological Approaches*. Santa Fe, NM: School for Advanced Research Press.

Pandey, Gyanendra. 1990. *The Construction of Communalism in Colonial North India*. New Delhi: Oxford University Press.

Pinch, William R. 1996. *Peasants and Monks in British India*. Berkeley: University of California Press.

Planning Commission. 2012. New Delhi: Press Information Bureau, http://planningcommission.nic.in/news/press_pov1903.pdf.

Poulantzas, Nicos. 2000. *State, Power Socialism*. New York: Verso.

Prakash, Gyan. 1990. *Bonded Histories: Genealogies of Labor Servitude in Colonial India*. Cambridge: Cambridge University Press.

Prasad, H. Pradhan. 1973. "Production Relations: Achilles' Heel of Indian Planning." *Economic and Political Weekly* 8(19): 869–872.

————. 1980. "Rising Middle Peasantry in North India." *Economic and Political Weekly* 15(5): 215–219.

Quigley, Declan. 1993. *The Interpretation of Caste*. New York : Oxford University Press.

Raheja, Gloria. 1988. *The Poison in the Gift: Ritual Presentation and the Dominant Caste in a North Indian Village*. Chicago: University of Chicago Press..

Rao, Anupama. 2009. *The Caste Question: Dalits and the Politics of Modern India*. Berkeley: University of California Press.

Rao, M. S. A. (ed.). 1978. *Social Movements in India*. New Delhi: Manohar.

————. 1989. "Caste, Ethnicity, and Dominance." In Frankel and Rao (eds.), *Dominance and State Power in India*, Vol. 1. New Delhi: Oxford University Press.

Robinson, Marguerite. 1988. *Local Politics: The Law of the Fishes: Development through Political Change in Medak District, Andhra Pradesh*. New Delhi: Oxford University Press.

Rudolph, Lloyd, and Rudolph, Susanne. 1967. *The Modernity of Tradition*. Chicago: University of Chicago Press.

————. 2001. "Redoing the Constitutional Design: From an Interventionist to a Regulatory State." In Kohli (ed.), *The Success of India's Democracy*. Cambridge: Cambridge University Press.

Sadhu, Amit, and Bharutwaj, Sandeep. 2003. "Developing Municipal Bond Markets in India." In Morris (ed.), *India Infrastructure Report: Public Expenditure Allocation and Accountability*. New Delhi: Oxford University Press.

Sawshilya 2000. "Administrative Culture in Bihar." In Sharma (ed.), *Administrative Culture in India*. New Delhi: Anamika Publishers.

Saxena, N. C. 2003. "Implementation of Poverty Alleviation and Food-Based Schemes in Bihar." Supreme Court Commission on Food Security.

Schumpeter, Joseph Alois. 1976. *Capitalism, Socialism, and Democracy*. London : Allen and Unwin.

Scott, James. 1985. *Weapons of the Weak: Everyday forms of Peasant Resistance*. New Haven, CT: Yale University Press.

Searle-Chatterjee, Mary, and Sharma, Usurla (eds.). 1994. *Contextualising Caste: Post-Dumontian Approaches*. Oxford: Blackwell Publishers.

Shah, Mihir. 2008. "Structures of Power in Indian Society: A Response." *Economic and Political Weekly* 43(46): 78–83.

Sheth, D. L. 1996. "Changing Terms of Elite Discourse: The Case of Reservation for 'Other Backward Classes.'" In Sathyamurthy (ed.), *Region, Religion, Caste, Gender and Culture in Contemporary India*, Vol. 3. New Delhi: Oxford University Press.

Singh, T. P. 1997. "Factors Affecting the Political Economy of Underdevelopment in Bihar." In Sinha (ed.), *Bihar Economic Revival*. Patna: Economic Association of Bihar.

Sivaramakrishnan, K., and Agrawal, Arun. 2003. *Regional Modernities: The Cultural Politics of Development in India*. Stanford, CA: Stanford University Press.

Spencer, Jonathan. 2007. *Anthropology, Politics and the State: Democracy and Violence in South Asia*. Cambridge: Cambridge University Press.

Spivak, Gayatri Chakravorty. 1988. "Can the Subaltern Speak." In Nelson and Grossberg (eds.), *Marxism and the Interpretation of Culture*. London: Macmillan.

Srinivas, M. N. 1962. *Caste in Modern India, and Other Essays*. Bombay: Asia Publishing House.

Tanabe, Akio. 2007. "Towards Vernacular Democracy: Moral Society and Postpostcolonial Tranformation in Rural Orissa." *American Ethnologist* 34:(3):, 558–574.

Thakur, Sankarshan. 2000. *The Making of Lalu Yadav and the Unmaking of Bihar*. New Delhi: HarperCollins.

———. 2006. Subaltern Saheb: Bihar and the Making of Laloo Yadav. New Delhi: Picador.

Thorner, Alice. 1982. "Semi-Feudalism or Capitalism? Contemporary Debate on Classes and Modes of Production in India." *Economic and Political Weekly* 17(49): 1961–1968.

Touraine, Alain. 1981. *The Voice and the Eye: An Analysis of Social Movements*. Cambridge: Cambridge University Press.

Tsing, Anna. 1993. *In the Realm of the Diamond Queen: Marginality in an Out-of-the-Way-Place*. Princeton, NJ: Princeton University Press.

Vishwas, A. K. 1998. *Understanding Bihar*. New Delhi: Blumoon Books.

Wadley, Susan. 1994. *Struggling with Destiny in Karimpur, 1925–1984*. Berkeley: University of California Press.

Wallerstein, Immanuel. 1974. "The Rise and Future Demise of the World Capitalist System: Concepts for Comparative Analysis." *Comparative Studies in Society and History* 16(4): 387–415.

West, Harry. 2008. "'Govern Yourselves!' Democracy and Carnage in Northern Mozambique." In Paley (ed.), *Democracy: Anthropological Approaches*. Santa Fe, NM: School for Advanced Research Press.

Wilkinson, Steven I. 2004. *Votes and Violence: Electoral Competition and Ethnic Riots in India.* Cambridge: Cambridge University Press.

Witsoe, Jeffrey. 2006. "Social Justice and Stalled Development: Caste Empowerment and the Breakdown of Governance in Bihar." *India in Transition: Economics and Politics of Change.* University of Pennsylvania: Center for the Advanced Study of India.

―――. 2011. "Corruption as Power: Caste and the Political Imagination of the Postcolonial State." *American Ethnologist*: 38: 1.

Wood, Ellen Meiksins. 1995. Democracy against Capitalism: Renewing Historical Materialism. Cambridge: Cambridge University Press.

World Bank. 2005. *Bihar: Towards a Development Strategy.* New Delhi: World Bank.

Yadav, Yogendra. 1997. "Reconfiguration in Indian Politics: State Assembly Elections 1993–1995." In Chatterjee (ed.), *State and Politics in India.* New York: Oxford University Press.

―――. 2000. "Understanding the Second Democratic Upsurge: Trends of Bahujan Participation in Electoral Politics in the 1990s." In Frankel, Hasan, Bhargava, and Arora (eds.), *Transforming India Social and Political Dynamics of Democracy.* New Delhi: Oxford University Press.

Yalman, Nur. 1960. "The Flexibility of Caste Principles in a Kandyan Community." In Leach (ed.), *Aspects of Caste in India, Ceylon, and North-West Pakistan.* Cambridge: Cambridge University Press.

Yang, Anand. 1989. *The Limited Raj: Agrarian Relation in Colonial India, Saran District.* Berkeley: University of California Press.

―――. 1998. *Bazaar India: Markets, Society, and the Colonial State in Gangetic Bihar.* Berkeley: University of California Press.

Index

Advani, L. K., 58–59, 131
agriculture, 176; agro-capitalism, 17, 39–40,
  49, 178; capitalism and, 210n31; caste
  associations and, 31–33, 36, 40, 41; colonialism and, 26, 39 (*see also* colonialism);
  commercialization of, 172, 210n30; cooperatives and, 93–99, 168; costs of, 173,
  179–80; credit and, 158; democratization
  of, 174, 180; direct cultivation, 144, 169–
  74, 177; efficiency of, 223n14; farmers
  and, 210n20; feudalism and, 39; Great
  Depression and, 31; green revolution,
  25, 41, 49, 173, 222n7; irrigation, 168,
  172–73; labor markets, 49, 171, 177; land
  development banks, 94–99; land rents
  and, 158, 174; large-scale, 159; minimum
  wage, 65, 176, 177, 223n8; mode of production debate, 39; NAFED and, 95;
  PACS and, 215n21; passive revolution
  and, 49; peasant farms, 223n14; political
  society and, 110; Rajnagar and (*see* Rajnagar); returns from, 173, 177, 179, 180;
  RJD and, 98–99, 185; sharecropping,
  39, 174; silent revolution and, 169; state
  institutions and, 179–81; territoriality
  and, 110; women and, 36; yields from,
  180–81, 180t, 215n8; *zamindars* and (see
  zamindars). *See also specific places, per-
  sons, topics*
All India Services, 89
Ambedkar, B. R., 65, 106, 207n23
Annexure One castes. *See* Extremely Backward Castes
Asian Development Bank, 194

Babri Masjid dispute, 201
backward-caste movements, 36, 188–89; aims
  of, 44; ambiguities in, 44; Annexure One
  and, 48, 191; Backward Classes Federation, 45, 46; bureaucracy and, 87–108; categorization and, 44; Chandapuri and, 44–
  45; Congress and, 40, 42, 46, 52, 207n20;
  contradictions within, 66; cooperatives
  and, 96–97; Dalits (*see* Dalits); democratization and, 51, 187, 188; development
  and, 43–45; EBCs and, 65, 76, 191, 201,
  213n40; equality and, 43; forward castes
  and, 44; green revolution and, 25; hegemony and, 44; identity and, 19, 36, 48, 78;
  institutional opportunities and, 43; interventions of, 67–68; Janata Dal and, 58,
  64, 67, 70 (*see also* Janata Dal); JP movement and, 55, 210n1 (*see also* JP movement); *kshatriya* status and, 36; Lalu and
  (*see* Yadav, L. P.); Lohia and, 42, 43, 48,
  189; militants and, 21; Mishra and, 192;
  Muslim-Yadav alliance, 201; Nitish and,
  195; OBCs and (*see* Other Backward
  Classes); patronage democracy and, 187;
  populism and (*see* populism); reservation opportunities and, 43, 45; RJD and,
  76, 77, 108, 187, 191 (*see also* Rashtriya
  Janata Dal); Sanskritization and, 35, 54,
  143, 150, 179, 223n13; social base of, 58;
  socialism and, 42, 45–50, 58, 105; Social
  Justice Pariwar and, 128; untouchability,
  171; Uttar Pradesh and, 201; Yadav leadership, 64. *See also specific groups, organizations, topics*